RACIAL JUSTICE
—— and the ——
CATHOLIC CHURCH

RACIAL JUSTICE
—— and the ——
CATHOLIC CHURCH

BRYAN N. MASSINGALE

ORBIS BOOKS
Maryknoll, New York 10545

Founded in 1970, Orbis Books endeavors to publish works that enlighten the mind, nourish the spirit, and challenge the conscience. The publishing arm of the Maryknoll Fathers and Brothers, Orbis seeks to explore the global dimensions of the Christian faith and mission, to invite dialogue with diverse cultures and religious traditions, and to serve the cause of reconciliation and peace. The books published reflect the views of their authors and do not represent the official position of the Maryknoll Society. To learn more about Maryknoll and Orbis Books, please visit our website at www.maryknollsociety.org.

Grateful acknowledgment is made to Random House for permission to publish excerpts from the poetry of Langston Hughes: "Harlem (2) ["What happens to a dream deferred..."]," "I, Too," from *The Collected Poems of Langston Hughes,* by Langston Hughes, edited by Arnold Rampersad with David Roessel, associate editor, copyright ©1994 by the Estate of Langston Hughes. Used by permission of Alfred A. Knopf, a division of Random House, Inc.

Queries regarding rights and permissions should be addressed to Orbis Books, Maryknoll, NY 10545-0302.

Manufactured in the United States of America.

Library of Congress Cataloging-in-Publication Data

Massingale, Bryan N.
    Racial justice and the Catholic Church / Bryan N. Massingale.
    p. cm.
    Includes bibliographical references and index.
    ISBN 978-1-57075-776-1 (pbk.)
    1. Racism – Religious aspects – Catholic Church. 2. Race relations – Religious aspects – Catholic Church. 3. Christianity and justice – Catholic Church. 4. Social justice – Religious aspects – Catholic Church. I. Title.
BX1795.R33M37 2010
282'.7308996073 – dc22

                            2009043396

In memory of my parents,
whose love and dreams
made this work possible

Contents

Preface

THIS BOOK HAS BEEN long in the making. It grows out of a struggle that is both personal and professional: the integration of my experiences as an African American and my Catholic faith. Over the years, the articulation of this struggle has taken many forms. Yet the fundamental and abiding conviction has been that there is a valuable and essential contribution that the black experience — the experience of creating meaning and possibility in the midst of the crushing ordinariness of American racism — can make to Catholic faith and theology.

When I began my graduate studies in the mid-1980s, one of my mentors cautioned me about focusing on issues of race. He observed, "If you do that, people will pigeonhole you and think that is all you can do." I received this advice with external politeness and respect, though inwardly I wondered: "But if I don't, who will?"

My professor's warning has proven to be more accurate than I would wish. Though I have taught courses across the range of Catholic moral theology and have lectured on issues ranging from terrorism to just war, from homosexuality to health care ethics, my published writings do focus on the issue of racism. This has led to a certain "pigeonholing," as my professor feared. Yet it is a risk that I have chosen to assume for two main reasons.

First, because of the existential concern I expressed above, namely, if my Catholic faith has nothing significant to say about a social evil that impacts my life every day in ways both small and large, hidden and blatant, then I and millions of other Catholics of color are fools and wasting our time. This compels me to give an account for the "reason for my hope," that is, to continue to engage in passionate and reasoned reflection demonstrating that there is no necessary contradiction between Catholic faith and an effective concern for racial justice and equality — despite the sad counterwitness of its concrete practices and omissions.

There is a second reason for assuming the risk of being a black Catholic ethicist who focuses on racial issues: a concern for the integrity and adequacy of the church's agency for justice. Virtually every social challenge facing the United States — education, care for the environment, access to health care, poverty, capital punishment, immigration reform, workers' rights, HIV/AIDS, criminal justice, right to life, concern for women — is entangled with or aggravated by racial bias against people of color. Racism is one of the central human rights challenges facing the country; it is the subtext of almost every social concern in our nation. It is my conviction — one that has only grown stronger with sustained study and reflection — that "Catholic failure to engage adequately the pivotal issue of racial injustice decisively compromises its theology of justice and renders its praxis of justice ineffective."[1]

This book, then, seeks to explore both the contributions and limitations of Catholic social reflection on racial justice. It addresses the question: Does Catholic faith have any relevance for the struggle for racial justice and equality in twenty-first century America? My aim is twofold: to develop a Catholic approach to racial justice more adequate to a nation, church, and world of increasing diversity and pluralism; and to demonstrate how a serious reckoning with the African American experience would enable Catholic social ethics to address some of its deficits and lacunae.

A word about the focus of this study. I concentrate on exploring racism from the perspective of the historic and continuing divisions in the United States between those social groups designated as "black" and "white" Americans.[2] I grant that a study that focuses upon these two racial groups is somewhat inadequate, especially given the increasing racial and ethnic diversity of the U.S. population. I also do not deny the existence or importance of racial tensions between or among other racial groups. Yet I contend that the estrangement between black and white Americans has shaped American life in decisive ways not matched by either the estrangement between whites and other racial/ethnic groups, or the tensions among the "groups of color."

In this, I agree with sociologist Joe Feagin, who characterizes the relationship between blacks and whites as "archetypal," meaning "it is the original model on which whites' treatment of other non-European groups" was patterned. Thus other racial and ethnic groups upon coming to this country were defined by their place within the racial ladder with whites on the top rung and blacks on the bottom. He further argues that the relationship between blacks and whites is archetypal in the sense that no other racial group has proved so central to the "white-controlled economy," white social life, and indeed the "white sense of self."[3] Moreover, those who have studied America's changing racial demography note that while our society is becoming more racially complex than a simple "white/nonwhite" divide, dark skin color or "anti-blackness" yet remains the pivotal element that determines a group's position in American social life. That is, "white" and "black" remain the critical reference benchmarks for measuring a social group's place in our public life.[4]

Historically and culturally, the attitudes, beliefs, and behaviors of white Americans toward blacks have most plagued and decisively formed us as a nation. This division is still the paradigm of racial injustice and thus merits privileged attention.

Yet there are serious obstacles to a forthright engagement with the issue of racism. I have taken to introducing lectures on racism by stating that there are three obstacles to overcome:

+ *We don't know what we are talking about* — that is, we lack clarity and agreement as to what constitutes "racism" in a so-called "post-racist" society;

+ *We don't know how to talk about it* — especially in mixed-race settings. The various racial and ethnic groups talk about "race" among themselves and in "safe" company. But we don't know how to talk about race productively in an interracial situation, where we often are inhibited by concerns of not wanting to appear insensitive, ignorant, or intolerant; and

◆ *We really don't want to talk about it* — that is, most Americans are very reluctant — even unwilling — to address the core reason for racial tensions and inequality in the United States, namely, the fact that a specific racial group benefits from our nation's racial hierarchy. We don't want to talk about the core issues that an honest discussion of racial injustice or racial disparity would entail, fearing the personal and social changes that such honesty would demand. Therefore, most prefer to tinker at the edges of the problem, basically saying, "Let's be nice to each other," rather than address the terrible truth and harsh reality of what we mean by racial injustice and racism. This is an especially difficult discussion for many (if not most) white Americans who (1) lack any first-hand experience with racial discrimination (except perhaps as perpetrators); (2) thus tend to minimize the occurrence or reality of racial discrimination; (3) lack awareness of how they benefit from the racial harms endured by others; and (4) are loathe to redress a system that benefits them.[5]

This is the reason for the failure of so many attempts at interracial "dialogue." We cannot have an honest engagement with racial injustice without addressing the unequal social status that results from it and is the reason for it. Why we need to overcome this hesitancy and address the core dynamic that feeds systemic inequality among the races is part of the reason for this book.

Another obstacle to overcome in discussions about race is their emotional charge. I have taught a course entitled "Christian Faith and Racial Justice" for several years. Much of what I write stems from my classroom experience. Inevitably, at some point in the course I have to suspend my planned lecture to allow space for the students to acknowledge and deal with the powerful emotions that are triggered by what they are learning. With the possible exception of homosexuality, no other issue engages us so emotionally and viscerally as that of racism. I have also discovered that until these emotions are acknowledged, no real learning or transformation can occur. The students become so overwhelmed that they literally shut down and tune out any further information or reflection. So at the beginning of this book, I want to acknowledge some of the emotions that may occur in its reading.

Discussions about race in the United States often are marked by unease, tension, anxiety, fear, anger, and confusion. For some, facing the reality of racism surfaces many *fears,* such as a fear of not being heard or understood; a fear of being blamed; a fear of the personal changes that might be required for a more faithful discipleship. Some feel *defensive* when the talk turns to racism; they do not want to be made responsible for wrongs that they lack a direct role in causing. Others feel *embarrassed* or *ashamed* as they confront a terrible history of human degradation and suffering perpetrated by members of their race. *Anger* is another common response in racial discussions, especially on the part of those who have been most directly harmed by this insidious social evil.

An examination of racism can also cause a sense of deep *sadness* as we come to realize the depths of human wrongdoing and tragic evil. Discussions of race can also lead to a sense of *weariness* and *discouragement;* after so much struggle and pain, there can seem to be too little progress to show for all of our efforts. Oftentimes we can feel *overwhelmed, paralyzed, and helpless* in the face of racism's seeming intransigence. Some approach the whole issue with *denial,* either willfully blind to or naively unaware of the ongoing reality of racial injustice. Finally, some feel that raising the issue of racism is counterproductive and needlessly *divisive;* they argue that we should focus upon what unites us rather than calling our attention to the divisions that exist among Americans.

These emotions are real. Confronting racism is difficult and challenging work. My aim in raising this issue to the forefront of our consciousness is not to foster division, but to heal a tragic brokenness in our society and church. Racism is an evil that afflicts us all. Though we are scarred in different ways and in varying degrees, no one living in the United States is immune from racism's terrible damage. We all are wounded by the sin of racism. Rather than promoting division, we are called to a solidarity in healing and struggle. The central question for us is this: *How can we struggle together against an evil that harms us all, though in different ways?* The central message of Catholic Christian faith is this: *The wounds of racism are real and deep, but healing is possible.* Thus I invite you to undertake this study, despite its difficulties and risks, sustained by Christ's assurance that the truth — however painful — will indeed set us free.

Acknowledgments

T HIS PROJECT REPRESENTS thoughts and ideas gathered over the
span of many years. Thus my debts are manifold. To engage
in public thanksgiving is both a joy and a risk: a joy to recognize
those who have been part of this project's success and a risk because
of the fear of leaving unnamed those who deserve mention. Such a
lapse only indicates a failure of memory, not a lack of gratitude.

I thank first of all my students over the years, especially at
St. Francis Seminary in Milwaukee, Marquette University, and the
Institute for Black Catholic Studies. They have been the laboratories
in which many of these ideas were tried, tested, and refined.

My colleagues in the Black Catholic Theological Symposium
have provided a forum in which many of my thoughts received
a maiden voyage. Their friendship is a sustaining one as we create
together a black Catholic theology. I especially thank C. Vanessa
White, Shawnee Daniels-Sykes, and M. Shawn Copeland for reading the fifth chapter and offering valuable insights.

Numerous academic and professional venues sponsored occasions for the presentation of my perspectives. I highlight the Black
Theology Session of the Catholic Theological Society of America,
the joint meeting of the Black Catholic Theological Symposium
and the Academy of Catholic Hispanic Theologians of the United
States, and the National Black Catholic Congress. Special mention
needs to be given to the Los Angeles Religious Education Congress, which provided a great forum for refining these ideas with
a nonprofessional audience of committed Christian catechists and
activists.

Among the many leadership groups in the Catholic Church with which I have worked, Catholic Charities USA and the Ethics Conference of the Catholic Health Association have been particularly supportive of my work in the area of racial justice. Special thanks to Father Clarence Williams, who brought my work to the attention of Catholic Charities USA and has been a constant source of support, encouragement, and prodding.

The administration of the Klinger College of Arts and Sciences at Marquette University helped this project through a research grant to supplement my sabbatical during which a significant part of this work was drafted.

I have been blessed with many friends who over the years have supported this project through their incessant questions, "How's the book? Where's the book?" Thanks Jim Dammeir, Brian Mason, Stephanie Russell, and José Gonzalez. Here it is!

Among my blessings I count the collaboration with my editor at Orbis Books, Susan Perry. She has been not only a professional colleague, but a friend whose belief in the merit of my ideas never flagged. Her dogged insistence that they deserved a wider audience has been the prod I needed to see this project through to completion.

My family, especially my sisters and brothers, have graced me with their love and support. As the research for and writing of this work unfolded, we have helped both of our parents make their transition to the eternal rest that awaits God's faithful ones. My appreciation to them is conveyed in this book's dedication.

Chapter One

What Is Racism?

THIS IS PERHAPS the most important chapter of this book. To know that Christians are to shun and struggle against racism is intuitively obvious. But to know what is meant by "racism," especially in a so-called "post-racial" society, is another matter. What exactly are believers called to reject and combat? Part of what makes racism such a difficult issue to address is that most Americans lack an adequate understanding of its depth, extent, and true nature. Thus, this chapter's question is critically important, for one's perception of this social evil will influence decisively one's theological interpretation, ethical guidance, and pastoral strategies.

In this chapter, I will situate the contemporary concern about racial justice in light of the major shifts in race relations now underway in the United States, changes occasioned by the election of the first African American as our president and the significant racial/ethnic demographic transition now underway. I will then consider what I call the "common sense" understanding of racism: Person A, usually but not always white, does something negative to Person B (usually but not always black or Latino) because of the color of his or her skin. This reality is real, but inadequate to deal with the racial quagmires we continue to experience in the United States.

Using the understanding of "culture" developed by Bernard Lonergan, I will demonstrate how racism is a culture, that is, part of the range of meanings and values that define a human group. Racism then refers to the underlying "set of meanings and values"

1

attached to skin color, a way of interpreting skin color differences that pervades the collective convictions, conventions, and practices of American life. This understanding of racism as a culture helps to explain its stubborn tenacity. This culture also has interpersonal and systemic effects — not the least of which is the justification of systems of racial privilege and advantage.

AN EXPLANATION OF TERMS

One of the challenges present in discussions about race and racism is that the terminology used to refer to the various racial and ethnic groups is fluid, evolving, contested, and rarely emotionally neutral. Among such terms are "white," "people of color," "nonwhite," and "racial/ethnic minority." For the sake of clarity and understanding, I want to clarify how I use these terms in this book.[1]

The term "white" refers to the dominant cultural group in our country. Originally, this group was primarily of Western European descent. It is important to note that "white" is a fluid category that has come to include over the years ethnic groups from other parts of the world. For example, the U.S. Office of Management and Budget (1999) defined "white" as "a person having origins in any of the original peoples of Europe, the Middle East, or North Africa." The U.S. Census Bureau further explains that "white" encompasses those who wrote on their census forms entries such as "Irish, German, Italian, Lebanese, near Easterner, Arab, or Polish." "White," then, does not refer to a "race," but rather to a social group that has access to political, social, economic, or cultural advantages that people of color do not share.

The terms "people of color" and "nonwhites" are collective terms that refer to all other racial and ethnic groups in U.S. society. While these terms make reference to skin color, they refer much more to social groups that, for the most part, find themselves without easy access to the political, social, economic, or cultural advantages enjoyed by those designated as white.

It should be further noted that "race" is a troublesome term, as is the idea that human beings constitute or can be divided into discrete and racially distinct social groups. The U.S. Census Bureau's understanding is important for the discussion in this work. It notes: "These categories are *social-political constructs* and should not be interpreted as being scientific or anthropological in nature."[2] In other words, "race" is a term of limited *scientific* usefulness, at best. Yet the enduring *social significance* of physical and cultural differences among human groups gives rise to the moral concerns at the heart of this project.

Difficulties also surround the use of the terms "minority" and "minority group" when referring to people of color collectively, or to African Americans, Latinos, Native Americans, or Asian Americans specifically. Among the issues raised with this usage is the fact that the term is not consistently employed to mean a "numerical"[3] minority; rather, it often carries connotations of power, prestige, value, and/or inclusion — or the lack thereof. However, no commonly accepted substitute for these terms has yet emerged, and their use is still widespread in social science literature. I try to account for this difficulty by using the modifiers "racial" or "ethnic" before the word "minority," while acknowledging the limitations of this approach.

PRELUDE AND CONTEXT: THE ELECTION OF AN AFRICAN AMERICAN PRESIDENT

"I thought I would never see the day!" This sentiment was echoed over and again by millions of African Americans, both on November 4, 2008, and on January 20, 2009. I myself felt a wondrous mixture of stunned disbelief, joy, and pride as the Obama family took the stage at Chicago's Wrigley Park on that late autumn night after being introduced as the "next First Family of the United States." Shortly after the news networks made the announcement of his election official, my cell phone began to ring. The first call was from my sister. In the midst of her joy, a wistful tone: "I wish Mom and Dad were here to see this." Another sentiment commonly voiced throughout black America.

The night of the inauguration, after a marathon day in front of the television incessantly flipping channels to follow every event of that historic day, I paused for a moment of quiet reflection. I wrote in my journal:

> I am overwhelmed and full of AWE at the momentous, seismic, epochal, unprecedented, ground-shifting nature of what we are experiencing in this country. For the first time in my life, I cried as I sang the National Anthem; I at last felt included in "America." This is not a *new* face of America, as this dark-skinned, nutmeg-hued man assumes one of the world's most important positions of leadership. For the darker face has always been here, but rarely acknowledged, at least not in celebration. Rather, what we witnessed today was the public recognition of that face — and its talent, beauty, and contribution. We, America, don't know how to act in this "brave new world." But here we are. I *cried*. I'm happy. I'm in stunned disbelief and amazement at the power of God and this new thing being done in our midst: the culmination of so many who kept faith in America through our darkest days, years, and centuries. Because it took almost 400 years to get here ... through the horrors of slavery, civil war, Jim Crow, and civil rights ... through nightmares of despair, humiliation, and exclusion ... through trials of hurt, death — and hope. Through our most enduring sin and stubborn stain, maybe we have begun to overcome.

Yet Race Still Matters in America

For many, Obama's achievement represents the fulfillment of Martin Luther King's dream: a black man whose ambition is bounded not by the color of his skin but by the content of his character. They view Obama's election for the nation's highest office as an affirmation of the fundamental soundness of the American project and the decency of the American people. Some even take this to be a moment of racial redemption, a sign that America has finally transcended its ugly racial past. Others see this as an occasion of racial vindication, that is, indisputable evidence that we live in a "color-blind" society where one's progress is no longer limited by skin color, but only by the strength of one's own drive, effort, and initiative. They also hold that with racism's demise we no longer need affirmative action policies, which are at best passé and at worst reverse discrimination. Obama's ascendency, according to these narratives, hails the arrival of a "post-racial" society, a descriptor, it should be noted, that Obama himself has never adopted.

There is much that is remarkable about this moment. It is a watershed event in our national history. The momentous nature of this development is demonstrated by the fact that the U.S. president is not only the leader of the government and the nation's chief executive, but also its "head of state." The presidency, in a real way, stands in our nation in the same relationship as Britain's monarchy. As "head of state," the president is the chief public representative of the United States, the living embodiment of the nation's values, ideals, and character. The president is an important, even primal, symbol of who "we" are, leading us both in public joy and celebration (as when welcoming a returning Olympic team), and in collective grief and mourning (as in the aftermath of 9/11). This symbolic charge of representing — indeed, *in-bodying* — who we are as a nation and people is what many mean when they take measure of a candidate and ask whether he or she is "presidential."

Thus, Obama, the ultimate "Other" — a descendent of those marked for slavery, considered subhuman for most of their history, and deemed as "having no rights that a white man is bound to respect"[4] — has now been deemed to be "presidential," that is, the personification of the country and its values. A black body is now the embodiment of "America." By any measure, this is a seismic moment in American life.

However, before we uncork the champagne in an explosion of national celebration and self-congratulation, let's take a deeper look.

Consider how race has framed, haunted — even "colored" — Obama's presidency from the very beginning of his quest for the nomination. Recall the first questions asked about him and his candidacy: "Is he black enough?" "Is he too black?" "Is the nation ready for a black president?"

Then the concerns became: "Is he an angry black man, à la the Reverend Jeremiah Wright?" Is he the (illegitimate) beneficiary of political affirmative action, as suggested by those who avowed that his race had been an advantage to his campaign? Why is he "black" if his mother's white? Why were most white primary voters in Pennsylvania and West Virginia who stated that race was an important consideration for their choice unwilling to vote for a black man?

Then consider the following events, all of which occurred within days of his election and the first two hundred days of his presidency:

* It has been widely reported that Obama has received more death threats than any previous presidential candidate, president-elect, or president. He received Secret Service protection eighteen months before the election, earlier in the campaign than any previous presidential candidate. The Secret Service has openly acknowledged that the "historic nature of his presidency poses 'unique' challenges with which to contend."[5]

* On campuses across the country, reports surfaced after the election of students writing anti-Obama comments, including one that said, "Let's shoot that [N-word] in the head."

* In Standish, Maine, a sign inside the Oak Hill General Store read: "Osama Obama Shotgun Pool." Customers could sign up to bet $1 on a date when Obama would be killed. "Stabbing, shooting, roadside bombs, they all count," the sign said. At the bottom of the marker board was written, "Let's hope someone wins."

* The day after his election, second- and third-grade students on a school bus in Rexburg, Idaho, chanted "assassinate Obama."[6]

* A national political leader, Newt Gingrich, described then Supreme Court nominee Sonia Sotomayor — the first person

of Hispanic ancestry to be named for the highest court — as a "Latina woman racist." Though he later retracted his comment, this was typical of the vitriol heaped upon her on the part of overwhelmingly white conservative activists.[7]

◆ There has been a resurgence of race-based hate groups and militia movements. The Southern Poverty Law Center has documented an alarming increase in the number, membership, recruitment efforts, and vitriolic rhetoric of white supremacist organizations and armed right-wing paramilitary militia groups. These armed bands, they note, "are just one part of an explosion of extremist rage in America — a backlash to the Obama election and the progress we're making toward social justice and tolerance." They further document what they call a "remarkable rash of domestic terror incidents since the presidential campaign, most of them related to anger over the election of Barack Obama." These incidents include cross burnings and violent attacks, as well as assassination plots and threats. The rage in these groups stems from, they conclude, increased nonwhite immigration and a decline in the percentage of whites in America.[8]

◆ Thinly veiled racially charged protests over health care have gained strength. Veteran Congressman John Dingell of Michigan commented, "I haven't faced crowds this angry since I voted for the Civil Rights Act of 1964."[9] The scene is the summer of 2009, as "town hall" discussions about health care reform across the nation are overwhelmed by vehement, boisterous, and angry crowds of mostly white middle-class citizens. I am struck by the connection made between the two events: the Civil Rights Act granting a semblance of legal equality to a long downtrodden black minority, and efforts to ensure a floor of decent health care for the vast majority of the poor and vulnerable. It manifests the racial undercurrent present in the health care debates by a portion of the white middle-class who apparently feel threatened by "something" they cannot clearly name. Maybe they sense (perhaps rightly) that things are changing, that the social order and the cultural codes they have taken for granted are shifting in fundamental, decisive, and seismic ways.

• In April 2008, a local Mississippi high school holds its first integrated school prom, ending decades of officially sponsored separate dances for white and black students. However, in March a group of white parents organized and held the usual separate "white prom," vowing that their children would never dance with blacks. (The exact words used by one parent were, "No nigger's going to be rubbing up on my daughter.") In the spring of 2009, a group of white parents organized and held a second unofficial "white-only" prom.[10]

My point is obvious, even belabored: Obama's presidency reveals that despite the indisputable changes in race relations of the past fifty years, it is also indisputable that race still matters. Race is far from being an insignificant reality in American life. It remains our deepest national obsession; it is still a principal and all too often decisive lens through which we filter our perception and understanding of the world. We continue to live in a highly racialized society, that is, "a society wherein race matters profoundly for differences in life experiences, life opportunities, and social relationships."[11] We are a nation "that allocates differential economic, political, social, and even psychological rewards to groups along racial lines; lines that are socially constructed."[12] Despite the obvious and welcome changes from the harsh and often savage brutalities of enforced segregation, it yet remains true that "the color question is pervasive in our lives, and it is an explicit tension or at least subtext in countless policy debates."[13]

Obama's presidency, then, does not mark the end of our racial dysfunction. Rather, it is dramatic proof that we are far from being a "color-blind" society. His quest and the discussions around it demonstrate that African Americans must still contend with and negotiate through a complex minefield of entrenched racial obstacles that whites do not have to consider. Even now, Obama runs the risk that any small misstep can transform him from being an acceptable racial "exception" to being the embodiment of white

America's racial fears about black men. Or, to put this point more colloquially, using the words of a CNN political pundit: "There's a reason why all of our presidents have looked like me. And Obama is rolling a huge stone up a steep hill."[14]

Thus a most important reality that this event tells us about "us" is that pronouncements concerning a "post-racial" America are premature at best; at worst, they are ideological evasions of reality. "Color-blindness" is a naive illusion. Obama's presidency does not herald the arrival of a racial promised land. In this nation race still matters.

THE BROWNING OF AMERICA AND RACIAL RESISTANCE

What accounts for this eruption of racial animus and hostility? Why would Obama's election be such a catalytic occurrence that commentators contend that some in the United States have become mentally or emotionally "unhinged" by this event? A deeper look at such questions requires us to probe the discomfort and unease that exist among some over the changing faces and voices of America.[15] The resistance encountered to genuine racial equality stems, in no small degree, from a deep anxiety among some quarters of white America to the nation's changing demography.

Any discussion of racial justice today must take account of the seismic shift occurring in the composition of our population. We are becoming more racially and culturally diverse than ever before. At least one out of three Americans is now "Latino or nonwhite." The Census Bureau reports that almost half of the nation's children under the age of five are members of racial minorities. Many of our nation's urban centers are now so-called "majority-minority," meaning not only that people of color are the majority of the population, but also that no single racial or ethnic group constitutes a numerical majority. Because of immigration patterns and differing birthrates among the various racial and ethnic groups, it appears likely that by the middle of this century (if not sooner), whites will no longer be the majority race in the United States. Indeed, it is probable that our country will have no single racial majority group.[16]

Not only is American society becoming more multiracial and multicultural, it is also more religiously diverse. In May 2001, National Public Radio noted that there are now more Muslims than Jews living in the United States. Indeed, the Muslim population is more numerous than many Christian denominations, whether singly or combined. This same source further reports that Hindus and Buddhists also are an ever-more significant presence in our social life.

Thus the landscape of U.S. society is being, and already has been, decisively altered. Our schools and workplaces are becoming ever more racially, ethnically, and religiously diverse in ways many might never have imagined, dreamed, hoped, or desired. It is increasingly difficult — even false — to assert without qualification that the United States is a "white Christian nation." But if not, then who, or what, is really "American"?

We are no longer a white Christian nation, and many white Christians are anxious. A March 2008 Pew study found that 56 percent of high school educated voters see newcomers as threatening, compared to less than a third of those with a college degree. This leads some to argue that while antiblack racism is still quite alive, as the face of America is changing, so is the face of American racism. Race still matters because for many Americans, dark skin now is associated also with a dangerous "foreignness" that is alien — if not hostile — to genuine "American" identity.

This provides a context for understanding how racial anxieties about Obama have been and continue to be discussed in coded reference to his "foreignness." Consider the following incidents:

- Someone at a rally late in the campaign said, "I don't trust him. He's an Arab." (Recall Senator McCain's response, "No, ma'am, he's a decent family man." Apparently, "Arab" and "decent" are mutually exclusive).

- Throughout the campaign, and continuing to this day, there is a sentiment voiced to the effect that "he doesn't see America the way we do" (as if it is self-evident who "we" are and how "we" see America).

- A September 2008 Pew survey found that "white voters who haven't graduated from college...were twice as likely to think that Obama is a Muslim as those who have."

- A persistent yet false e-mail circulated rumors that Obama took his oath of office as a senator on the Koran.

- An anxious reservation is conveyed in the following sentiment: "His name is just too much like Osama."

- Finally, a recent manifestation of this trend is the oft-proven false but maddeningly persistent belief that Obama was born in Kenya. Thus he is not a native-born U.S. citizen and therefore was illegally elected and exercises no legitimate authority.[17]

These events demonstrate how it is more acceptable to express reservations about Obama's so-called "foreignness" than to express a direct racial prejudice.[18] "Foreignness" and "Muslim" have become placeholders for "race" and "black."

It is tempting to dismiss these incidents as either naive or ignorant bigotry, as beyond the serious consideration of thoughtful persons. But to do so would miss the deeper point: Obama has become a walking "ink blot," a living Rorschach test upon which a number of whites project their deep-seated fears, resentments, and anxieties over no longer being a "white Christian nation." Obama, again, becomes important not only for who he is in himself, but for what he is revealing about us.

Obama, in his heritage and outlook, represents an inexorably changing American identity. His is the face of our inevitable future. That someone who is so "Other" — with the strange name, dark skin, and unusual background — is now the symbolic embodiment of what it means to be "American" is a confirmation of some people's worst fears. It is not surprising, then, that this evokes from some a kind of "tribalism," that is, a defense of self- and group interests — what is "ours" — against those "others" who are seen as a threat to one's entitlements.[19] This carries the danger of social fragmentation and division, if not worse. A noted social commentator expresses this fear:

> My biggest fear, as this nation moves into an inevitable browning, or hybridization, is that there will be a very powerful minority, overwhelmingly composed of Euro-Americans, who will see themselves in significant danger as a consequence of the way democracy works: winner-take-all. And they will begin to renege on some of the basic principles that created the United States and made it what it is.[20]

Thus Obama's presidency forces us to confront the changing faces and voices of America, that is, the new national identity in the process of becoming. For some, this is profoundly disorienting, a source of visceral fear and existential unease. Many, it seems, are experiencing *culture shock*. I use the term "culture shock" quite deliberately and intentionally. It describes the anxiety and other feelings (such as surprise, disorientation, uncertainty, and confusion) felt when people have to operate within an entirely different cultural or social environment, such as in a foreign country. It grows out of the difficulties of assimilating the new culture, in knowing what is appropriate and what is not.

This seems an apt description of what lies behind many of the reactions that an Obama presidency has aroused. Many white Americans are experiencing "culture shock" in their own homeland, as the country is being transformed into something that is strange, unfamiliar, "foreign," and threatening. They react with confusion, anger, and even disgust; for example, consider the sometimes voiced sentiment: "I resent having to speak Spanish in my own country." They feel that America is being morphed into something they don't understand, and desire even less. Such feelings of unease, disorientation, confusion, and resentment are often manipulated all too easily by the unscrupulous and the demagogues who always arise in times of cultural upheaval and uncertainty.[21] This anxiety is projected onto Obama — hardly surprising, given the symbolic role of the presidency in this country and his strange name, dark skin, and unusual background.

This emerging multiracial and multicultural society is an America we have never been, and, for some, it is a source of visceral fear and existential unease that motivates passive (and possibly active) resistance. Confronting the possibility of social tribalism, then, is absolutely essential to any adequate understanding of the dynamics of our political moment and justice struggles that we face. Obama's presidency, and the public discourse and the reactions it continues to arouse, make manifest the latent anxiety among many: Whose country is this? Who are we — and what is America? — if we are not white and Christian? This is another reason why race still matters.

RACISM AND CULTURE

All of these considerations are germane to addressing the question, "What is racism?" For the answer to that question must be one that accounts for the diffuse anxiety on the part of those who view the election of a black man with a dismay bordering on rebellion. The response to that question should also help explain the persistence of racism despite momentous progress and seismic change. This reflection must also enable us to understand the paradox of undeniable racial progress coupled with apparently intractable opposition to full racial equality and inclusion.

To understand this new era of race relations, the persistence and intransigence of racial inequality, and the challenges we face in this moment, we must have a deeper understanding of racism than what I call the "commonsense" understanding that prevails among the vast majority of Americans. This understanding could be expressed as follows:

> Person A (usually, but not always, white) consciously, deliberately, and intentionally does something negative to Person B (usually, but not always, black or Latino) because of the color of his or her skin.

Note the following characteristics of such an understanding:

- It focuses on interpersonal transactions or behaviors, that is, upon individuals — or at most, small groups with clearly identifiable actors — acting negatively toward other individuals who are racially different.

- It focuses on conscious, deliberate actions, that is, someone intentionally chooses to act in a negative manner toward another.

- It focuses upon the harm that another experiences because of race-based actions, rather than the advantages that may accrue to those doing the harm.

- Finally, while it acknowledges that whites may be the "default" perpetrators, this social group is not the only one that can engage in such behaviors (which is the basis for the often heard rejoinder, "But blacks and Latinos are just as racist as whites").

Thus the commonsense understanding discusses racism as personal acts of rudeness, hostility, or discrimination usually but not always directed against persons of color.

It needs to be acknowledged that such an understanding encompasses no small amount of racially motivated bias. No one disputes the fact that acts of blatant insensitivity still stain our social fabric. Most fair-minded people grant that acts of racial hostility and callous bigotry still occur. Members of any racial group can, and sadly too often do, act unjustly toward those they consider racially different.

Nonetheless, such an understanding does not account for the anxiety we see in U.S. society over the election of an African American as its head of state. A focus on individual behaviors and attitudes does not adequately explain the existence of a racialized society, where race is a principal lens for social interpretation and understanding. A preoccupation with the discrete acts of individual actors cannot explain the persistence and pervasiveness of racial discrimination in hiring, such that white ex-offenders are more likely to be hired for entry-level jobs than black applicants with no criminal record (what one author calls "race trumps criminal records").[22]

Individual acts of racial animus — even when perpetrated by persons of color — cannot alter the fact that in the United States, one racial group is socially advantaged and the others endure social stigma.

In short, an emphasis upon personal attitudes and actions — what social psychologists call prejudice and discrimination[23] — cannot explain the persistence of racism despite undeniable changes. There appears to be something "more," an underlying dynamic that remains constant despite significant watersheds and shifts, and that morphs to assume new forms and manifestations. What is this "X" that remains constant, impervious even to the election of a black man to the highest office of the land and his selection as the symbolic embodiment of the nation's values? And what dynamic accounts for the resistance to and rejection of that very black embodiment? To respond to such questions, we need a fuller and more robust concept of racism than the "commonsense" understanding allows.

My answer, in brief, lies in the realization that racism is a *cultural* phenomenon, that is, a way of interpreting human color differences that pervades the collective convictions, conventions, and practices of American life. Racism functions as an ethos, as the animating spirit of U.S. society, which lives on despite observable changes and assumes various incarnations in different historical circumstances. Analyses that focus only or principally upon interpersonal dynamics (what person A does to person B) miss the more important and pivotal cultural setting that not only facilitates such acts, but makes them understandable and intelligible.

I advance this insight by first developing what I mean by "culture," and then describing the "culture of racism."

Toward an Understanding of Culture

Developing an adequate understanding of culture is a complex undertaking, as there seems to be no standard uniform definition. The prominent anthropologist Clifford Geertz describes culture as "a system of inherited conceptions expressed in symbolic forms by means of which [humans] communicate, perpetuate, and develop their knowledge about and attitudes toward life."[24] The noted

Canadian theologian Bernard Lonergan provides the following succinct definition: "A culture is simply the set of meanings and values that inform the way of life of a community."[25] Culture thus denotes a system of meanings and values, expressed in symbolic form, that conveys and expresses a people's understanding of life. Culture is the set of attitudes toward life, beliefs about reality, and assumptions about the universe shared by a human group.

Note that culture in this sense is more basic and fundamental than society, social institutions, or social policies and customs. Culture expresses the meaning of society, the value of the patterned ways of social interaction humans construct, and the significance of the ways in which we live and order our communities.[26] Simply put, culture provides the meaning of the social. Lonergan declares, "Over and above mere living and operating, [humans] have to find a meaning and value in their living and operating. It is the function of culture to discover, express, validate, criticize, correct, develop, [and] improve such meaning and value."[27] Shawn Copeland concisely explains Lonergan's distinction between a "society" and its "culture" this way: society is "the way human persons live together in some orderly and predictable fashion"; culture is "the meaning of that way of life."[28]

To put this another way, culture provides the ideological foundation for social, political, and economic policies. The cultural meaning or significance of social life, Lonergan notes, "is felt, intuited, and acted out" and "communicated" in symbolic forms. That is, the underlying meanings and values of social life are expressed and conveyed through "rites and symbols, language and art." Thus he concludes that "culture stands to social order as soul to body"[29]; that is to say, culture is the spirit that animates social institutions and customs, makes them intelligible, and expresses their meaning and significance.

I want to emphasize several observations:

• First, cultures are *shared* or group realities. An individual cannot have a "private" culture. One's culture is also shared by others who belong to a given social group.

◆ Second, cultures are *learned* communal beliefs and values. The set of meanings and values that animate a social group are "transmitted from generation to generation through learning."[30] This learning happens both formally and informally, through conscious instruction and tacit understanding, by intentional training and unconscious socialization.

◆ Third, cultures are *formative,* that is, they shape the personal identities of a community's members, as they express their way of being in the world and their understanding of their place within it. Even though people create culture and it is in a state of constant development, culture also shapes behavior and consciousness within a human society. It conditions our thoughts, values, and actions. Lonergan's formulation is instructive: *"All human doing, saying, thinking, occurs within the context of a culture* and consists in the main of using the culture. It is within culture as it is historically available that provides *the matrix within which persons develop* and that supplies the meanings and values that inform their lives."[31]

◆ Fourth, a group's set of meanings, values, and beliefs about life are expressed *symbolically.* That is, culture is carried and expressed through visible markers (for example, art, music, language, clothing, literature, and dance). As Lonergan puts it, "Meaning is embodied or carried in human intersubjectivity, in art, in symbols, in language, and in the lives and deeds of persons."[32] Such symbols are not only badges of difference and markers of tribal membership. They are also the icons of a people's identity, or representations of the *soul* of a people.

This last point is extremely important. Discussions about culture, cultural differences, and cultural sensitivity often focus solely on the externals, that is, what we can see, hear, taste, touch, or smell. We too often focus only on the symbols, symbolic carriers, or social patterns and do not attend to the set of assumptions, meanings, and values about life that these symbols express or convey. This is a very shallow notion of culture.

For example, I lived as a student in Rome for three years. During this time, I became fairly proficient in the Italian language; I could distinguish and appreciate many kinds of pasta; I became adept at negotiating the bewildering Roman traffic; I mastered Italian telephone and social etiquette; and I even grew accustomed to the Italian pronunciation of my name. Nonetheless, I never considered myself "Italian" — nor was I ever mistaken for one. Despite my extended stay in Italy, I never arrived at a point where I felt that I truly understood the Italians. There is something about the Italian sensibility, something about the Italians' approach to life, something about how they understand themselves, that will always elude and mystify me — no matter how detailed my mastery of the external symbols or carriers of their culture.

My point is quite simple: mastering the external symbols of a culture does not make one a member of that culture. And attention solely to the external carriers or patterns of a culture gives one a very limited understanding of its adherents.

This is because culture, at its core, is something internal. It is a people's soul, a set of meanings and values that is an individual's and a social group's identity. It is the frame of reference through which they look at the world, the template or lens through which they interpret life. Culture shapes consciousness. This is why cross-cultural encounters — and especially times of cultural change or imposition — are occasions of personal and group trauma (that is, "culture shock"). One's frame of reference is disrupted and one's sense of self is disoriented, even threatened. Culture, then, is more than what one eats, wears, and drinks. Culture is not principally a way of acting, but a way of being. Culture comprises totality of the way a group is in the world. The external symbols give meaning, direction, and identity to a people in ways that touch not just the intellect, but most especially the heart.

Thus in order to understand the cultural differences and distinctiveness of black and white Americans, we cannot merely list or attend to the external differences in speech, customs, dress, time, art, and literature that mark these groups. We must go deeper and try to understand the "soul" of these groups, that is, the set of meanings and values that informs their ways of life. I now turn to the task of articulating the "soul" of these respective cultures. This exercise will help make Lonergan's insights more concrete and also bring us closer to the core of the reality of racism.

The "Soul" of African American Culture

If culture is the set of meanings and values that informs a people's attitude and stance toward life, what set of meanings and values constitute African American culture?[33] This is obviously a complex question. I admit at the outset that my response will not be a comprehensive one; my hope is to stimulate further reflection upon this important topic.

I begin by acknowledging that African Americans are a diverse people. We are not a monolithic cultural entity. We live in urban, rural, and suburban settings. We are among the poor, the working class, the middle class, and even the wealthy. We are unemployed, factory workers, farmers, and professionals. We are Catholic, Protestant, Muslim, Jewish, and unchurched. We are northern, southern, and western. We are male and female. Our loving relationships encompass a variety of sexual orientations and expressions. Our musical tastes encompass Leontyne Price, Wynton Marsalis, Whitney Houston, Boys-II-Men, and Tupac Shakur. Black life in America evidences a plurality of lifestyles and cultures.

Can one, then, speak of a common African American culture without negating our legitimate diversity? I believe that we can. This culture is rooted in a common experience that black folk cannot avoid in the United States: the experience of racial prejudice, discrimination, rejection, and hostility — both subtle and overt — based upon the simple fact of our physical blackness. The following statement articulates this experience well:

> No matter what part of the country black people come from, they are beset with indignities traceable to the single fact that they are black. However well-to-do economically or however extensive their formal training, however correct their behavior, black people can never protect themselves from the fact

that they are not accepted as they would be if they were white
and had the same achievements.[34]

In fact, the historical event that melded the diverse African
peoples brought to this country into an identifiable community in
the United States was that of slavery and its aftermath: the experience of having one's humanity denied, questioned, or attacked.
What was common to all was the experience of being regarded and
treated as less than fully human. In the provocative words of Audre
Lorde: "To survive in the mouth of this dragon we call america, we
have had to learn this first and most vital lesson — that we were
never meant to survive. Not as human beings."[35]

Because of this common experience, African Americans share
a common history. Black history, according to James H. Cone, is
a "record of joy and pain" that chronicles both "the history of
white inhumanity" toward black persons, and "the record of [black]
resistance against a condition of bondage."[36] Out of this shared
history emerges a common culture — conveyed in music, poetry,
dance, prose, speech, and dress — that articulates the unbearable
pain, the unimaginable joy, and the unbreakable beauty of carving
out one's humanity in an atmosphere of racist insanity.

If one were to try to capture the "soul" of African American
culture in a word, perhaps it would be *struggle.* Here I agree with
the thoughts of law professor Roy L. Brooks, which merit extensive
citation:

> If a residual racial perspective that cuts across class lines and
> other intra-racial differences does inhere in African Ameri-
> cans, surely it consists of at least two ingredients. *One is
> the expectation of struggle,* that is, the belief that whether
> an African American wants simply to get through the day or
> to tackle more complex endeavors (obtaining a quality edu-
> cation, finding and holding a good job, successfully raising a
> family), he or she should expect to encounter no dearth of
> artificial, racial barriers and must be prepared to recognize
> and deal with them effectively. I doubt that this vision of exis-
> tence is *fundamental* to the way white Americans approach

their lives, or, if it is, that it is as *pervasive* among whites as it is among African Americans. . . . *The second ingredient is the belief that society ("the system" or "the Man") is more foe than friend,* a theme echoed by African American writers and social activists from the days of slavery to recent times.[37]

If this analysis is correct, then the external manifestations of black culture are symbolic representations of a basic stance toward life: the fundamental and pervasive struggle to be recognized, welcomed, and accepted as a human being. This entails a passionate quest for freedom, equality, and dignity in a racially hostile milieu. I argue that this fundamental struggle for humanity is the "soul" of black culture. Even if one does not believe that it exhausts the whole of black culture, no one can deny that "struggle" is a constitutive part of it. One simply cannot understand black people if one does not understand the pervasive sense of struggle that informs their lives and identity.

The "Soul" of White Culture

What, then, is the set of meanings and values that informs the way of life of white Americans? In other words, what does it mean to be "white?" Here we face two difficulties. First, as with African Americans, white Americans are not a cultural monolith. White Americans also exhibit a wide diversity of lifestyle and cultural expressions.

Second, for the most part white Americans do not think of themselves as "white" or as belonging to a "white culture." For most white Americans, the phrase "white culture" is meaningless. The few white authors who advert to this issue note, "Most whites have not thought much about their race. Few, upon being asked to identify themselves by attributes would name whiteness among their primary characteristics."[38] The emerging research in the field of "white studies" confirms a phenomenon that I have often noted in classes and workshops I have conducted. When asked what their racial/cultural identity is, many whites will state an ethnic background (for example, a hybrid of German/Irish) — but then relate that this ethnic background is not a significant part of their personal identity. Most whites will describe themselves as "American" — which is significant because if "American" is their specific cultural identity, what does that make people of color? Few in my experience spontaneously describe themselves as "white." As the sociologists Feagin and Vera observe, "Apparently, for most whites, being white means rarely having to think about it."[39]

This is an extremely significant observation. Not thinking of oneself as "white" and the easy equation of "white" with "American" are keys to determining the "soul" of white culture. "White" denotes a frame of reference that is *unquestioned*. It is unquestioned because it is *invisible* and *unnamed*. It is unquestioned and invisible because it is the *norm* by and against which all other frames of reference (that is, cultures) are measured. Much as a fish is unaware of water, so whiteness — for white folk — exists on the fringe of consciousness because it is so "normal," obvious, and "just the way things are." That is why it is so easy for white people to equate "white" and "American." For white Americans, whiteness is "reality."

Hence, the "soul" or essence of white culture is a worldview that — when it adverts to itself — sees itself as the measure of what is real, standard, normative, and/or normal. White culture is a perspective that measures, but is seldom measured; studies, but is rarely studied; analyzes, but is not often analyzed; evaluates, but is typically not evaluated. Let me make this point clear with an example. When I was a student for the priesthood, the annual evaluation by the seminary's faculty often raised the concern about how I, as a black person, would fit into a white parish. But never were questions raised about how a white parish would accept me, nor of how the overwhelmingly white seminary community handled living with a black man. This is because "whiteness" studies, but is rarely studied; and evaluates, but is seldom evaluated — at least by whites themselves.

Because it purports to encompass reality, white culture does not have to be aware of itself unless those who are "other" challenge its presumption (or pretense) of being normative or standard. Hear the following perceptive observation offered by a white woman:

White is transparent. That's the point of being the dominant race. Sure the whiteness is there, but you never think of it. If you're white you never *have* to think about it.... And if white folks remind each other about being white, too often the reminder is about threats by outsiders — nonwhites — who steal white entitlements like good jobs, a fine education, nice neighborhoods, and the good life.[40]

Is there a historical or paradigmatic event that melded the diverse group of European ethnicities and social classes into an identifiable white group? Many scholars point to two: First, the coalition forged between the white southern elite and the white poor before, and most especially after, the Civil War. Derrick Bell, among others, avows that the southern elite skillfully manipulated white skin privilege to keep the white poor and black poor from forming a common cause. Poor whites in the South often fared no better than most black folk. Both were victims of an exploitative system that benefited an aristocratic minority. However, poor southern whites, because they possessed the benefits associated with white skin, enjoyed the consolation of knowing that they were not "niggers." This social status, despite their poverty, provided them with a psychological cushion and legal protections not enjoyed by black Americans. Thus "white" became understood as a culture of advantage and privilege uniting whites across class lines.[41]

A second historical event that melded the various white groups together in a common culture is the assimilation process by which southern and eastern European immigrants became members of the dominant group and thus considered "white." The historical details of this process are too complex for presentation here. Suffice it to note that by 1940, the Census Bureau ceased separate classifications for southern and eastern European immigrants, subsuming them under the general heading of "Caucasian (White)."[42]

In summary, Ruth Frankenberg offers this succinct "definition" of "whiteness":

First, whiteness is a location of structural advantage, of race privilege. Second, it is a "standpoint," a place from which white people look at ourselves, at others, and at society. Third, "whiteness" refers to a set of cultural practices that are usually unmarked and unnamed.... Among the effects on white people both of race privilege and of the dominance of whiteness are their seemingly normativity and their structured invisibility.[43]

So, if a key component of black culture is "the expectation of struggle," then a core element of white culture is *the presumption of dominance and entitlement,* that is, the presumption of being the norm or standard that measures all other frames of reference and to which all "others" should conform. To put this another way, white culture is a particular frame of reference or understanding of reality that does not acknowledge its particularity.

   "The struggle to be recognized and accepted as human in a racist society" versus *"the presumption of dominance and measure of normativity"*: these are the set of meanings and values that undergird the cultural products of black and white Americans. They also give us an important window into the dominant frame of reference that undergirds the meanings and values present in American public life and the personal identities of many white Americans. This perspective, that is, understanding racism as a cultural set of meanings and values informing a particular way of life, enables us to better grasp how a focus on culture helps us attend to the deeper roots of this social evil.

The Culture of Racism

Understanding culture as the set of meanings and values that inform a people's way of life enables us to get beneath the various interpersonal manifestations of racial animus and discrimination and thus better understand "racism" and its insidious tenacity. In the United States (and Western societies in general), racism functions as a culture, that is, a set of shared beliefs and assumptions that undergirds the economic, social, and political disparities experienced by different racial groups. This set of meanings and values provides the ideological foundation for a racialized society, where society's benefits and burdens are inequitably allotted among the various racial groups. This set of meanings and values not only answers questions about the significance of social patterns, customs, and policies. As a culture it is also formative; racism is a communal and learned frame of reference that shapes identity, consciousness, and behavior — the way a social group understands its place and worth.

In a perceptive analysis, theologian Gary Chamberlain articulates the cultural significance of racism in terms strikingly similar to Lonergan's understanding. Defining racism as a "symbol-system," he argues:

> In order to understand the depth of racism in American society and among practicing Christians, to grasp its persistence despite all rational arguments against it, racism is viewed as a substitute religion. . . . In this sense, racism is a symbol-system which functions as an unconscious, unreflective meaning system resting upon symbols of color and sex which are deeply embedded in the fears and anxieties of white Americans. The terms *white, black, mixing, mingling, blood* take on symbolic meanings and identity functions which reflect a world-view as strong or stronger than the Christian symbols of *cross, bread, wine, resurrection, brotherhood, family of man.*[44]

Chamberlain continues by positing that racism functions as an identity formation system that shapes the inner awareness and self-understanding of white Americans:

> Racism in American history has answered questions of meaning and identity for a people engaged in a struggle to determine who they were and why they existed as they did. . . . Blacks historically have told whites who they are not and what their place is not, a contrast identity. Racist symbols, institutionally expressed, gave meaning, motivation, and identity to white Americans' existence.[45]

Hence, he contends that racism is a symbol system that malforms, conforms, and deforms us into an alien identity radically at odds with authentic Christian belief, so much so that most whites are unaware of how their identity is shaped by this consciousness. As a consequence, note how Christianity itself becomes coopted, malformed in order to conform it to an alien identity.

Chamberlain's insight was expressed more colloquially in an earlier section. Recall the observation offered by a white woman who reflected on the invisibility of white identity until it is challenged by nonwhite others:

> White is transparent. That's the point of being the dominant race. Sure the whiteness is there, but you never think of it. If you're white you never have to think about it.... And if white folks remind each other about being white, too often the reminder is about threats by outsiders — nonwhites — who steal white entitlements like good jobs, a fine education, and the good life.[46]

This woman thus demonstrates how the cultural symbol "white" functions as a privileged racial "contrast identity," one that defines itself in opposition to that which is "other." And on the basis of this group identity, her racial group is "entitled" to social advantages and benefits.

The Reality of Unconscious Racism

Deeper insight into this understanding of racism as a culture — that is, as an underlying symbol system that (1) justifies race-based disparities, and (2) shapes identity and consciousness — comes from considering the phenomenon of "unconscious racism" as developed by critical race scholars. I focus on the ideas of a seminal advocate to this school of thought, Charles R. Lawrence.

In brief, "unconscious racism" connotes how race can operate as a negative — yet not conscious, deliberate, or intentional — decision-making factor, due to the pervasive cultural stigma attached to dark skin color in Western culture. Race functions as a largely unconscious or preconscious frame of perception, developed through cultural conditioning and instilled by socialization.

The core insight of "unconscious racism" is conveyed in the following paragraph. Though lengthy, it merits citation and reflection:

> Americans share a common historical and cultural heritage in which racism has played and still plays a dominant role. Because of this shared experience, we also inevitably share many ideas, attitudes, and beliefs that attach significance to an individual's race and induce negative feelings and opinions about nonwhites.... At the same time, most of us are unaware of our racism. We do not recognize the ways in which our cultural experience has influenced our beliefs about race or the occasions on which those beliefs affect our actions. In other words, a large part of the behavior that produces racial discrimination is influenced by unconscious racial motivation.[47]

Put more simply, because a racialized set of meanings and values permeates all of our society's cultural products, we learn our culture's "racial code" almost by osmosis. We absorb it tacitly through the everyday process of socialization and learning what it means to be an "American." So much so that this racial code can function on a level beneath our conscious awareness. This is what happens when a person who is otherwise well meaning and without conscious prejudice spontaneously acts or thinks in a racially negative way. "Where did that come from?" she may think in dismay or embarrassment. Such a reaction betrays the influence of the tacitly learned and absorbed racial meanings inherent in our culture.

Unconscious racism, then, denotes the influence of a cultural frame or lens that we have learned and act out of in unintentional and preconscious ways. It is a shorthand for the concrete effects that result from a racial conditioning that is transmitted through unconscious socialization, or what Lawrence calls "tacit understandings":

> Culture — including, for example, the media and an individual's parents, peers, and authority figures — transmits certain beliefs and preferences. Because these beliefs are so much a

part of the culture, they are not experienced as explicit lessons. Instead, they seem part of the individual's rational ordering of her perceptions of the world. The individual is unaware, for example, that the ubiquitous presence of a cultural stereotype has influenced her perception that blacks are lazy or unintelligent [or more prone to violence]. Because racism is so deeply ingrained in our culture, it is likely to be transmitted by *tacit understandings:* Even if a child is not told that blacks are inferior, he learns that lesson by observing the behavior of others. These tacit understandings, because they have never been articulated, are less likely to be experienced at a conscious level.[48]

The tacit, covert, hidden character of such racial bias, motivation, and conditioning is critical to an understanding of unconscious racism's insidious, pervasive, and largely unacknowledged impact:

> *A crucial factor in the process that produces unconscious racism is the tacitly transmitted cultural stereotype.* If an individual has never known a black doctor or lawyer or is exposed to blacks only through a mass media where they are portrayed in stereotyped roles of comedian, criminal, musician, or athlete, he is likely to deduce that blacks as a group are naturally inclined toward certain behavior and unfit for certain roles. *But the lesson is not explicit: It is learned, internalized, and used without an awareness of its source.* Thus an individual may select a white job applicant over an equally qualified black and honestly believe that this decision was based on observed intangibles unrelated to race. . . . Even the most thorough investigation of conscious motive will not uncover the race-based stereotype that has influenced his decision.[49]

Just as culture shapes one's consciousness and conditions one's thoughts, values, and actions, so too does racism shape behavior and belief. Two examples illustrate this point. Recall the research cited above in conjunction with the undesirability of black male applicants even when the alternative is a white male with a criminal record. Researcher Devah Pager acknowledges that most employers consciously want to do the right thing. Yet the problem is that they often "rely on instinct when hiring," with the result that latent biases influence the hiring process. She states, "One of the things I observed [is that] employers will ask black applicants upfront whether or not they had a criminal background. That suggests that there are some automatic associations between race and criminality. When employers are confronted with a young black man, some employers might automatically think that this young man may have a history of criminal involvement."[50]

Another example illustrating the influence of unconscious racism comes from its impact on voter decisions during the 2008 presidential election. This is well articulated in the following posting from a blogger on CNN's "political ticker":

> As a white male in a white state who has seen more black people on COPS than in real life, I have to say it does feel odd sometimes that I'm supporting Obama with every ounce of my being. But when I think of how irrational it would be to give into that weird feeling in favor of a man ... all because he is white ... well, that just isn't a prejudice I can live with. That's why I'm voting for Obama, no matter what COPS has led me to believe about minorities.[51]

Note how strange or weird he reports feeling when acting contrary to the dominant meanings and values that have formed him as he learned the racial code inherent in our culture. Yet also note how this influence, while formative, need not be determinative. One can choose to act out of another cultural frame or set of values. We will discuss this possibility in depth in later chapters.

Lawrence concludes that racism is a much more complex reality than our current system of jurisprudence recognizes. He declares, "requiring proof of conscious or intentional motivation as a prerequisite to ... [a] recognition that a decision is race-dependent ignores much of what we understand about how the human mind works. It also disregards the ... profound effect that the history of

American race relations has had on the individual and collective unconscious."⁵²

Katrina as a Case Study of "Cultured" Unconscious Racism

Let us further consider the culture of racism and its formative influence in light of some events that occurred in the aftermath of Hurricane Katrina. Because of the culture in which we live and the socialization we have received, "race" provides a major lens through which we witnessed, processed, and evaluated this event. Let us take but one example, yet a particularly emblematic one. The Associated Press published two photos of people in identical situations in the flooded waters of New Orleans. The first, of a black young man, carried the caption, "A young man walks through chest-deep flood water after looting a grocery store in New Orleans." The second showed two white men, with the caption, "Two residents wade through chest-deep water after finding bread and soda from a local grocery store after Hurricane Katrina came through the area of New Orleans." The people are engaged in identical actions, yet one is described as "looting," the other as "finding."

After a storm of protest ensued, the photos were removed from the Associated Press website. But the incident is telling. Clearly racial bias was at work. But was it deliberate and/or intentional? More than likely not. We need not, and must not, limit ourselves to a choice between deliberate conspiracy, racial innocence, or blatant bigotry. Using the concept of unconscious racism, Angela Davis explains the photo controversy by noting the widespread and pervasive association of dark-skinned people with crime and danger:

> One unconscious phenomenon that contributes to, or forms the basis of, this unconscious racism is the association of crime with black and brown people....It is that association and these unconscious beliefs that result in the captions on these photographs, and that causes so many to care more about

black people stealing televisions than white people causing the death of black lives through their neglect. And because these beliefs are unconscious, they are so difficult to eliminate or even address.[53]

This association of blacks with crime and criminality had effects far more devastating than biased captioning. It fueled frenzied reports of lawlessness, mayhem, murder, and rape occurring at the Superdome, the Convention Center, and throughout the city. Yet subsequent investigations showed little credible evidence of such behaviors. These nonverified rumors were simply reported as facts by the media. Racial bias? To be sure. But not necessarily intentional. Unconscious bias seems especially prevalent in chaotic or ambiguous conditions. As Lawrence notes, "In ambiguous social situations, it will always be easier to find evidence supporting an individual's assumed group characteristics than to find contradictory evidence."[54]

But attributing this reporting to unconscious bias is not to dismiss its often dire consequences. As a result of such erroneous news coverage, rooted in unconscious racial associations, public sympathy for Katrina's survivors was replaced by "anger and disdain."[55] Rescue efforts and food drops were suspended out of a fear of getting shot; police and the National Guard were given license to "shoot to kill"; suburban police forces turned back blacks fleeing the city at gunpoint, fearing that "they would turn their city into another Superdome." The sheriff of neighboring St. Tammany Parish openly admitted telling his deputies to engage in racial profiling and targeted policing, out of a conviction that people of color were more likely to be engaged in criminal activity than whites. He stated: "Now I don't get into calling people names and all that fact, but if you're gonna walk the streets of St. Tammany Parish with dread locks and 'Chee Wee' hairstyles, then you can expect to be getting a visit from a sheriff's deputy."[56] All of this because of the influence of unconscious racism, which causes us to see or fear danger in situations involving blacks that would not evoke such reactions in circumstances involving whites.[57]

There is yet another impact or effect of unconscious racism that needs to be noted, what Lawrence calls "racially selective sympathy and indifference." By this he means, "the unconscious failure to extend to a minority the same recognition of humanity, and hence the same sympathy and care, given as a matter of course to one's own group."[58] This manifestation of unconscious racism is important for understanding Jesse Jackson's assertion, made at the height of the storm: "America has a high tolerance for black suffering."[59] "Racially selective sympathy and indifference" also renders intelligible (though not excusable) the apparent negligence of public officials who knew that many would not be able to leave the city in the event of a catastrophe, yet did not care enough to develop comprehensive plans for their evacuation. Again, note that this was not necessarily a conscious decision, but perhaps due to the unnoted effects of socialization in a culture of racism. Certain lives thus become easier to ignore or, put another way, certain lives have a higher claim upon public energy and concern. "Racially selective sympathy and indifference" was also evidenced in the evacuations of white tourists from hotels and certain hospitals while the black and poor languished.[60]

Thus the events surrounding Katrina illumine both how and to what extent racial bias is still a major force in U.S. life. But it is a type of racism that is unacknowledged and easily denied, for it is largely unconscious or outside of personal awareness. Selective indifference and sympathy, rooted in tacit racial beliefs, underlies a great deal of society's neglect of poor persons of color.

Lawrence concludes that racism is a much more complex reality than is commonly recognized:

> Racism is a set of beliefs whereby we irrationally attach significance to something called race. . . . But racism in America is much more complex than either the conscious conspiracy of a power elite or the simple delusion of a few ignorant bigots. It is part of our common historical experience and, therefore, *a part of our culture. It arises from assumptions we have learned*

to make about the world, ourselves, and others, as well as
from the patterns of our fundamental social activities.[61]

In summary, racism functions as an ethos — as a pervasive symbol system of meaning, identity, and significance — much more than
as a set of discrete, consciously motivated acts. Racism, understood
as a pervasive symbol system of meaning, gives us the framework for
comprehending the significance of personal acts of racial animus. It
is a system of meaning that rests upon the fears and anxieties of
white Americans and is expressed in the cultural symbols, social
order, and public policies of the country. Racism is a cultural
phenomenon, a way of interpreting human color differences that
pervades the collective convictions, conventions, and practices of
American life. It significantly forms the identity of the dominant
group, that is to say, "the matrix in which persons develop and that
supplies the meanings and values that inform their lives."[62]

This understanding of racism as an identity-shaping culture
explains the diffuse yet palpable "culture shock" and intense resistance encountered among not a few white Americans at the election
of an African American president. Such an event, and the major
demographic changes underway, are a threat to their sense of identity and shake the foundations upon which they believe the country
was built. For many white Americans are ensnared, entangled,
and enmeshed — malformed, conformed, and deformed — by a
value-laden web of racial significance and meaning that it is largely
invisible and outside of their conscious awareness.

TO WHAT END?
THE JUSTIFICATION OF WHITE PRIVILEGE

This analysis helps us now appreciate *why* racial justice is resisted
in American life, the persistence of racism despite obvious changes,
and why racial tribalism is an ever-present threat. Recall that for
Lonergan, "culture stands to social order as soul to body, for
any element of social order will be rejected the moment it is
widely judged inappropriate, meaningless, irrelevant, useless, just

not worthwhile."[63] That is, culture animates social institutions and customs and expresses their meaning and significance. Culture provides the ideological foundation for social, political, and economic arrangements, which will be changed only when they are seen as contrary or foreign to the underlying cultural ethos. Hence, we must now consider the purpose of social arrangements that arise out of a culture of racism and endure despite major shifts and challenges.

This obviously is a complex matter. In what may be the most comprehensive examination of current race relations by an official body, the National Research Council concluded that the attitudes of the majority of whites toward blacks are fundamentally "ambivalent." Despite endorsing in principle the concepts of equal opportunity and respectful treatment, this body noted that "most whites do not yet accept blacks as social equals."[64] The Research Council's description of this fundamental ambivalence is worth citing in full:

> Black-white relations are important in determining the degree to which equal opportunity exists for black Americans. Whites desire equality of treatment in social institutions and in governmental policy; however, many whites are less likely to espouse or practice equality of treatment for blacks in their personal behavior. Thus, *at the core of black-white relations is a dynamic tension between many whites' expectations of American institutions and their expectations of themselves.* This state of affairs is a significant improvement from 45 years ago. . . . But the divergence between social principle and individual practice frequently leads to white avoidance of blacks in those institutions [e.g., housing, employment, and education] in which equal treatment is most needed. The result is that American institutions do not provide the full equality of opportunity that Americans desire.[65]

As a result of this fundamental racial ambivalence, most whites, while endorsing equality of opportunity in the abstract, endorse it far less when equal treatment results in:

* close or frequent social contact;

* or involvement of significant numbers of blacks;

* or blacks being promoted to positions of significant power and decision making.[66]

The Research Council's conclusions resonate quite well with the insights offered by Martin Luther King Jr. in his last major text. Toward the end of his life, he provided what I consider a classic description of the fundamental racial ambivalence in contemporary America:

> Negro and white have a fundamentally different definition [of "equality"]. Negroes have proceeded from a premise that equality means what it says, and they have taken white Americans at their word when they talked of it as an objective. But most whites in America in 1967, including many persons of goodwill, proceed from a premise that equality is a loose expression for *improvement.* White America is not even psychologically organized to close the gap — essentially it seeks only to make it less painful and less obvious but in most respects to retain it.... *The great majority of Americans are suspended between ... opposing attitudes. They are uneasy with injustice but unwilling yet to pay a significant price to eradicate it.*[67]

What this suggests is that the opposition to racial equality — for the most part — no longer is rooted in deliberate malice or an explicit espousal of white superiority. This is a major and significant change from the not too distant past. Most Americans today are committed to the values of interracial decency and respect. However, opposition to full equality now takes the form of various strategies employed to justify and defend *white privilege, entitlement, and social dominance.*[68] Again, the observations of the *Common Destiny* study are cogent:

> [Today] differential treatment of blacks infrequently takes the form of blatant hostility and overt discrimination. Differential

treatment is most likely to occur when it allows someone to avoid close interracial contact; *it prevents the establishment of interracial relations of equal status or black dominance*, especially in employment and housing; and it is possible to find a nonracial explanation for differential treatment. For example, blacks who find little difficulty gaining entry- and even middle-level employment positions frequently encounter barriers to upper-level positions that would involve *significant authority over whites or the need to interact with them in social settings* like private clubs.[69]

White privilege, then, is the reason for the ongoing presence of racism and the resistance that efforts to unseat it encounters. Racism, understood as an underlying set of meanings, values, and beliefs, provides the ideological justification for "constellations of political and economic power."[70] The concrete forms of these social arrangements have varied in U.S. history, taking the forms of slavery, colonialism, Jim Crow segregation and humiliation, overt discrimination, and token presence. Racism's manifestations change, sometimes dramatically. But at its core, racism always involves the use of skin color differences for the purpose of assigning social rank or privilege. What results, then, is a system of racially conferred — and denied — privilege, advantage, benefits, and status. Racism connotes a social context where color differences are used for saddling ostracism and stigma upon some, and conferring advantage and benefit to others. In a racist society, "white" is more than a skin color. It is a social status that gives those designated as white "the ability to enjoy privileges and benefits which flow from it."[71]

The Nature of White Privilege

Most of us are trained to see how racism disadvantages or burdens people of color. Racism obviously results in inferior and unjust treatment for many. We are not so accustomed to see how racism results in unfair advantages or benefits for the dominant racial group. "White privilege" shifts the focus from how people of color are harmed by racism to how white Americans derive advantages because of it. White privilege is the flip-side and inescapable corollary of racial injustice. Racial injustice comes about to preserve and protect white privilege.

"White privilege" refers to the reality that in U.S. society "there are opportunities which are afforded whites that people of color simply do not share."[72] These advantages range from greater ease in hailing a taxi and moving into whatever neighborhood they can afford, to easier access to positions of social influence and political power, to the presumption that their race will not work against them when seeking employment and in other social situations. Being racially advantaged might be unwanted or undesired by individual white Americans. In fact, some white Americans are distressed when they become aware of the reality of white privilege. Regardless of an individual's desires, an "invisible package of unearned assets" is enjoyed by white people because of the racial consciousness that is subtly pervasive in our social customs and institutions.[73] White privilege illustrates how pervasive beliefs about the inadequacies of people of color become expressed by or entrenched in our society's institutional policies, social customs, cultural media, and political processes. These social habits and policies then function to reinforce the individual white person's beliefs about a sense of entitlement and to instill in racial minorities a sense of inferiority.

The Genesis of White Privilege: A Case Study

The privileged status of whiteness did not "just happen." It has been intentionally constructed over a long period of time. White privilege is the result of social policies, institutions, and procedures that deliberately created a system to advance the welfare of white Americans and impeded the opportunities of persons of color.[74]

Among the most important effects and manifestations of white privilege are the economic advantages that have been conferred upon white Americans by public policy and political power throughout our history. Racism inevitably causes economic disadvantages and burdens for groups of color. Here are several key events and movements that illustrate the links between race, economic impoverishment, and economic opportunity — events that both burdened people of color seeking to escape poverty and eased the way for white Americans desiring to advance their economic fortunes.

+ *The institution of slavery.* Slavery means exploited labor; the labor of enslaved Africans was essential for creating wealth for others from which they often derived no benefit. Slavery resulted in the creation of wealth not only for the white slaveholding elite, but for all who benefited from and participated in a "slavery-centered" economy (for example, merchants, bankers, fishermen, shipbuilders, traders, auctioneers, bounty hunters, and immigrant farmers).[75]

+ *The Indian Removal Act of 1830.* By this act of Congress, Native Americans were forcibly removed from their lands and resettled in territory that was of no interest to whites. Their property was then made available for white settlers. This stolen land became the basis for white economic enrichment that could be passed on as an inheritance to future generations. This economic disenfranchisement also led to the impoverishment of future generations of Native Americans.[76]

+ *The Supreme Court Decision of* Plessy v. Ferguson *(1896).* This decision enshrined the realities of racial segregation, second-class citizenship, and "separate but equal" facilities in our national life. Among the many pernicious effects of this decision was the creation of inferior educational opportunities for African Americans. They and other communities of color endured severely restricted access to quality education. Segregated schools were poorly funded in comparison to their white counterparts. This created a deficit of educational attainment — the effects of which are still with us — that translated into economic disadvantage in the labor market and compromised participation in higher paying and socially prestigious professions.[77]

+ *The exclusion of Asian Indians from eligibility for U.S. citizenship.* In 1923, the U.S. Supreme Court (*U.S. v. Bhagat Singh Thind*) ruled that while Asian Indians were indeed "Caucasians" by race, they could not be considered "white." The result was that many Asian Indians were stripped of their naturalized citizenship. This meant that they were unable to legally own property; many had their assets taken from them and given to whites.[78]

* *The exclusion of domestics and agricultural workers from the Social Security Act of 1935.* At the height of the Depression this law created a new public policy that established a basic level of economic security for many of the country's workers. However, by excluding domestics and agricultural workers, this act effectively denied Social Security pensions and benefits to 75 percent of black workers.[79]

* *The provisions of the Wagner Act (1935), allowing unions to exclude African Americans from union membership.* This legislation granted new legal protections and recognitions to labor unions and gave many working-class whites access to higher wages and benefits. However, because the act also allowed unions to exclude blacks from union membership and its benefits, it legally protected white laborers from competition in the job market, creating economic opportunities reserved for whites and further maintaining the existence of a lower paid, exploited labor pool of color.

* *The failure of the Federal Housing Administration (1940s and 1950s) to grant loans to even minimally integrated neighborhoods.* This agency provided low-cost government-guaranteed loans to working-class families, enabling mass home ownership and the accumulation of wealth that could be passed on to heirs. Ninety-eight percent of these loans were given to whites; blacks were granted less than 2 percent. The refusal to grant loans to integrated neighborhoods was a practice known as "redlining."

Many more historical examples can be cited. These suffice to demonstrate how white privilege was deliberately created and often state-sanctioned. They demonstrate how pervasive beliefs about the inadequacies of people of color — the underlying cultural set of meanings and values — become expressed by or entrenched in our society's institutional policies, social customs, and political processes for the purpose of maintaining white group privileges and advantages.

A Personal Reflection on White Privilege

Racism and white privilege are not abstractions or sociological theories. They harm — and benefit — real people. I have just documented how the privileged status of whiteness was socially constructed and officially sanctioned and how this resulted in economic advantage for some and a burden for others. The story of my family illustrates this well. My father was trained as a carpenter; he received his associate's degree in carpentry from Milwaukee's technical college in the mid-1950s. Yet he was never employed as a carpenter nor did he ever practice his trade. For he was refused admission into the local carpenter's union, due to that union's informal but iron-clad exclusion of blacks from membership. He was relegated to the ranks of unskilled laborers: working as an orderly in the county mental hospital, stocking shelves at a local department store, and sheltering his family in the local housing projects. He forfeited not only the higher salary that should rightfully have been his, but also the accumulated capital that could have come from home owner-ship and investment, which could also have been a legacy for his children and their descendants. Racism translated into economic dis-advantage and exploitation. That's real. It has affected not only me, but many others in this nation and continues to do so.

But my family's story also illustrates the reality of white privilege. For some person, some other family, some racial group, benefited from my father's exclusion as a competitor for a valued job. Some other family was able to purchase a home and benefit from the economic stability which that resource conferred. Some other family was able to pass on that value in an estate to its heirs, providing them with a "leg up" in life — perhaps the seed money for a college education, for a first house, or for a business opportunity. And some members of those families are also readers of this work.

This, then, is white privilege: the uneven and unfair distribu-tion of power, privilege, land, and material resources favoring white people. White privilege is not an abstraction; it is real. White privilege is the range of unearned (and at times, unwanted) advantages that come simply from possession of an attribute our society prizes, namely, the status of being considered "white." When I say members of those families who benefited from my father's exclusion are now readers of this text, I am not saying that they (or you) are bad people. The individuals may not have chosen it, realized it, or even desired it. They may not have had a prejudiced bone in their bodies. But the advantages are real nonetheless, as is the damage of racial injustice. We will never adequately deal with the reality of racial injustice, and its generational effects, unless we name its causes and attack its sources.

In summary, today the continuing resistance to racial equality, despite undeniable progress, can be largely explained by a fundamental ambivalence on the part of the majority of white Americans: their desire to denounce blatant racial injustices, and yet preserve a situation of white social dominance and privilege. To say it plainly, most Americans are committed to both interpersonal decency and systemic inequality. Racial equality encounters ongoing resistance because this nation is still committed to maintaining relationships of white cultural, political, and social dominance, that is to say, a culture of "white supremacy."[80]

CONCLUSION

The goal of this chapter was to articulate an understanding of racism that is more adequate than the "commonsense" one: Person A deliberately, consciously, and intentionally acting in a negative way to Person B because of his or her skin color. Such an understanding cannot account for the pervasiveness of racial discrimination despite momentous changes nor for the deep anxiety that many feel in the face of the changing racial demography of the United States.

Racism has never been solely or principally about insults, slurs, or mere exclusion, as demeaning and as harmful as these are. These are but the symptoms of a deeper malady. Racism entails more than conscious ill will, more than deliberate acts of avoidance, malice, and violence perpetrated by individuals. Though such events are still of concern, they do not take us to the heart of the matter. For despite measurable progress in combating individual prejudice and blatant discrimination, the systemic obstacles and barriers that stymie the life chances of persons of color still endure, and race remains a principal lens for interpreting and understanding U.S. society.

Racism, at its core, is a set of meanings and values that inform the American way of life. It is a way of understanding and interpreting skin color differences so that white Americans enjoy a privileged social status with access to advantages and benefits to the detriment, disadvantage, and burden of persons of color. It is the set of cultural assumptions, beliefs, and convictions that justify the existence of a "kinder, gentler" racism, that is, one that advocates interpersonal decency, kindness, and respect for all while it yet protects white systemic advantage and benefit.

U.S. Catholic ethical reflection, if it is to be adequate and effective, must adopt a structural and systemic approach to racism. This means approaching this social evil as a cultural phenomenon, that is, as an underlying color symbol system that (1) justifies race-based disparities; (2) shapes not only behavior, but also one's identity and consciousness; and (3) often operates at a preconscious or nonrational level that escapes personal awareness. Effective moral analysis and action require understanding racism as a culture of white advantage, privilege, and dominance that has derivative personal, interpersonal, and institutional manifestations. In the words of David Wellman:

> Racism is not simply about prejudice.... Racism can mean culturally sanctioned beliefs which, regardless of the intentions involved, defend the advantages whites have because of the subordinated positions of racial minorities.... Thus racism is analyzed as culturally acceptable beliefs that defend social advantages that are based on race.... Racism today remains essentially what it has always been: a defense of racial privilege.[81]

Chapter Two

An Analysis of
Catholic Social Teaching
on Racism

I N THE PREVIOUS CHAPTER, I argued for a more cultural and
systemic understanding of racism. I contend that racism is a
deeply entrenched symbol system of meanings and values attached
to skin color that provides group identity, shapes personal consciousness, and justifies the existence of race-based economic, social,
and political disparities. This approach better accounts for its various manifestations in contemporary U.S. society. We now turn to
the task of analyzing Catholic engagement and reflection on racial
justice in light of this cultural understanding.

Perhaps the most remarkable thing to note concerning U.S. Catholic social teaching on racism is how little there is to note. Since
the beginning of the modern civil rights movement with the 1954
Brown school desegregation decision, the U.S. Bishops' Conference
has issued only three statements solely devoted to racial justice in the
name of the entire body of bishops (1958, 1968, and 1979). None
of these is marked by the depth or rigor of social analysis that one
finds in many of their other social justice statements (for example,
the landmark pastoral letters on the challenge of peace and economic
justice). During this time, the church's universal magisterium, specifically the Pontifical Council for Justice and Peace, has developed
only two documents that are devoted to this topic (1988 and 2001).

43

All of these statements are rather "thin," both in their length and the theological reflection and analysis they offer. Furthermore, since the publication of the 1979 document, *Brothers and Sisters to Us,* fewer than 18 percent of U.S. archbishops and bishops have issued individual or collective statements concerning the sin of racism.[1]

Other than these few documents, what the bishops themselves call the "radical evil" of racism is mentioned only in incidental and passing ways in official Catholic social teaching, including relatively recent resources such as the *Compendium of the Social Doctrine of the Church.* To say that racial injustice is not a major concern of Catholic social teaching would be an understatement. In the words of the foremost proponent of black theology, James H. Cone, "It is amazing that racism could be so prevalent and violent in American life and yet so absent in white theological discourse."[2]

In what follows, I will offer an exposition and analysis of the three major pastoral statements issued by the U.S. Roman Catholic hierarchy in the last half of the twentieth century, roughly corresponding to the beginning of the modern civil rights movement. These constitute the official response and position of the Catholic Church in America to the presence of racism and the evils that it causes. The historical milieu and ecclesial context of each statement will be sketched, the main features of the document's content summarized, and the aftermath and effects of the statement will be noted.

I will also examine more recent statements issued by individual bishops in the United States, showing the principal characteristics and moral analysis found within them. Finally, I will offer a critique of these documents in the light of the understanding of racism presented in the previous chapter, a black liberationist hermeneutic, and the experience of black Catholic membership.

PROLOGUE:
A CONTEXT FOR THIS DISCUSSION

To situate this body of teaching, I will discuss some historical markers that illustrate the importance of this topic and some recurring dynamics in the Catholic approach to racial injustice.

The Browning of the Catholic Church

Along with the rest of the nation, the Catholic Church in the United States is undergoing a dramatic shift in its demographic composition. At least 46 percent of its members are people of color.³ In many dioceses, Hispanics constitute the largest single group of Catholics — if not an outright majority. Every Sunday in this country, Mass is celebrated in dozens of languages; among these are English, Spanish, Italian, Chinese, Korean, Hmong, Vietnamese, and Polish. U.S. Catholics are increasingly diverse in our racial and ethnic heritages, in our languages and skin colors, in our ways of perceiving life and celebrating our faith. By God's grace, the church in the United States is rapidly becoming a microcosm of the world's peoples.

Yet the diversity of the Catholic Christian community is not always seen as a cause for celebration; too often it is a source of tension and discomfort. The enduring residential segregation of U.S. society is mirrored in the racial and ethnic composition of Catholic parishes, which are often geographically based and thus reflect the racial and economic disparities of our nation's neighborhoods. Many persons of color can tell stories of how they received a rude welcome when visiting a so-called "white" parish. Some even report they were refused the "sign of peace" as the community prepared to approach the altar to receive the Eucharist.⁴ In addition, many Catholics are uneasy when they are asked to worship in multicultural or multilingual ways. So often one hears complaints such as, "Why do we have to sing in Spanish?" "Don't they have their own church?" "Gospel music isn't really Catholic, is it?" Rather than rejoicing in the God-given diversity of the human family, too often Catholics reflect the racial attitudes and divisions of U.S. society.

Moreover, even though almost half of its members are persons of color, this reality is not reflected in the church's leadership. The conference of bishops, the members of diocesan staffs, the senior executives of Catholic agencies and organizations, the major superiors of religious orders, and the faculties of Catholic seminaries and educational institutions are still predominately — even overwhelmingly — white.

Sadly, the words of the few Catholic African American bishops, stated over twenty years ago, remain too relevant today: "Blacks and other minorities still remain absent from many aspects of Catholic life and are only meagerly represented on the decision-making level.... This racism, at once subtle and masked, still festers within our Church as within our society. It is this racism that in our minds remains the major impediment to evangelization in our community."[5]

Pope John Paul's Challenge and Its Reception

The next historical marker is the bold summons that Pope John Paul II gave to our country during his last pastoral visit to the United States in January of 1999. In St. Louis, while challenging Catholics to be "unconditionally pro-life," he declared:

> As the new millennium approaches, there remains another great challenge facing this community...[and] the whole country: *to put an end to every form of racism, a plague which ...[is] one of the most persistent and destructive evils of the nation.*[6]

Thus spoke the Holy Father in 1999. However, the pontiff's prophetic call was not universally embraced by the Catholic faithful. Indeed, a major Catholic commentator speaking on EWTN, the Catholic cable network program, immediately after the pope's address, lauded John Paul's uncompromising stances concerning the death penalty and euthanasia but noted that the pope's "curious remarks about racism" demonstrated "how ill-served the Holy Father is by his advisors, since racism is no longer a pressing social issue in the United States."

This moment is important for two reasons. First, this particular cable network (EWTN) is the self-styled "media presence" of the U.S. Catholic Church. That such statements could be aired on a network renowned for its orthodoxy, and that they were not officially repudiated or challenged, suggests that standing against racism is not a major marker of Catholic identity or orthodoxy. Second, this event illustrates a recurring dynamic in the U.S. Catholic engagement with racism, namely, that the church of Rome has been more vigilant, solicitous, concerned, and forthright regarding racial injustice and the plight of racial minorities in the United States than have U.S. Catholics and their leaders. Rome has shown a willingness to confront racial inequality in a way that the U.S. church has yet to muster.[7]

The Controversy over the Federated Colored Catholics

The final historical marker concerns the controversy over the existence of the Federated Colored Catholics, a group founded by the black Catholic layman Thomas Wyatt Turner in 1924. One of the group's major concerns was to develop a black voice for the concerns of black Catholics within their church. As Turner declared, "Too often issues related to the colored are discussed without any contribution from the people themselves."[8] In a series of conventions held between 1924 and 1932, this group pressed for an end to Negro exclusion "from the normal life of the Catholic Church in America"[9] manifested in racially segregated churches and barriers to admission to Catholic schools, organizations, and hospitals.

At its 1930 convention in Detroit, the Federated Colored Catholics articulated these aspirations in the following declaration:

We wish to earn a decent livelihood; free from interference based upon merely racial attitudes.

We desire to educate all our boys and girls in Catholic schools, from the primary school to the university, according to each one's native ability.

We desire admission to Catholic institutions, [such as hospitals, parishes, and the Knights of Columbus], . . . to which, as Catholics and human beings, we may legitimately lay claim.

We wish as Catholics to insist upon the sacredness of human life. We condemn every violation of law in the taking of life, no matter what the crime. [This is a reference to the widespread practice of brutal and sadistic lynching of blacks, principally men].

We wish to enjoy the full rights of citizenship, in direct proportion to the duties and sacrifices expected of our group, and cheerfully rendered by us to our country in peace and in war.

We wish all our fellow citizens... to be freed from the obsession that Negroes' progress is harmful to American civilization; and to recognize... that the good of one group is the good of all.

We do not wish to be treated as "a problem," but as a multitude of human beings, sharing a common destiny and the common privilege of the Redemption with all humankind.[10]

However, this program — indeed the organization itself — ran into stiff opposition from the leading white Catholic "liberals" of the time. The most prominent among them, Father John LaFarge, gave voice to a major objection, namely, the attempt to bring "unified, mass pressure to bear upon the Church in order to obtain recognition of their rights." For LaFarge (who, I hasten to note, was among the most progressive white voices on racial matters of this period) and other white liberal Catholics, the tone of demand found in the black leaders' statement made them equate a group dedicated to Negro solidarity with a "separatist organization." The controversy centered over two questions. First, whether it was better to fight for the rights of Negroes in the church through activism, or to promote better race relations through discussion and education? Second, what was the role of white clergy in this black organization: to encourage black leadership or be a force for white paternalism? LaFarge's position is quite clear. He wrote, "Although the Negro is the victim of discrimination, he does not necessarily know the answer or the cure."[11]

LaFarge did more than just write. In 1932, he orchestrated a constitutional revision, led by a group called the Clergy Conference on Negro Welfare, which changed the organization's name from the Federated Colored Catholics to the Catholic Interracial Council. Turner was removed as the head of this new group. The new group's leadership was effectively decided and controlled by white clergy. LaFarge then articulated the group's new approach: "Direct assault will not dislodge [racial] customs and taboos. The idols will bow out only when people have become sufficiently enlightened to wish to remove them of themselves. Hence, basic to the situation is a program of education, in the sense of public relations for the truth."[12]

Indicative of this new approach is a manifesto issued by a group of twelve white New York college students in 1933. LaFarge gave extensive presentation and enthusiastic praise to their resolutions:

To maintain that the Negro as a human being and as a citizen is entitled to the rights of life, liberty, and pursuit of happiness and to the essential opportunities of life and the full measure of social justice.

To be kind and courteous to every colored person, remembering the heavy yoke of injustice and discrimination he is bearing.

To say a kind word for him on every proper occasion.

Not to speak slightingly or use nicknames which tend to humiliate, offend, or discourage him.

To remember that the Catholic Church and the Catholic program of social justice have been called "the greatest hope of the colored race."

To recognize that the Negro shares my membership in the Mystical Body of Christ and the privileges that flow therefrom and to conduct myself in accordance therewith.

To give liberally on the Sundays of the year when the collections are devoted to the heroic missionaries laboring among the Negro group.

To become increasingly interested in the welfare of the Negro; to engage actively in some form of Catholic Action looking to the betterment of his condition, spiritually and materially.[13]

Comparing the two sets of resolutions, one cannot help notic-
ing the stunning contrast. The second reflects an attitude of benign
paternalism, seeing blacks as a group in need of white sympathy
and services. They are considered to be a "missioned to" people
who are not acknowledged to have a sense of agency or initiative.
Indeed, as we saw in the deliberations of the white clergy, there is
a real suspicion — if not fear — of black leadership or initiative. To
anticipate a contrast to be developed later, these white liberals evidence great *sympathy* for the plight of the victims of social injustice,
but little real *compassion*.

Most important, the first manifesto from the black Catholic leaders calls for systemic changes. It critiques the institution of racial
segregation and advocates genuine racial equality with whites. The
white resolutions have no call for systemic change. Rather they
focus on treating black individuals with courtesy, decency, and
respect. The contrast could not be more glaring: one approach advocates social transformation; the other calls for good manners. One
presses for justice; the other counsels kindness.

Understanding this dynamic is key for appreciating what is to
follow. For LaFarge's approach of combating racism through good
manners, education, reason, and interracial dialogue becomes the
dominant approach of the U.S. Catholic Church, an approach that
endures even until today. This orientation is a constant in the history
of Catholic engagement with racism, and it is important to note that
it represents the thinking of the most progressive or enlightened
white Catholics, until very recently.

With this context, let us now examine the various statements of
the collective body of Catholic bishops.

DISCRIMINATION AND
THE CHRISTIAN CONSCIENCE (1958)[14]

Perhaps the watershed event in the history of twentieth-century
American race relations is the landmark decision of the Supreme
Court in 1954, *Brown v. Topeka Board of Education.* In this deci-
sion, the Court rejected the doctrine of "separate but equal" in

the area of education. It declared that segregated facilities of their very nature are "inherently inferior" and called upon educational facilities to be integrated "with all deliberate speed."

This Supreme Court decision is indicative of the historical and social climate of the 1958 bishops' statement. Racism, as evidenced in prejudicial and discriminatory attitudes, customs, and behaviors, enjoyed the protection and favor of the law. Especially — though not exclusively — in the South, unequal treatment between blacks and whites was mandated even in the most ordinary circumstances of life such as eating meals in a restaurant, visiting a public park, or traveling on a bus.

The overt racism of daily social interactions was also manifest in the political and economic spheres. Fear of reprisals and physical violence from the Ku Klux Klan and White Citizens Councils kept all but a small fraction of the eligible black population from registering to vote. Black representation in the major professions of law and medicine was woefully inadequate and in some states virtually nonexistent — and these few persons were severely limited as to their clientele and the places where they could practice. Segregated housing patterns were the norm. While housing and neighborhood patterns were not always regulated by law, the effective use of "block busting" and racial steering techniques resulted in a de facto segregation almost as rigid and blatant as a de jure system.

With the 1954 Supreme Court decision, an era of attempts to crack this system of hard-core segregation began in earnest. Martin Luther King Jr.'s nonviolent methods of economic boycotts and peaceful demonstrations achieved the desegregation of Montgomery's buses. Efforts were made to desegregate school systems; often these were met with violence, as in the case of Little Rock in 1957.

It was in this context of a nation attempting to come to grips with the challenge of desegregation and the upsetting of longstanding cultural customs that the American bishops issued their 1958 statement. In this document, the bishops voiced their concern that the "transcendent moral issues" involved in the quest for racial justice and equality had been forgotten or obscured. Noting that this was a multifaceted problem that had been analyzed from the disciplines of law, history, economics, and sociology, the bishops declared that "the time has come...to cut through the maze of secondary or less essential issues and to come to the heart of the problem. The heart of the race question is moral and religious" (187–88). Thus the bishops' intention was to address the moral and religious aspects of the question, in particular the need for an individual conversion or change of "poisoned attitudes" toward our fellow men (188).

There are four doctrinal bases upon which the bishops based their moral judgment of compulsory segregation: (1) the "universal love of God for all mankind" revealed especially in the expiatory death of Jesus for all; (2) Jesus' mandates to love one's neighbor and "to teach all nations," implying that all men are brothers and sisters and neighbors to one another; (3) the intrinsic universality of the Christian faith, which "knows not the distinctions of race, color, or nationhood"; and (4) the natural moral law "that God has implanted in the souls of all men," which teaches that each human being "has an equal right to life, to justice before the law, to marry and rear a family under human conditions, and to an equitable opportunity to use the goods of this earth for his needs and those of his family" (188–89).

Upon these foundations the bishops established two principles to govern the behavior and attitudes of Christians in the realms of race relations: (1) the equality of all peoples in the sight of God, rooted in the fact of humanity's common creation, redemption, and eternal destiny; and (2) the obligation to love our fellow human beings. This Christian love, the bishops stated, was not "a matter of emotional likes or dislikes...but a firm purpose to do good to all men..." (189).

In light of the above reasoning, the bishops reached the main conclusion of their statement. It was their judgment that enforced segregation could not be reconciled with the Christian view of the human person. For segregation "in itself and by its very nature imposes a stigma of inferiority upon the segregated people" and as a matter of historical fact it "has led to oppressive conditions and the denial of basic human rights for the Negro" (190).

In this document, the bishops made no specific recommendations or proposals for action. They merely called upon all to "act quietly, courageously, and prayerfully" and urged that any concrete plans for action be based on "prudence," which was defined as that virtue "that inclines us to view problems in their proper perspective" (191–92). They deplored both "gradualism" and the "rash impetuosity" that leads to "ill-timed and ill-considered ventures" (192). They commended instead a "method of quiet conciliation" (187). Clearly the bishops had no intention of making this document a bold clarion call to action. Catholics were not being urged to become proactive agents of racial justice. Rather, the bishops hoped that the faithful would "seize the mantle of leadership from both the agitator and the racist." While they stated their position firmly and clearly, a calm, balanced, reasoned tone pervades the document. It is a cautious and deliberately crafted statement of the policy and position of the Catholic Church on the matter of racism and especially mandatory segregation.

In general, the immediate response of the Catholic press to this statement was positive. Words such as "strong," "impressive," and "historic" were used to describe it. But the document had little secular significance or influence. There are at least two reasons for this. A major reason lies in the tardiness of the Catholic response — over four years *after* the Supreme Court's decision — as compared with the earlier statements of twenty-one other major American Christian denominations. The Catholic Church was the only religious body whose national assembly first issued a statement on the topic as late as 1958; all the other major Christian bodies had issued statements by early 1957, with some having done so as soon as 1954. To put it bluntly, the Catholic Church was very "late to the party."

The second reason stems from the lack of specificity in the Catholic response as compared to similar documents by Protestant bodies. The Protestant statements tended to be more concrete, calling for support of the Supreme Court decision, the integration of church facilities, and the effective extension of the Negro's right to vote. Many contained explicit condemnations of the Ku Klux Klan, White Citizens Councils, and violent, lawless attacks on integration efforts. None of these realities are even mentioned in the Catholic document. Despite their judgment that compulsory segregation was incompatible with Christian belief, there was no call to desegregate Catholic facilities or fraternal organizations. In contrast to the Protestant statements, the Catholic response could only be seen as general and vague; consequently it was easily dismissed as being merely a pious exhortation.[15]

A possible — indeed probable — explanation for both this tardiness and lack of specificity is that this statement was issued reluctantly under pressure from Rome and over the objections of leading U.S. church authorities. John Cronin, a priest then working at the National Catholic Welfare Conference, was the principal drafter of the statement. Years later, he published an account of the circumstances surrounding the document's genesis. He relates how Rome was insistent that the bishops issue a letter on racism, and indeed Cronin had one ready in draft form. But the chair of the Conference's Administrative Board resisted, fearing "it would create division among the bishops." The day before he died, Pope Pius XII sent a cablegram to the apostolic delegate in the United States, "ordering the American bishops to issue the statement at once." After Pius's death, the delegate held an emergency meeting with the American cardinals preparing for the conclave to elect a new pope. Cronin states, "They decided to suppress the cablegram as unofficial, since it lacked the papal seal." Cronin relates that if it were not for the forceful interventions of Cardinal O'Boyle of Washington, D.C., prevailing over the lingering recalcitrance and obstructions of other American cardinals, the statement in all likelihood would not have been issued.[16]

One should also note that the statement apparently had little impact upon efforts to deal with racism within the church itself. William Osborne describes his 1967 work, *The Segregated Covenant,* as "the story of the slow and unsteady implementation of the bishops' declaration" of 1958.[17] Osborne based this conviction upon the following observations: the membership lists of civil rights groups (for example, CORE and the NAACP) were under-representative of the Catholic population; Catholic youth were "notoriously absent" from the sit-ins and freedom rides of the civil rights movement; Negro Catholics were refused admission to Catholic schools and even hospitals; a separate Negro Catholic Church "existed in every major city in the United States"; there was a serious scarcity of Negro priests; and the rank and file of Catholic people "exhibited no distinguishable attitudes or practices vis-à-vis civil rights" from the rest of the population. The strong impression one has is that the average Catholic had not read the 1958 statement — much less agreed with it.[18] Thus at the end of his study, Osborne concludes:

> The position of the Catholic Church on discrimination in employment, housing, and access to public accommodations is clear and convincing. But this is the policy statement of an organization: it is not to be mistaken for the response of the Catholic people, nor even of the bishops or clergy. As this study reveals, there are still several large dioceses where these problems receive only marginal attention, if any at all.[19]

Such were the effects and aftermath of the Catholic bishops' 1958 statement.

THE NATIONAL RACE CRISIS (1968)[20]

> Now — ten years later — it is evident that we did not do enough; we have much more to do.... It became clear that we failed to change the attitudes of many believers. (175)

Ten years later, the Catholic bishops again found it necessary to address themselves to the racial problems and tensions of the United States. As the quote above indicates, there was the realization that their previous statement did not do what was intended. American Catholics did not respond to the nuanced, careful, and reasoned articulation of church teaching on matters of race. What events moved the bishops to this realization and caused them to address the racial situation one more time?

There are perhaps three factors that are essential components of the historical and social context of this statement. The first is the "long, hot summer" of 1967 when racially motivated rioting and civil disturbances rocked many major urban centers. Newark, Detroit, and Washington, D.C., were among the hardest hit. These urban rebellions stoked fears of racial insurrection in the nation. In the wake of these disturbances, the Presidential Advisory Commission on Civil Disorders (popularly called the Kerner Commission) was formed to discover why the rioting occurred and what could be done to avoid future racial disturbances.

The release of the Kerner Commission's report in March of 1968 is the second significant event leading up to the publication of the 1968 Catholic statement.[21] The Kerner Report was a devastatingly direct, honest, and dire exposé and assessment of the explosive and volatile nature of the nation's racial situation. The major findings of the Kerner Commission were:

This is our basic conclusion: Our nation is moving toward two societies, one black, one white — separate and unequal.

Discrimination and segregation have long permeated much of American life; they now threaten the future of every American.

To pursue our present course will involve the continuing polarization of the American community and, ultimately, the destruction of basic democratic values.

... White society is deeply implicated in the ghetto. White institutions created it, white institutions maintain it, and white society condones it.

White racism is essentially responsible for the explosive mixture which has been accumulating in our cities since the end of World War II.

The most fundamental [cause of the mood of violence in 1967] is the racial attitude and behavior of white Americans toward black Americans.

The Kerner Commission's report is given extensive presentation because of its impact upon the bishops' deliberations on the matter of race. It established in an undeniable and irrefutable fashion the pervasiveness and urgent seriousness of the country's race problem.

A third component of the social-historical matrix of this statement was the assassination of Martin Luther King Jr. on April 4, 1968. The killing of this civil rights figure was a clear sign to many of how deeply rooted racial tensions were in America and the distance the country had yet to travel toward achieving a solution to its racial problems. His death triggered another wave of rioting and civil disturbances in over sixty-two cities, which raised the fear that the country would have to endure another "long, hot summer." Furthermore, his death opened the possibility that more militant "Black Power" advocates would seize the leadership of the civil rights movement.

Not only is the historical context important for understanding this document; there was also a significant development within the U.S. church itself: the publication of a statement from the National Black Catholic Clergy Caucus (NBCCC) in April of 1968. This inaugural meeting of the NBCCC was the first national gathering of the country's black Catholic clergy and marked the first attempt in many decades of black Catholics to speak to their church from the perspective of their black experience. Joseph A. Francis, a participant in that 1968 meeting, who later served as auxiliary bishop of Newark, describes the mood of this convocation:

> We had been told for such a long time and in so many ways by so many persons that we were second rate, that we were less than equal and would never amount to anything in society and in the church. . . . We were determined to set out on a course of self-determination which would not only prove our detractors and oppressors wrong and benefit all of our people, including our oppressors, but would impress the Catholic Church, in which we believed and which we loved, to take us seriously and begin to place [us] in our rightful positions of leadership and ministry.[22]

This historic assembly approved a statement that shocked the Catholic community. In perhaps its most famous phrase, the black clergy described the Catholic Church as "a white racist institution." They called upon the church to recognize that a profound change had occurred in the attitude of the black community, manifested in the demand that "black people control their own affairs and make decisions for themselves." (Note the echoes of Thomas Wyatt Turner!) The black priests also described the increasing alienation and estrangement that was taking place between the black community and the Catholic Church due to the church's "past complicity with and active support of [the] prevailing attitudes and institutions of America." The statement concluded with this warning:

> ... unless the Church, by an immediate, effective and total reversing of its present practices, rejects and denounces all forms of racism within its ranks and institutions and in the society of which she is a part, she will become unacceptable in the black community.[23]

Thus the bishops, meeting in late April of 1968, were faced with a societal and ecclesial context that they could not ignore. Because of the critical situation of the nation, something more than the cautious approach used in 1958 would be necessary. As an article published in the National Catholic Reporter on the eve of their gathering put it: "The essential decision facing the bishops is: 'Shall words be supplemented with action?' "[24]

One of the most striking differences between the 1958 and 1968 statements is their tone. The tenor of the latter document is strong and urgent; it is readily apparent that this statement was written in an atmosphere of crisis. (Hence, even the title of the statement, The National Race Crisis, is significant). There is a strong undercurrent of fear present — fear of social upheaval and destruction:

> When will we realize the degree of alienation and polarization that prevails in the nation today? When will we understand that civil protests could easily erupt into civil war? ... There is no place for complacency and inertia. The hour is late and

the need is critical. Let us act while there is still time for collaborative peaceful solutions. (178)

Another noticeable difference between the two documents is the negligible doctrinal base or theoretical justification found in the 1968 statement for its conclusions. The bishops in 1968 were not so much concerned with giving a highly reasoned articulation of their position as they were with making their flocks aware of the dire need to act decisively. What little doctrinal justification that is present is mentioned in an almost offhand way: the eradication of racism would enable people to "live with equal opportunity to fulfill the promise of their creation in the image and likeness of God" (176) and enable Christians to demonstrate that "love of neighbor which is the proof of love of God" (177).

In two very noteworthy ways, this document advances the positions taken in the previous one. First, it contains an explicit acknowledgment of Catholic culpability in the genesis of the current race crisis. The document states: "Catholics, like the rest of American society, must recognize their responsibility for allowing these conditions to persist. . . . In varying degree, we all share the guilt" (175). Second, this statement takes a much broader view of the problem of racism. It recognizes that racist attitudes and behaviors "exist, not only in the hearts of men but in the fabric of their institutions" (175). Thus a concern is shown not just for individual race prejudice but for institutional racism as well. Indeed, as will be seen, most of the bishops' recommendations concern the institutional manifestations of racism.

The bishops' understanding and analysis of the race problem amount to a virtual endorsement of the findings of the Kerner Report. In fact, explicit reference to the Commission occurs four times in the document. They accept the Commission's views that the nation is becoming rapidly polarized into two separate and unequal societies and that white racism is essentially responsible for the "current social crisis" (175, 176). Thus the bishops conclude that the national race crisis "is of a magnitude and peril far transcending any which the Church in America or the nation has previously confronted" (177).

Unlike its predecessor, this document makes several concrete and strongly urgent recommendations for action. Within the Catholic community, the bishops first called for the "total eradication of any elements of discrimination in our parishes, schools, hospitals, [and] homes for the aged" (176). Second, an Urban Task Force was established within the United States Catholic Conference to direct and coordinate all Catholic efforts in this field. Dioceses were strongly urged to establish similar programs on the local level (176–77). In the wider societal arena, the bishops stated that quality education for the poor was "a moral imperative"; called upon the private sector to provide employment for Negroes, stating that should it fail to do so "it becomes the duty of the government to intervene"; and strongly urged the "strict implementation . . . of both the letter and the spirit" of the federal Open Housing Act to advance integrated and fair housing.

Despite the significant advances that this statement made over that of 1958, it nonetheless did not receive unqualified approval and acceptance. In an editorial entitled "B Plus for Effort," the *National Catholic Reporter* called the bishops' priorities "dubious" in light of the fact that the Urban Task Force was allotted only $28,000 — as compared to several hundred thousand for a study of clerical concerns (namely, priestly celibacy) and $2.2 million for the Catholic University of America. Yet it commended the bishops for treating not just ecclesiastical problems but social issues as well. The editorial concluded:

> Most of all, it was heartening to learn that the greatest part of the bishops' discussion was on race and poverty. The announced result was not instantly impressive. . . . But it seems to us that a new direction is being set.[25]

Newsweek provided detailed coverage of the document's proposals. It also reported the "strong dissatisfaction" of "militant Negro priests" with the document's recommendations. A spokesman was quoted as saying: "the Catholic Church is primarily a white racist institution. There's a fantastic gap between our thinking and the thinking of the bishops. " The spokesman is further reported as saying that the only way to bridge the gap was to recruit more Negro priests and increase black representation in the church's hierarchy.[26]

Indeed, perhaps the most significant development of this era was the creation of several black-identified groups within the Catholic Church. In addition to the NBCCC, the National Black Sisters' Conference, the National Black Lay Caucus, and the National Black Seminarians' Association came into existence during this time. In fact, within two years after the publication of the black clergy statement, the National Office for Black Catholics (NOBC) was established. Headquartered in Washington, D.C., this office functioned as the coordinating agency for the various black groups and institutionalized black reflection, advocacy, and presence within the U.S. Catholic experience.[27]

In summary, the 1968 race statement advances in several ways the position of 1958. It was a much more comprehensive and timely response to the social-historical context, evidenced an understanding of the institutional aspects of racism, showed an appreciation for the findings of the social sciences in its analysis of the racial situation, and addressed itself to the racism within the Catholic community. Yet note how it took a strong external stimulus in the form of several urgent social and ecclesial crises to compel the bishops to act. While further research is needed to confirm this hypothesis, my studies thus far lead me to believe that the U.S. bishops act corporately on racism only in response to external pressure from Rome and/or grave crises in church or society. Perhaps the main weaknesses of the document are its lack of doctrinal foundation and theological reflection and the absence of sufficient financial commitment for its successful implementation.

BROTHERS AND SISTERS TO US (1979)[28]

Racism is an evil which endures in our society and in our church. Despite apparent advances and even significant changes in the last two decades, the reality of racism remains. (381)

In these opening words of this response to America's racial dilemma, the Catholic bishops state their reason for yet another pastoral letter: the fact that racism still remains a major human rights challenge. Despite changes in the nation's laws, the granting of voting rights, and the elimination of enforced segregation, the bishops were forced to conclude that "too often what has happened has been only a covering over, not a fundamental change" (383).

What was the historical and social situation that moved the bishops to make these observations regarding the presence of racism in America and to issue a third pastoral letter? In the late 1970s the nation entered a new phase in its history of race relations. Having overcome the problem of de jure, or legally sanctioned, discrimination and segregation, it now had to come to grips with the far more difficult matter of de facto discrimination, in other words, the racism that results from the very operation of social institutions and systems (such as education, finance, and justice) and from the accumulated effects of a history of racial oppression. De facto segregation cannot be eradicated simply by passing a law against it; overcoming it requires positive actions and innovative programs.

Thus the late 1970s were a time of school desegregation controversies. Busing often met organized and violent resistance, especially in Boston and Louisville. This was an era of affirmative action plans that were efforts to extend preferential treatment to minorities in order to compensate for deficiencies caused by past racial discrimination. This was also a time of intense legal debates over the use of quota systems designed to achieve this goal and the existence of so-called "reverse discrimination." Moreover, this was a time of economic recession, with the poor — who were disproportionately black, Hispanic, and Native American — being the hardest hit. Finally, the 1970s saw the rise of right-wing extremist groups such as the Ku Klux Klan and the neo-Nazis. Through demonstrations, vocal opposition to desegregation efforts, and mass distribution of hate literature, they increased the level of racial tension throughout the South and in several northern urban centers. *U.S. News & World Report* attributed the rise of these groups to (1) a backlash at the steady gains in the South by blacks since the 1960s; (2) a widespread dissatisfaction with busing and affirmative action programs; and (3) mounting anxiety over the nation's economic troubles, especially inflation and unemployment, which caused poor and lower-class whites to perceive black gains as a threat.[29]

Ecclesial developments within the Catholic community provided another impetus to reexamine and rearticulate the church's racial teachings. As part of the Catholic contribution to the celebration of America's bicentennial, the bishops initiated a process of nation-wide consultation on issues of justice in the country. Regional hearings solicited testimony that would be used by delegates at a national gathering (held in Detroit in 1976) as the basis for a five-year action plan for the Catholic Church in the United States. Black Catholics were an integral part of this "Call to Action" process. For example, at a regional hearing held in Newark in 1975, Brother Joseph Davis, then executive director of the National Office for Black Catholics, gave a powerful, eloquent, and blunt assessment of the Catholic Church and race relations:

> In analyzing the church's own documents, it is obvious that the church has always perceived . . . its primary constituency as the white, European immigrant community. On several significant occasions, when the Catholic Church had the opportunity to depart from the structures of racism so rigidly imposed by the dominant society [and] to affirm the humanity and dignity of black people . . . it has invariably backed off in deference to the sensitivities of the white Catholic community.
>
> There are no complex, unfathomable, complicated reasons why there are so few black Catholics in this country. . . . It does not take a great deal of analysis to understand why the church has had such a minimal response by black people to its initiatives.
>
> Documentable history does not demonstrate the *credibility* of the institution, especially if interpreted in the light of the gospel. Among the Christian institutions of this nation, the Roman Catholic Church has the poorest record of promoting indigenous leadership among blacks, or allowing the

cultural adaptation which could produce the greatest harmony between the church and the people.[30]

Based upon such testimony, the delegates at the Detroit conference in 1976 adopted a resolution on "Ethnicity and Race." Formulated by a coalition of blacks, Hispanics, Native Americans, and whites, it was presented by Eugene Marino, then the black auxiliary bishop from Washington, D.C. — and one of only four black men who were members of the American hierarchy. This statement noted that while church teaching on racial equality was clear, the response of the American Catholic community "is in fact a mockery of this teaching." It strongly recommended the appointment of more racial and ethnic minority bishops. Moreover this assembly specifically urged the national body of bishops to recognize the persistent reality of racism within society and the church by issuing "a pastoral letter on the sin of racism in both its personal and social dimensions" within two years.[31] The bishops of the United States accepted this recommendation and incorporated it into their five-year plan. Joseph Francis, the newest black member of the conference of bishops, was assigned to chair the drafting committee.

Some of the main themes of this pastoral letter are:

1. *The persistence of racism despite statutory changes.* The bishops challenged the popular view that racism was no longer a problem in American life, a view that caused the sense of urgency of the 1960s to yield to "an apparent acceptance of the status quo" (383, 384). They declared that "too often what has happened has been only a covering over, not a fundamental change," for an "unresolved racism" still permeated social structures and individual attitudes.

2. *The covert existence and subtle nature of contemporary racism.* In several places, the document pointed out that racism existed "beneath the surface" of American life, manifested in racially disparate unemployment figures, prison populations, and housing patterns. While noting that "crude and blatant" expressions of racial prejudice were now socially unacceptable, they nevertheless

maintained that racism was still evidenced in "the indifference that replaces open hatred" (384, 385).

3. *The link of racism to economic injustice.* The bishops held that racism and economic oppression were "distinct but interrelated forces." Their analysis of the situation found that racial minorities were being asked to bear a disproportionate share of the burden of a changing economy characterized by "limited resources, restricted job markets, and dwindling revenues." Furthermore, the bishops stated that economic pressures "exacerbate" latent racial tensions, especially when poor whites are forced into competition with racial minorities for limited job opportunities (383).

4. *The institutional character of racism.* This pastoral letter continued the approach of its predecessor in noting not only the personal but also the structural dimensions of the race question. It furthered and strengthened the previous position by being more specific as to the meaning of institutional racism:

> The structures of our society are subtly racist, for these structures reflect the values which society upholds. They are geared to the success of the majority and the failure of the minority. ...Perhaps no single individual is to blame. The sinfulness is often anonymous, but nonetheless real. The sin is social in nature in that each of us, in varying degrees, is responsible. All of us in some measure are accomplices.... The absence of personal fault for evil does not absolve one of all responsibility. We must resist and undo injustices we have not caused, lest we become bystanders who tacitly endorse evil and so share in guilt for it. (384)

5. *Ecclesial racism.* While not going into specifics, the bishops did acknowledge that the Catholic Church had often been perceived as a racist institution and needed to confess a share in the sins of the past: "Many of us have preached the Gospel while closing our eyes to the racism it condemned. We have allowed conformity to social pressures to replace compliance with social justice" (386).

6. *Doctrinal bases for the Catholic stance.* The bishops based their condemnation of racism on four tenets of Christianity: (1) the

commitment to evangelization, which was defined as "bringing consciences, both individual and social, into conformity with the Gospel" (383); (2) the doctrine of creation, which proclaims that all men and women bear the imprint of the Creator and as children of God are brothers and sisters to one another (383, 385); (3) the mystery of the incarnation, which reveals the truth of the dignity of each human being (383); and (4) the teaching of scripture that "all people are accountable to and for each other" (Mt 25:31–41) (385).

Because of these tenets, the bishops reached definitive and unambiguous ethical conclusions: "Racism is a sin: a sin that divides the human family, blots out the image of God among specific members of that family, and violates the fundamental dignity of those called to be children of the same Father." And again: "Racism is not merely one sin among many; it is a radical evil that divides the human family and denies the new creation of a redeemed world" (387). This is the first time the body of bishops forthrightly declared that racism is sinful.

7. *Recommendations for action.* Like the 1968 statement, this pastoral letter gave specific guidelines for action and even went beyond its predecessor by making its suggestions more concrete and detailed. The bishops saw the need for action on three fronts — the personal, ecclesial, and societal. The bishops exhorted *individuals* not only to reject racial stereotypes, slurs, and jokes, but also to learn how social structures inhibited the economic, educational, and social advance of the poor. The *church* itself was called to a comprehensive self-examination and renewal by: (1) insuring that its parishes became places of welcome and inclusion for people of all races; (2) developing liturgies that respected, fostered, and incorporated the gifts of the various races; (3) recruiting, training, and promoting ordained, religious, and lay leaders of color; (4) continuing and expanding Catholic schools in the nation's inner cities; and (5) implementing in every diocese and religious institution an effective affirmative action program that would surpass the efforts of secular institutions.

Concerning *social change,* the bishops issued guidelines of only a general nature, calling for a fight to achieve the dual goals of racial and economic justice (387–88). Finally, these church leaders exhorted *all* to confront the "irrational fear" at the base of racial hostility and animosity (387–88). Through such measures, the bishops hoped to alleviate and curtail the "unresolved racism" that continued to plague American life.

Thus *Brothers and Sisters to Us* is a strongly worded document that forcefully and unequivocally condemns racism in its contemporary manifestations as an evil and a sin. As such, it offered great promise of a new beginning in the Catholic story of race relations. Indeed, shortly after the issuance of this statement, Bishop Marino commented: "By stating clearly the mandate of Christ for those dispossessed because of race, the pastoral of the American bishops offers a splendid foundation on which to build an agenda for the 1980s."[32] Some strides were made: more black men were ordained to the episcopacy, and many dioceses and religious communities increased their efforts to recruit women and men into the priesthood and religious life. Efforts were made to encourage liturgical adaptation and inculturation with black cultural heritage.[33] Many dioceses established offices for black Catholic concerns and ministry.

However, the publicity given this document was very limited. Most media and ecclesial attention given to the 1979 assembly of bishops did not highlight the pastoral letter on racism, but rather the bishops' failure to endorse inclusive language in the liturgy. Thus, many — if not most — Catholics were (and still are) unaware of the document's existence. In 1984, Father Edward Braxton (currently bishop of Bellville, Illinois), a prominent African American Catholic theologian, noted that the pastoral letter "is not implemented, preached, studied or even printed in many places."[34] And on the fifth anniversary of *Brothers and Sisters to Us*, Bishop Joseph Francis addressed the American bishops' annual assembly and said:

It would be comforting to millions of people of all races if I could relate that the pastoral on racism has made a significant difference in the racial attitudes and practices of sisters and brothers in the Catholic Church in the United States of

America. I fear that it has not. In fact, I have often called it the "best-kept secret in the U.S. church."

Had our words been taken seriously by clergy, religious, and laity, millions of blacks and other racial minorities in our country...would really have something to celebrate on this fifth anniversary. How encouraged we would be if this pastoral on racism had received the same kind of publicity and acceptance as the pastoral on war and peace.[35]

The passing of the years has only deepened the disappointment of the black Catholic community with the reception of this statement. In a reflection issued on the tenth anniversary of *Brothers and Sisters to Us*, the Bishops' Committee on Black Catholics concluded:

The promulgation of the pastoral on racism was soon forgotten by all but a few. A survey...revealed a *pathetic, anemic* response from archdioceses and dioceses around the country. ...The pastoral on racism had made little or no impact on the majority of Catholics in the United States....In spite of all that has been said and written about racism in the last twenty years, very little — if anything at all — has been done in Catholic education; such as it was yesterday, it is today.[36]

To mark the twenty-fifth anniversary of *Brothers and Sisters to Us*, the Catholic bishops commissioned a study to discern its implementation and reception.[37] While it is written in official language and strives to put the best face on the situation, one cannot but discern that it paints a disheartening, if not dismal, picture of the Catholic community's relationship with African Americans. Among the findings are the following:

◆ Since the publication of *Brothers and Sisters to Us*, only 18 percent of the nation's bishops have issued statements condemning the sins of racism. (Moreover, my own research reveals that most of these statements were written by only a handful of bishops. Furthermore, most deal only with personal attitudes of deliberate racial malice and not with systemic racism or white privilege).[38]

* Most Catholics (64 percent) had not heard a homily on racism or racial justice in the past three years. That is, it was not preached on even once over the entire three-year cycle of the Sunday lectionary.

* The report notes the lack of black representation among the church's leadership on all levels: bishops, priests, sisters, deacons, lay pastoral ministers, and diocesan directors of religious education. African Americans are less than 3 percent of the total in every category of leadership (that is, less than their proportion of the U.S. Catholic population)...and less than 1 percent in many (for example, priests, sisters, and seminarians). Thus, despite the clear commitment of *Brothers and Sisters to Us* to vocational recruitment and retention, twenty-five years later the leadership of the church's chanceries, diocesan offices, parish staffs, schools, institutions of higher education, and Catholic organizations is still overwhelming white.

* The document notes that "many diocesan seminaries and ministry formation programs are inadequate in terms of their incorporation of the history, culture, and traditions of black Americans."

* Only 44 (or 33 percent) of dioceses have Offices for Black Ministry (OBMs). (It is unclear if this number includes Multicultural Offices that are mergers of various racial and ethnic groups under one umbrella.) Furthermore, in 2009, that number is certainly reduced due to additional closures and mergers since the report was issued.

* Over half of these OBMs report that they lack the financial resources needed for effective ministry in the black community.

* One-third of the OBMs report that the black laity are either "never" or "hardly ever" involved in planning or decision making for black Catholics.

* Most disturbing, the report notes that "White Catholics over the last twenty-five years exhibit diminished — rather than

increased — support for government policies aimed at reducing racial inequality."

Thus this official investigation details the significant lack of compliance with the church's own recommendations for action contained in *Brothers and Sisters to Us*. It concludes that the "Church's statements condemning racism have not had their intended effect of reducing the pervasiveness of racist attitudes over the last twenty-five years." Hence, the promise of *Brothers and Sisters to Us* is still largely a "dream deferred."

ANALYSIS OF RECENT STATEMENTS BY INDIVIDUAL BISHOPS

At the chapter's beginning, I noted how in addition to these three pastoral letters on racism issued by the entire Catholic episcopal conference, a small number of bishops have issued their own statements addressing this social evil. In a previous work, I extensively presented and analyzed these documents.[39] For the sake of completeness, I will summarize that work here and then briefly will consider three more recent statements by individual Catholic prelates.

In looking at statements issued by the few bishops who addressed this matter since the publication of *Brothers and Sisters to Us,* one notes the following characteristics:

1. The substantive concerns of these bishops lie with the more obvious and visible actions of racial hatred and exclusion. Even when they articulate an awareness of covert and systemic forms of racism, their attention is primarily focused upon the voluntary, conscious, and deliberate actions of individuals. What one does not find is an examination or critique of the underlying cultural beliefs or myths that facilitate, engender, and legitimate these racist behaviors.[40] Racist beliefs are seen as commonly held personal stereotypes; they are not examined as reflections of endemic cultural patterns. Thus these episcopal statements implicitly convey an understanding that reduces racism to demonstrable manifestations

of personal racial prejudice. The bishops' understanding of racism privileges personal and interpersonal manifestations of racial bias over those that are systemic and structural.

2. They are primarily moral exhortations and appeals to conscience. They employ a parenetic style of argumentation; in other words, the basis for the moral appeal or duty proposed is often presupposed and left implicit.[41] These episcopal interventions are admonitions rooted in faith convictions that are assumed to be intuitively obvious and shared by those being addressed. Thus the warrants for the bishops' stance on racism are seldom argued for or explained in detail. In addition, the bishops employ a strategy of moral suasion in their ethical argumentation. That is, they assume their audience's goodwill and acceptance of the basic faith tenets that they delineate. They also direct their appeals principally to individuals. Thus the bishops presume that if the incompatibility of racist behaviors with Christian faith is pointed out, this will lead to personal conversion, which will result in social transformation. But the inherent limitations and constraints imposed on an individual's freedom, knowledge, and moral agency by what one prelate admits is an "enormity" of "cultural entrenchment" are neither acknowledged nor addressed.[42]

3. In keeping with their understanding of racism and policy of moral suasion, almost all recommend some form of self-examination akin to the traditional examination of conscience, that is, an honest inventory and acknowledgment of the racial prejudices and fears that all too often motivate the behavior of Catholics. The faithful are to avoid using racial slurs and telling racial jokes; they also are to challenge such behaviors among their family members, friends, and co-workers. Parents are asked to instill in their children the values of racial tolerance and an appreciation for ethnic diversity. Individuals are asked to cultivate interracial and cross-cultural friendships. Catholic schools and teachers are invited to develop curricula that foster cultural respect and toleration. Priests are asked to preach regularly about the issue of racism. Churches should offer liturgies of racial reconciliation; prayers for racial justice should be a regular part of Sunday worship. Catholic parishes are to be "safe places"

for interracial dialogue and open sharing; they also are to offer hospitality to those who are racially and ethnically different. One has the impression that the basic summons is for Catholics to treat those who are racially different with respect, decency, and civility. This is consistent with the view that racism, being primarily a manifestation of personal prejudice, can be eradicated by practices that foster individual conversion and interpersonal goodwill.

This is the dominant perspective found in the documents of the few church leaders who chose to address this issue in the latter part of the twentieth century. Since that time, three other bishops have issued statements on racial justice in the early part of this century: Cardinal Francis George (Chicago, 2001), Bishop Dale Melczek (Gary, Indiana, 2003), and Archbishop Alfred Hughes (New Orleans, 2006).[43] The following are among the principal characteristics of these statements:

1. All of these statements, without slighting the personal manifestations of racial bias, stress a more structural understanding of racism. Hughes teaches that racism "involves not only individual prejudice but also the use of religious, social, political, economic or historical power to keep one race privileged." George speaks of "patterns of social and racial superiority" that are created "consciously or unconsciously" to "privilege people like themselves." Melczek's analysis is particularly masterful, rooting individual manifestations of racial animus in the influence of a pervasive culture — "shaped by those who represent the dominant power" — that forms a "racialized self."[44]

2. These statements explicitly name and address the reality of white privilege. That is, they focus not only upon the harms suffered by people of color by this social evil, but the benefits and advantages that whites gain because of society's endemic racial bias. They also note how this systemic advantage and benefit is largely invisible to white Americans. George goes so far as to note how white privilege "often goes undetected because it has become internalized and integrated as part of one's outlook on the world by custom, habit and tradition." Hughes states that for white people "everything is

normal because white people often do not see the advantages inherent in simply being born into society with physical characteristics valued by that society."[45]

3. These documents acknowledge in forthright and direct ways this faith community's complicity in the racism of U.S. society. Hughes laments that the Catholic Church's response to racial injustice has been "uneven" and "not a high priority." Melczek and George highlight Catholic complicity in "white flight" from urban areas and how racial fears have shaped the current realities faced by our nation's cities. George relates how "Catholics mixed parish loyalty with racial prejudice in a desperate, always unsuccessful, effort to 'save' particular neighborhoods by preventing the entrance of black people." These events and the mass exodus of whites out of integrated neighborhoods set the stage for the current reality of what George calls "spatial racism," that is, the visible chasm of isolation in segregated housing patterns that fuels social neglect and indifference.[46]

4. Finally, these statements espouse a wider range of responses to combat the social evil of racism. Without omitting calls for dialogue, education, and cross-cultural awareness, they also call for strategies such as proactive hiring to insure that the religious workforce and its management reflect the racial and ethnic diversity of the community; advocacy of fair wage, housing, and employment practices; working with other social agencies to provide low-cost housing; and continuing participation in antipoverty programs.

Thus from this presentation of the statements of individual Catholic prelates we can form three conclusions: (1) the vast majority of U.S. bishops have not addressed this issue since the issuance of *Brothers and Sisters to Us* in 1979; (2) the few who have mainly continue the dominant trend of approaching racism as conscious and deliberate acts of omission and commission performed by individuals; and (3) the contributions of George, Melczek, and Hughes show that more adequate systemic approaches to the malady of racism — while a minority view among church hierarchs — are consistent with Catholic faith convictions.

CRITICAL OBSERVATIONS CONCERNING CATHOLIC SOCIAL TEACHING ON RACISM

No presentation of the position and teaching of the Catholic Church on race and racial justice would be complete without taking note of the deficits that affect its adequacy and effectiveness. Awareness of the limitations present in the tradition will set the stage for making proposals for future action and reflection.

First, unlike other major pastoral letters on social justice issues, including *The Challenge of Peace* (1983) and *Economic Justice for All* (1986), *Brothers and Sisters to Us* is not informed by sustained social analysis. There is no evidence of a formal investigation of the phenomenon of racism. The church's teaching on racism is uninformed by current social science. The evidence given for its claims is often more impressionist or anecdotal, and its conclusions are thus too often pious exhortations that do not persuade critical readers — especially those who do not share our faith presuppositions.

Second, the teaching lacks an extended theological or ethical reflection upon racism. While the bishops clearly believe that racism is contrary to Christian conviction and practice — and such a conclusion may be intuitively obvious — the theological warrants for this stance are not well articulated. A coherent presentation of why, *in the light of faith,* racism is contrary to the Gospel is missing. The faith reflection on this social evil is theologically thin, at best.

Third, the bishops developed no formal plan for implementing the teachings and exhortations of *Brothers and Sisters to Us* unlike the other two pastoral letters referred to above. There was a lack of initial publicity and no plan for ongoing catechesis. Because of this oversight, the pastoral letter on racism has had little impact upon the consciousness and practices of the vast majority of American Catholics. One can safely assert that even the existence of this document and its teachings are unknown to most Catholics. Research detailed above notes that the church's stance on racism is rarely taught or studied in our seminaries, formation programs, and catechetical institutions. Thus the bold words and conclusions of *Brothers and Sisters to Us* are unknown because they are often unspoken and unstudied.

These lacunae are serious enough. But there are more substantial deficits in the Catholic approach that must be considered.

First, Catholic teaching on race in America has neglected or slighted an essential step in social reflection, namely, listening to the voices of the victims and examining the situation from their perspective. Not only is this teaching uninformed by sustained social analysis; it also manifests a subtle but pervasive paternalism. Note the title of the latest collective statement: *Brothers and Sisters to Us*. This begs the question: Who's the "us"? The very title indicates that this is a document written for white Catholics and addressed to white Catholics. The Catholic racial justice tradition tends to speak *about* and *for* aggrieved African Americans; but it does not support or acknowledge black agency, meaning independent thought, action, and leadership.[47] There is no indication that African Americans themselves have a contribution to make toward either understanding or changing the climate of racial injustice. The American Catholic approach has been far more willing to prompt whites to concede rights to blacks than to encourage blacks to press for social justice. This cannot but render Catholic ethical reflection on racial matters inadequate and impoverished, if not even erroneous.[48]

The lack of a sustained social analysis of racism leads to another inadequacy or deficit: an *overly optimistic perspective* that fails to account for how deeply entrenched racial bias is in American culture. American Catholic teaching on race often presumes that it is addressing a rational audience of well-intentioned people, and thus assumes that racism can be overcome principally by education, dialogue, and moral persuasion.[49] Such assumptions are naive. They fail to take into account the insights of the social sciences regarding the depth of racism. Racism is not merely or primarily a sin of ignorance, but one of advantage and privilege. Privileged groups seldom relinquish their advantages voluntarily because of dialogue and education.

To put this another way, the church's past efforts have been impeded due to a fundamental misunderstanding of racism. Racism has never been principally about insults, slurs, or exclusion, as demeaning and harmful as these are. Racism entails more than conscious, deliberate, and intentional ill will or acts of avoidance, exclusion, or malice perpetrated by individuals. Individual bias and personal bigotry are real, but a limited slice of reality. Racism is an underlying cultural set of meanings and values, that is, a way of interpreting skin color differences so that white Americans enjoy a privileged social status with access to advantages and benefits to the detriment, disadvantage, and burden of persons of color. Racism, at its core, is a defense of racially based white social privilege.

The Catholic perspective on racial justice is inadequate because it fails to attend to the formative power of a racist cultural symbol system and consistently downplays the structural dimensions of racism. The cultivation of mutual interracial relationships, based upon courtesy and respect, is admirable and even necessary. However, such relationships are insufficient. Interracial courtesy, decency, and respect cannot overturn and dismantle the cultural stigmatization and structural disadvantage that lie at the core of America's racial quagmire. Authentic loving relationships can exist even in the midst of a socially unjust situation. Again, the major shortcoming of the Catholic approach to racial justice is that it is insufficiently attentive — if not blind — to the nexus of race and cultural power and social privilege, and the need to sever this linkage.

Thus to the extent that the Catholic approach to racial justice focuses upon deliberate, conscious, and intentional acts of individuals directed against persons because of their race or ethnicity and seeks to address them by moral appeals and suasion, to that extent it is inadequate to deal with what the bishops acknowledge is a "radical evil" and a "distortion at the heart of human nature." Such strategies do not take account of what theologian Bernard Lonergan calls "the flight from understanding" — the refusal of unwanted insight when such insight would entail changes that are costly, painful, or demanding.[50] And they do not give due recognition to the power of human sin. As St. Thomas Aquinas teaches, sin is fundamentally *unreasonable* — an "act against right reason" — and cannot be ameliorated by appeals to reason alone.[51]

Finally, and most significantly, American Catholic social teaching on race suffers from a *lack of passion*. As a corporate body and as individuals, Catholics espouse a number of beliefs, but not all of these are held passionately. For example, no one can doubt the passion with which the Catholic Church opposes abortion. If others know anything about Catholicism, they certainly know that the Catholic Church is against abortion. This position is articulated repeatedly, forcefully, and uncompromisingly. It is a position held fervently and passionately, even in the face of significant opposition and disagreement. Opposition to abortion is a major public marker of Catholic identity. Contrast this with the Catholic teaching on indulgences, which, though without doubt "official," is held dispassionately. For most, it is a belief of little commitment, priority, or importance.

My point is this: despite the bold words of *Brothers and Sisters to Us*, we must conclude that racial justice is not now — and never has been[52] — a passionate matter for most American Catholics. Indeed, the U.S. Bishops' Committee on Black Catholics noted how *Brothers and Sisters to Us* aroused a "pathetic, anemic response" from most Catholics.[53] The pastoral on racism has had little impact upon the consciousness and behavior of the vast majority of American Catholics. It is difficult *not* to conclude that Catholic engagement with racism is a matter of low institutional commitment, priority, and importance. If "passion" connotes commitment, involvement, and fervor, the Catholic stance on racism, in contrast, can be characterized as tepid, lukewarm, and half-hearted. Standing against racism is not a core component of Catholic corporate identity.

Hence, when viewed from the perspective of the black experience — that is, the perspective of those who most immediately endure the injustice of racism — there are serious shortcomings and deficits in the dominant approach in U.S. Catholic social teaching on racial injustice. This teaching is superficial in its social analysis of racism, naïve in its reliance upon rational persuasion, and blind to how the church's complicity in and bondage to a racialized culture compromises its teaching and identity. In short, Catholic reflection on racism is not radical enough to do justice to what the bishops themselves call a "radical evil."

A CONCLUDING
BLACK CATHOLIC REFLECTION:
"SOMETIMES I FEEL LIKE
A MOTHERLESS CHILD"

If standing against racism is not a priority for the Catholic Church and its approach to and engagement with this social evil is inadequate and ineffective, where does that leave a black Catholic believer? Such a question cannot be evaded by invoking the pretense of academic objectivity or intellectual neutrality.

I begin my response by invoking the memory of Sister Thea Bowman, a powerful preacher and charismatic teacher who was a mentor for many of us who are leaders in the black Catholic community today. In 1989, she stood before the bishops of the United States to address them about what it meant to be black and Catholic in America. She began her presentation by singing the slave spiritual: "Sometimes I Feel Like a Motherless Child."

> Sometimes I feel like a motherless child,
> Sometimes I feel like a motherless child,
> Sometimes I feel like a motherless child,
> A long ways from home. A long ways from home.
> True believer, a long ways from home, a long ways
>   from home.[54]

We do not know the names of the enslaved Africans who composed this song. But their feelings — unbearable pain, unspeakable grief, heartbreaking loneliness, and inconsolable sadness — have been immortalized and preserved in searing words and haunting melody. The experience of being uprooted from "home," and of being an alien in a land that yet is mockingly familiar, is what it means to be a "motherless child." One attempts to make one's way the best one can in a hostile world where one's family, experience, opinion, and very life simply do not matter. The plaintive and haunting moan, "Sometimes I feel like a motherless child," has become a classic vehicle for expressing an aching loneliness and estrangement too deep for words.

Sister Thea's insight as she began her presentation with this song was that the experience of black Catholics in this church is like that of a "motherless child." We are a part of a body of believers that oftentimes is called "Holy Mother Church." Yet if truth be told, this church has been less than a nourishing and supportive mother for many, if not most, black Catholic believers at some time or another. For us, this song of our ancestors conveys the pain, grief, hurt, and disappointment of belonging to a church wherein we too often feel orphaned and abandoned.

This is the existential import of the historical and theological analysis of Catholic engagement (or lack thereof) with racism rehearsed in this chapter. Beneath the intellectual articulation lies a sense of rupture, estrangement, and alienation. This fractured relationship stems from the realization, as articulated by the Black Catholic Clergy Caucus in 1968, that the U.S. Catholic Church is a "white racist institution." In light of what has gone before in this book, we can now better understand the significance of this insight.

Recall that I argued that the key component of black culture is "the expectation of struggle," and that a core element of white culture is the presumption of dominance, that is, the presumption of being the norm or standard to which all "others" should conform. Now we can better understand the phrase "white church culture" and what black Catholics mean when we say that the Catholic Church is a "white institution." It entails more than the obvious fact that a Western European culture has shaped the culture of the Catholic Church in the United States.[55] What makes this a "white" church culture is deeper than the cultural roots of its liturgical music and rubrics. It is the presumption that these — and *only* these — particular cultural expressions are standard, normative, universal, and thus really "Catholic."

Furthermore, it cannot be disputed that the U.S. Catholic Church has acted by omission and commission in ways that decisively allied it with the culture of racial domination and cause it to be identified as "white." It has done this explicitly (for example, the practice of slaveholding and refusing to admit persons of African descent to positions of church leadership and authority) and implicitly (such as its tacit acceptance of legal segregation and refusal to actively evangelize African Americans).[56] Thus the Catholic Church in the United States is a "white" institution, insofar as it promotes, defends, and partakes — however unwittingly — of the culture of dominance.

What makes the U.S. Catholic Church a "white racist institution," then, is not the fact that the majority of its members are of European descent (especially since in many places, they no longer are), nor the fact that many of its members engage in acts of malice or bigotry. What makes it "white" and "racist" is the pervasive belief that European aesthetics, music, theology, and persons — and only these — are standard, normative, universal, and truly "Catholic."

Let me make this point plain by considering two comments offered by church leaders during a meeting to discuss a proposed pastoral letter on racism:

+ "If we say what you want us to say, our people will get mad."

+ "My people won't understand *white privilege.*"

Others in attendance nodded their heads in agreement with these sentiments. I took notes on the observations offered, and then responded in this vein: "Thank you for your comments. They are more helpful than you realize. But I need some clarification. When you say, 'your people' will get mad, or 'your people' won't understand, who do you mean? After all, I'm sure that there are many black, Latino, and American Indian parishioners in your dioceses who not only will welcome this document, but also understand exactly what is meant. So, who are 'your people'?"

Silence. Because through their comments, these church leaders and officials inadvertently revealed a core reality of the U.S. Catholic

Church, that is, what they really believe yet seldom make explicit. Namely, that *"Catholic"="white."*

Consider some further examples. Several priests complained after an ordination where most of the ordinands were foreign-born Hispanics: "When are we going to get some more of our priests?" (Despite the fact that these were "their" priests, ordained for lifelong service to their diocese.) Or a bishop of a major urban see who commented, referring to the broad cultural diversity of his flock and its presbyterate: "I told the Nuncio that for my next diocese, I want to be assigned to one in the United States." Or a noted Catholic commentator who remarked during Pope Benedict's recent (2008) Mass in Washington, D.C., after a Prayer of the Faithful and Presentation of the Gifts marked by diverse languages and spirited Gospel and Spanish singing: "We have just been subjected to an overpreening display of multicultural chatter. And now, the Holy Father will begin the sacred part of the Mass."[57]

We must resist the temptation to see these as "isolated incidents," as nothing more than the utterances of flawed individuals. Such comments are more typical and widespread than many are willing to acknowledge. They illustrate the fundamental insight that in a white racist church, "Catholic" means "white." In U.S. Catholicism, only European aesthetics and cultural products are truly Catholic — regardless of the church's rhetorical commitment to universality.

Thus the U.S. Catholic Church is a white church not only by numbers (though this is changing), but also in its cultural self-identity. This is the deepest reason for why it has failed to undertake the actions and changes needed to effectively challenge or fundamentally alter the marginalization of its members of color. To do so would mean its self-destruction as a white institution. A white church will not — indeed *cannot* — be responsive to the existential concerns of African Americans and other groups of color, if by "white church" we mean a church identified with and complicitous in racial privilege and dominance. Recall that it is the essence of "whiteness" to be the arbiter of what is considered "real," and thus worthy of study, consideration, and attention. To the extent that the Catholic Church in the United States is a "white institution," it cannot adequately respond to the existential passions and religious questions of African Americans. It must deem such concerns as unimportant, irrelevant, insignificant, impertinent, or even dangerous, for they are a threat to the presumption of dominance. The U.S. Catholic Church has to remain "white" or undergo a radical conversion. This will not be easy. The church's "whiteness" is more deeply entrenched than we would like to believe.

"Sometimes I feel like a motherless child." How do black Catholics affirm the real experience of God found in a church still practically committed to white racial privilege? How do we sing of the Lord in a foreign land, that is, in a church that seldom affirms our full humanity? What in Catholicism resonates with the heartaches, groans, and cries of black peoples? What resources are available to the Catholic faith community to ground a more adequate and effective engagement with the evil of racism? These are the questions that will occupy — and haunt — us in this work's remaining chapters.

Chapter Three

Toward a More Adequate
Catholic Engagement

THE PREVIOUS CHAPTERS advanced an understanding of racism as a cultural system of meanings and values that answers questions of identity, status, and group position in a society. As the noted social scientist Gunnar Myrdal observed in his classic study:

> In this magical sphere of the white man's mind, the Negro is inferior, totally independent of rational proofs or disproofs. And he is inferior in a deep and mystical sense. This is a manifestation of the most primitive form of religion. There is fear of the unknown in this feeling, which is "superstition" in the literal sense of the word.... So the Negro becomes a "contrast conception." He is "the opposite race" — an inner enemy, "antithesis of character and properties of the white man." His name is the antonym of white.[1]

This set of meanings and values provides the foundation for justifying, maintaining, and defending a system of white social privilege, material advantage, and economic benefit to the detriment, disadvantage, and burden of persons of color. This understanding of racism poses a significant challenge to Catholic, indeed Christian, ethical reflection and practice. The dominant trend of Catholic racial discourse privileges a concern with conscious, deliberate, and intentional acts of racial malice of individuals — what I call the

"commonsense" understanding. Catholic racial reflection principally views racism as the external expression of individual bias or
personal prejudice. Such an understanding is woefully inadequate
and cannot but lead to impoverished theology and ineffective
pastoral practice. In line with the perspectives I advocate, Gary
Chamberlain, a Christian theologian, declares:

> Past efforts of the churches to deal with racism have been
> impeded by numerous misunderstandings. Generally racism
> was viewed as nothing more than prejudice.... Furthermore,
> the churches' inadequate approaches to racism rest upon a false
> understanding of the cause of the problem.... The churches'
> efforts to alleviate the suffering of the oppressed, as needed
> as they are, divert attention from the core of the problem, the
> oppressing agents, whether individuals or institutions, in white
> society.[2]

Thus the questions now become: What resources are there that
can deal adequately and effectively with this deeper understanding
of the evil of racism? What is in our possession that can mount an
effective counterattack or resist what the U.S. bishops themselves
admit is a "radical evil" and a profound distortion of identity at
the heart of humanity? How do church and society get beyond their
cultural captivity to white privilege? What alternative set of meanings and values — what counteridentity — are mediated by Catholic
Christian faith and its system of cultural symbols?

The goal of this chapter is to arrive at a more adequate theological and pastoral engagement with the social evil of racial
injustice. To do so, we will consider the current state of reflection on
racial reconciliation and then consider some fundamental themes in
Catholic social reflection that could be resources for more effective
thinking and practice. Among these are the sacraments of Baptism
and Eucharist; interracial solidarity and the option for the poor;
and lament and compassion as core practices and virtues.

A key assumption of this chapter, indeed of this whole project,
is that Christian faith has a valuable and essential role to play in
the effort to bring about a more racially just society. Despite the

scandalous counterwitness on the part of the churches, both as individuals and as institutions,[3] articulating a spirituality of racial resistance is important if for no other reason than it seems essential if people are to (1) negotiate the major shifts of identity and valuing needed to overcome the entrenched biases of our historical conditioning, and (2) undertake the material sacrifices needed for a more just distribution of social resources.

I have long been inspired and haunted by the successes and failures of the U.S. civil rights movement of the 1960s. In my research and meditation, the following observation continues to resonate deeply:

> The most significant, and at the same time perhaps the most perplexing, lesson is that racial healing and reconciliation require a context of shared beliefs and values.... [The civil rights movement] eventually lost anchor in the prophetic witness of the black church.... This proved devastating because *people are by and large not inclined toward radical acts of social relocation, economic redistribution, or racial reconciliation unless they can see their own life-stories as part of a larger theological narrative.*[4]

Given the deeply entrenched racism that is an endemic part of the American ethos, and the profound sense of cultural trauma already being experienced by many as the nation and the church move toward an inevitable "browning," a counternarrative that grounds another identity is absolutely critical to respond to the human need for identity and meaning. Situating our ethical strivings in the context of a larger, broader, and deeper narrative — within an alternate cultural set of meaning and value — is an important and even indispensable contribution that religious faith can make toward the goal of achieving a more racially just society.

THE CHALLENGE OF RACIAL RECONCILIATION

As mentioned above, for several years I have taught a course entitled "Christian Faith and Racial Justice." After attempting to gain clarity as to the nature of "racism," my students and I seek to discover how the Christian faith has been both complicitous in and subversive to the existence of racial hierarchy in American life. As an instructor, one of the challenges I face is providing resources from a Christian perspective that address the concept of racial reconciliation or healing. There are few published resources available from professional theologians or ethicists, and most of these are written from an evangelical faith perspective. The lack of serious and sustained reflection upon such an important issue is a major lacuna in theological ethics in general, and Catholic ethics in particular.

Hence, thinking about racial reconciliation is to engage in an adventure of theological pioneering. It skirts the frontiers of Christian ethical reflection by pondering questions such as:

+ How can we conceive of "reconciliation" in racial matters, where the "forgiveness" sought is not merely — or even principally — between antagonistic *individuals*, but between estranged racial *groups?*
+ What contribution does a Christian theo-ethical imagination bring to the effort to overcome longstanding and deeply entrenched racial antipathies and injustices?
+ How do we overcome the poisonous legacies of suspicion, mistrust, fear, animosity, and even hatred that constantly threaten our attempts at intergroup living?
+ How do we heal the caustic residue of unspeakable harm and violence so that new beginnings are possible?
+ How do estranged groups learn to live together in justice, and not merely coexist in the same place?
+ What contribution does our faith make to the new beginning we long for and so desperately need?

I propose to explore these questions by (1) coming to some clarity as to the meaning of "racial reconciliation"; (2) exploring the treatment of this topic in the body of racial reconciliation literature authored by American evangelical theologians and pastoral ministers; (3) probing the Catholic ethical tradition and its potential contribution to this issue; and (4) concluding with a summary of the work that lies ahead toward a more adequate theological understanding of racial reconciliation from a Christian perspective.

At the outset, I offer a caveat about the parameters of my approach. First, I intentionally limit this examination to the issue of racial reconciliation as it presents itself in the U.S. experience, and within that experience, to the racial tensions and divisions between the racial groups designated as "white" and "black." I grant that a study of American race relations that focuses only on these racial groups is somewhat inadequate. Yet the estrangement between these two groups has shaped American society in decisive ways not matched by either the estrangement between whites and other racial groups, or race-based tensions among the groups of color. The "black/white" divide continues to demand privileged attention.

Second, I hope to demonstrate that the issue of racial reconciliation is not — or ought not be — peripheral to the interests and concerns of Christian theologians and ethicists. The stain of racism in American society is our most perduring and intransigent social injustice.[5] Further, one can argue that almost every major social question or phenomenon in the United States today — whether education, crime, health care, poverty — is entangled with, and/or exacerbated by, historic racial animus and present-day discrimination against people of color in general and African Americans in particular. Thus healing or overcoming the social divisions between racial groups is not only of paramount importance for the nation; addressing this issue is also crucial for the adequacy and relevance of Christian social ethics.

What Is "Racial Reconciliation"?

Let's begin this effort of understanding racial reconciliation through an imaginative consideration of questions such as:

+ What would a racially just society look like?

+ What would an America free from the stain of racism be like?

+ What would be the racial composition of its classrooms, neighborhoods, professional schools, and occupations?

Far from being a distraction or trivial exercise, moral imagination (that is, "a playful suspension of judgment leading us toward a more appropriate grasp of reality")[6] is critically important. Envisioning an alternative future not only sheds light upon what is lacking in the present; it provides a framework for considering the course of action required to bring the desired future to fruition.

Yale law professor Harlon Dalton considers such questions and engages in a series of "thought experiments" to envision what he calls "a racial Promised Land," that is, an America free of the virus of racism.[7] One such racial utopia he calls "Beigia," an exact mirror image of the planet Earth, except all of the inhabitants of this world experience a sudden transformation of their skins into an identical shade of beige. Their hair, facial features, and body types are also changed in such a way as not to signify racial differences. Describing this world's inhabitants, Dalton quips, "It is as if someone mixed three parts Mariah Carey to one part Connie Chung."[8] Individual differences and familial resemblances still exist on Beigia, but do not fall into "racial" patterns. He extends the thought experiment by removing from the Beigians any memory of their previous racial identities. In this scenario, racial tensions and divisions are eliminated because the category of "race" as we know it (that is, human groups socially defined by apparent physical differences) has ceased to exist. Racial harmony and peace prevail through the cancellation of racial difference. Racial conflicts, then, are eradicated through the elimination of racial diversity. With no racial differences, there are also no racial tensions.

This thought experiment has a certain popular resonance. We often hear people say, "When I look at you (meaning a person of color), I don't see black." Or, "There is only one race: the *human* race." Or again, "We need to stop focusing on race, because deep down we are all the same." Or yet another phrasing: "Talk about race is so divisive. We need to focus upon what unites us and not what divides us." Such statements, while often well intentioned, nonetheless also convey a desire to get beyond race by ignoring racial differences.

Without discounting the significant benefits of living in a world free from the poison of racial bigotry and estrangement, Dalton believes that most people would find such a monochromatic world an undesirable place.[9] He posits two reasons. First, he worries that the lack of physical differences would make cultural distinctiveness harder to preserve. Granted that race and ethnicity are distinct realities, nonetheless he states that many people associate color difference with cultural heterogeneity. He fears that a lack of visible distinctiveness compromises a group's ability to resist what he calls the "homogenizing pull of American mass culture."[10] Second, and most significantly, stripping away all memory of racial identity also deprives us of an important dimension of what makes us who we are. Dalton argues that without "our past, whether noble or ignoble, painful or pleasurable, we cease to exist."[11] All of this militates against "Beigia" being a model of racial utopia or the goal of a process of racial reconciliation.

The significance of this thought experiment for Christian ethics is that an adequate account of racial reconciliation needs to provide a positive interpretation and embrace of racial difference and distinctiveness.

Dalton's next thought experiment considers another planetary duplicate, a racial utopia he calls "Proportia." In this utopia, every city, school, neighborhood, church, occupation, profession, sports team, civic and voluntary association in Proportia's United States has a racial composition of 75 percent white, 12 percent black, 9 percent Latino, 3 percent Asian, and 1 percent Native American.[12] Thus, in every aspect of American life, the racial composition of every group and association would mirror the racial distribution of American society as a whole.

Again, this utopian arrangement has a strong popular resonance. We often find appeals to this approach in our public discourse. A severe proportional imbalance of persons of color in positions of social influence is often taken as prima facie evidence of racial exclusion or detriment. Such reasoning, for example, underlies concern regarding the racial disparities present in the law clerks for the Justices of the U.S. Supreme Court,[13] and the fact that the major executives of Fortune 500 companies are overwhelmingly white males. Proportional representation, then, appears to offer some promise as a vehicle toward the goal of racial reconciliation and harmony.

Yet this "racial promised land" is also unsatisfactory. Besides the massive population shifts that would be required, proportional presence of racial groups in social institutions and settings does not guarantee an end to racial suspicion and animosity. Moreover, a rigid adherence to proportional representation fails to take into account or allow for genuine cultural differences or preferences.[14] For example, would we want to insist that a Gospel choir must have a membership that is 75 percent white, or that a professional basketball team be only 12 percent black, or that a math department could have only 2 percent of its students be Asians, or that an Irish dance troupe be 9 percent Hispanic?

But "Proportia" does point us to what is at the heart of racial tensions and animosities. Interest in proportional representation reflects a concern over racial exclusion from positions of power and social influence. Severe racial imbalances are a cause for concern when they compromise access to social prestige, political power, or cultural influence. In other words, anxiety over proportional representation reflects concern about a racial group's ability to be effective participants in U.S. society and public life.

Thus these thought experiments are helpful for understanding both the problem and the goal of racial reconciliation. What is problematic in American culture is not the presence of racial differences, but the linkage of power and prestige to racial difference. Color differences are not the problem. It is the meaning and value assigned to these differences — the use of color differences to advance or circumscribe, enhance or impede, the life chances and opportunities of a human group — that is problematic and socially divisive.[15]

Thus I contend that racial reconciliation is not concerned with the elimination of racial differences, but rather the elimination of the stigma and privilege associated with race. Racial reconciliation, then, is the process of healing the estrangement, division, and hostility between racial groups by overturning or severing the linkage between race and social, cultural, and/or political subordination and dominance.[16]

Note that this understanding of racial reconciliation privileges a concern for the systemic and cultural character of racism. It gives less attention to individual and interpersonal transformation. Some might question if such a focus is sufficient; I maintain that it is essential and critical. For until the nexus between race, power, and privilege is overcome, relations between racial groups cannot but be marked by resentment, suspicion, mistrust, and hostility.

Mainstream Evangelical Theology of Racial Reconciliation

With this understanding of racial reconciliation, we now turn to an examination of the theological approach adopted by American evangelical writers on this issue. The literature that stems from this faith tradition is of interest for two reasons. For one, evangelicals are a significant presence in American religious life, accounting for around 25 percent of the Christians in the United States.[17] Second, evangelical writers have produced a corpus dealing with racial reconciliation that is unmatched by any other Christian tradition.[18]

The designation "popular" characterizes most of this literature. That is, these works are directed toward a lay audience and presuppose no formal theological education. Much of it is also of the genre of "personal testimony," that is, the authors are giving an account of their personal faith journeys and the convictions to which this journey has brought them in order to inspire their readers to embrace a similar faith stance.

Another hallmark of much of this literature is its interracial authorship. Many of these major works are jointly authored by a white male and an African American male who speak of their journey from racial naïveté, hatred, and/or bitterness to a commitment to interracial friendship and racial reconciliation ministry.[19] Thus the authorship of the work gives testimony to the commitment they hope to engender in their readers.

Another distinguishing feature of this literature is a sense of urgency. Perhaps this can be explained by the fact that many of these works appeared in the aftermath of the Los Angeles racial riots of 1992, events that almost all of our authors specifically mention. These authors view the events of Los Angeles as a dire wake-up call to the church and a summons to the self-examination and repentance needed in order to avoid more cataclysmic events in the future.[20]

In their understanding of racial reconciliation, the following characteristics mark this literature:

1. There is a universal, emphatically stated conviction about the utter incompatibility of personal faith in Jesus Christ and practices of racial discrimination and attitudes of racial hatred. Perkins and Tarrants provide a searing statement of this conviction:

> If we are puzzled why so few professing Christians in America are concerned for racial reconciliation or the poor, part of the answer may be that they are not really Christians at all. One of the greatest challenges we face today is helping the "Christians" come to saving faith.
>
> But lack of true conversion is not the only problem in the Church today. Among many who are true converts of Jesus Christ, there is another problem: *lack of total commitment to Him....*
>
> In the broadest sense, then, racial alienation in the Church goes back to these two root problems — lack of true conversion and lack of total commitment.[21]

2. Another common characteristic is the belief that racial estrangement, especially between Christians, is evidence of the power of the demonic at work both in the world and in the church. The authors often speak of their conversion experiences from racial hatred, bitterness, and fear as an experience of "deliverance" or "release" from spiritual captivity or bondage.[22]

3. With very few exceptions, this literature understands racism as consisting of attitudes of racial hatred and personal actions of culpable omission and/or commission. While some authors advert to the concept of "institutional racism," the most attention by far is given to issues of personal culpability in racial divisions. An example

of this feature is found in the discussion of whether "blacks can be racist." The almost universal answer is a virtually unqualified "yes." The following gives a most cogent expression of this conviction:

> Therefore, according to this definition [i.e., racism understood as involving the power to dominate or oppress], white society (the dominant culture) is racist, but the black community is not, nor could be, racist. When translated to the individual level this means that the actions of the police who beat Rodney King were racist, but the actions of the mob against the white truck driver were not.
>
> As Christians we must categorically reject this conclusion. It denies all levels of personal responsibility. *Racism is first and foremost a condition of the heart.* ... Like all sin, racism is first personal, and every one of us — African-American, Euro-American, Hispanic, Asian, Native American — must deal personally with this sin in our own lives. ... Whites must admit responsibility; but blacks also must admit wrongful attitudes.[23]

4. Evangelicals believe that the remedy for racism is personal conversion and deeper adherence to faith in Jesus Christ, for only Christ can break the demonic hold of racism that grips churches and individuals. Moreover, in Christ reconciliation has already been gained for us. This literature consistently and repeatedly invokes Ephesians 2:13–16; it regards Christ's dissolution of the barrier separating Jew and Greek as descriptive of the present action of Christ breaching the wall of hostility separating black and white.[24]

5. A concrete measure of the authenticity of one's conversion is one's willingness to be an "ambassador of reconciliation" (the text invoked here is 2 Cor. 5:17–20). Such willingness is manifested by one's commitment to develop relationships of mutuality and friendship with members of another race. Evangelical racial reconciliation stresses the importance of cultivating deep interracial relationships as the means of remedying the racial divide that plagues American churches and society. This conviction is virtually universal:

One of Satan's primary tools to inhibit racial reconciliation and cross-cultural outreach is to make us very comfortable with homogeneity.... However, being Christ's ambassadors at home may mean sacrifice — sacrifice that relinquishes an established status or position to adopt a lesser position in order to develop a cross-cultural friendship.[25]

Indeed, these authors devote considerable space to articulating what they consider "biblical attitudes" that ground, facilitate, and characterize Christian interracial relationships. For example, Perkins and Rice develop these principles: *"admit"* that there is a separation or division; *"submit"* to the healing power of God; and *"commit"* to "an intentional lifestyle of loving our racially different neighbors as ourselves."[26] Washington and Kehrein's contribution devotes considerable space to explicating the principles of "commitment, intentionality, sincerity, sensitivity, interdependence, sacrifice, empowerment, and call."[27]

6. Finally, these evangelical writers typically do not devote much time or attention to public policy issues relative to race. For example, one finds little sustained reflection upon or analysis of affirmative action, criminal justice reform, welfare reform debates, or civil rights legislation. The overwhelming evangelical consensus is that society and church are transformed through personal conversion and the cultivation of interpersonal cross-cultural relationships. As Perkins and Rice declare, *"Civil rights* is a political concept; the *brotherhood* spoken of by biblical and contemporary prophets is a much higher calling."[28]

Two possible reasons may account for this stress upon the personal dimension and virtual neglect of the systemic issues. First, evangelical theology and faith emphasize the necessity of a personal relationship with Jesus Christ as Lord and Savior.[29] This endemic focus upon the experience of personal salvation facilitates a marked concern for the *individual's* responsibility and participation in all forms of sin, particularly that of racism.

Second, in some evangelical quarters, the legacy of the 1960s, including the civil rights movement, is viewed suspiciously as the product of liberal activists whose religious convictions were at odds with what they believe to be religious orthodoxy. For example, many evangelical leaders and believers were wary of Martin Luther King Jr., partly because of what they considered his theological liberalism, a concern that endures even to the present day.[30] This suspicion that systemic social change advances the agenda of theological liberalism provides another explanation for the evangelical bias toward individual and personal approaches to social ills.[31]

There is much that is admirable in the evangelical approach. These authors evidence a passion, commitment, and urgency for the cause of racial reconciliation that is sorely lacking in other Christian traditions, including the Catholic Church. The testimony of the risks that the authors have taken, the costs they have paid for their convictions, and the sacrifices they undergo to witness to racial fellowship are truly inspiring. My (mostly white) students seldom fail to be moved, and even amazed, by these works. For many, their encounter with these authors is an occasion for deepening or recovering their own faith convictions.

Yet I must conclude that the evangelical perspective on racial reconciliation is inadequate, principally because of its neglect of the structural and institutional dimensions of racism. The cultivation of mutual interracial relationships based upon spiritual principles is admirable and even necessary. Such friendships go a long way toward overcoming the deep-seated racial isolation of American society that fuels racial stereotypes, suspicions, and fears. However, such relationships are insufficient. Faith-based friendship — what our authors call "yokefellowship"[32] — cannot overturn and dismantle the cultural stigmatization and structural disadvantage that lie at the core of America's racial quagmire.

This approach's shortcomings stem from the following fact: authentic loving relationships can exist even in the midst of a socially unjust situation. For example, despite the friendship, commitment, and love that these interracial authors evidence for each other, they never address the reality that one of the pair would likely experience racially pejorative treatment when seeking housing or approval for a mortgage loan.[33] Housing discrimination is a structural reality that cannot be remedied solely by friendship. Moreover, faith-based friendship is quite compatible with the existing dominant American ethos, which, I argue, harbors both interpersonal decency and structural inequality when it comes to racism. Interracial respect and kindness, while necessary, are woefully inadequate to the task of undermining the set of meanings and values that justify white privilege, advantage, and benefit. Thus the major shortcoming of the evangelical approach to racial reconciliation is that it is insufficiently attentive — if not even blind — to the nexus of race and social/political/cultural power and privilege, and the need to dismantle this linkage.

An Alternate Understanding of Racial Reconciliation

What, then, are we to do? Recall that this is a task that lies at the frontier of social ethical reflection. We scarcely understand the dynamics of interpersonal reconciliation; healing the culturally rooted estrangements and resentments that divide peoples into opposing blocs and groups is vastly more complex. Some even avow that this task demands a "knowledge and wisdom we have yet to attain."[34] I now offer my best insights, realizing they are incomplete yet necessary fragments in this vitally important endeavor.

Recall that racial divisions are not the results of a mere misunderstanding, breakdown in communications, or absence of dialogue. Overcoming them requires more than the abilities of a mediator or facilitator skilled in dispute resolution.[35] Our racial divides stem from a history of abuse, neglect, and abandonment; from the legacies of exploitation and the realities of humiliation; in short, from an absence or miscarriage of justice. Overcoming them requires social transformation.

Thus, there can be no authentic reconciliation without a struggle for justice. This is why I have long been impressed with Eric Yamamoto's approach to interracial reconciliation, for he roots reconciliation in the quest for justice. He describes interracial justice as follows:

> Interracial justice entails hard acknowledgment of the historical and contemporary ways in which racial groups harm one another, along with affirmative efforts to redress justice grievances and [their] present-day effects. ... Interracial justice is integral to ... the establishment of "right relationships, the healing of broken relationships."[36]

Yamamoto's extensive research leads him to conclude that there are four dimensions required for such interracial justice to be a reality:

1. *Recognition,* that is, an acknowledgment of the humanity of the other and the historical roots of racial grievances and cultural sources of conflict;

2. *Responsibility,* which entails an assessment of group agency in imposing harms upon another community and consequently accepting responsibility for the attending racial wounds;

3. *Reconstruction,* that is, the active steps of healing the psychological and social wounds — for example, the loss of dignity and respect, the sense of inferiority and self-hatred — caused by racial injustice (which may include apologies, statements of regret, and the acceptance thereof); and

4. *Reparation,* which is the process of rectifying the material harms caused by racial injustice and white systemic advantage (such as economic disadvantages, social deprivations, and/or political exclusions). Yamamoto notes that this dimension guards against insincere or incomplete racial reconciliation efforts that are "empty apologies" or "mere talk."[37]

Inspired by these seminal insights, I highlight two processes as critical: telling the truth and affirmative redress.

Truth-telling

Common to every effort of social reconciliation is a recognition that deep social wounds cannot be healed without an honest examination of the reasons for and causes of the estrangement. The South

African "Truth and Reconciliation" process is widely considered the paradigm of such efforts.[38]

Yamamoto describes truth-telling as the process of "recalling history and its present-day consequences in order to release its grip."[39] Healing racial divisions, then, entails facing history and facing ourselves. It demands a truthful accounting and owning of responsibility, an acknowledgment of the complicity and indifference that fuel social ruptures, and confronting the inconvenient truths and naming the social falsehoods that enabled injustice to occur.

This insight is entirely consistent with the Catholic faith. Pope John Paul II, citing an ancient maxim, declared: "Truth is the basis, foundation, and mother of justice."[40] Moreover, in reflecting on the challenges of the new millennium, John Paul called for a "purification of memory" as a necessary condition for reconciled relationships between peoples. The International Theological Commission explained that this purification of memory "aims at liberating personal and communal conscience from all forms of resentment and violence that are the legacy of past faults ... because the consequences of past faults still make themselves felt and can persist as tensions in the present."[41] With specific reference to racial divisions, the Pontifical Council for Justice and Peace declares, "the weight of history, with its litany of resentments, fears, suspicions between families, ethnic groups or populations must first be overcome."[42]

In addition to a more honest account of historical roots of racial injustice, then, truth-telling requires a certain shifting or reframing of the social narratives, that is, the "stock stories" social groups tell themselves, both to challenge their selective and partial recollections and to make their present-day effects more obvious and apparent.[43] As an example of such a reframing, we can consider the experience of African American enslavement. Any serious reflection upon racial reconciliation in the U.S. context must squarely confront the legacy of slavery.[44] The slavery narrative, though, is too often invoked in a way that instills a sense of horror for past events, yet also excuses present concern (as in the somewhat typical retort, "It's not my fault; I never owned any slaves!"). This fundamental American story needs to be retold in a way that illustrates its present reality and effects.[45] For slavery's horror does not lie only in events of brutality, cruelty, and dehumanization of a not so distant past. The horror of slavery *continues in the present* through a rarely acknowledged legacy, as Dalton explains:

> Slavery continues to shape our lives more than a century after abolition because the link it forged between Blackness and inferiority, Blackness and subservience, Blackness and danger, has survived to this day. Slavery's enduring legacy is that our "subhumanity" has been deeply imprinted in the American psyche. The resulting mental imprint continues to shape the way people think about race to this very day.... Slavery lives on in our lives; not as broken bones or clanking chains, but as a largely unconscious way of framing how we are seen, how we see ourselves, and how we relate to the world around us.[46]

In other words, the institution of black chattel slavery both expressed and continues to shape our nation's cultural consciousness. "The set of meanings and values that informs" our public life, forged in the crucible of slavery, indelibly links "blackness" with being "less than white" and thus suited for less than fully equal treatment. Some of the still enduring effects of this legacy are seen in the following account:

> Prejudice against black people in American culture gets expressed among Los Angeles white residents who will hire a newly arrived Latino immigrant from Mexico before they will hire a "fifteenth-generation" black resident of the United States. "They trust Latinos. They fear or disdain blacks.... Latinos, even when they are foreign, seem native and safe, while blacks, who are native, seem foreign and dangerous.... *This is what slavery has done to us as a people*, and I can scarcely think of it without tears."[47]

Thus concern about slavery is not so much centered upon an apology for the *past*, but for the sake of a more truthful acknowledgment of the *present*. Slavery's legacy as an African stigmata of inferiority needs to be forthrightly addressed and articulated in any adequate account or process of racial reconciliation in America.[48]

The importance of truth-telling means the struggle for racial justice is often a contest or clash between competing and divergent social narratives. Thus the effort of reconciling social divisions entails debunking the "comfortable fictions" — the deliberate distortions, misleading euphemisms, selective recollections, and self-serving presentations — that societies employ to mask the presence of injustice or make its existence tolerable. Facing history and ourselves, telling the truth of our situation, acknowledging our responsibility and complicity, and declaring who profited and how from these estrangements are essential to healing the wounds of racism.

Affirmative Redress

In agreement with Yamamoto, by "affirmative redress" I mean healing the psychic wounds, material harms, and economic disadvantages inflicted by racial injustice and its resulting social chasms.[49] Reparation repairs damaged social relationships by removing the systemic barriers that impede a racial or ethnic group's full participation in social life and the unambiguous recognition of their equal humanity. These include equitable and fair access to political participation, education, housing, medical care, employment, and promotion. The goal of affirmative redress is to rectify the harms caused by a long history of race-based unjust enrichment and unjust impoverishment.

Note again the consistency of this insight with religious faith. Catholic morality has long recognized the responsibility to repair the harm or injury done to another. Note the traditional injunctions about making restitution, an obligation rooted in the principle that "when injustice is done it must be repaired."[50] The Catholic magisterium recently has applied this insight on just restitution to the specific issue of racial grievances and the question of reparations. This teaching recognizes that various forms of racial reparation are possible, including monetary compensation, formal apologies and statements of regret, and symbolic gestures (such as monuments and memorials to the victims of an injustice).[51] As the U.S. bishops succinctly express this faith conviction, "Social harm calls for social relief."[52]

It is in this context that I address one form of affirmative redress, certainly not the most important but a particularly symbolic and neuralgic one in the U.S. context, namely, affirmative action. "Affirmative action" is an umbrella term given to a variety of practices that seek to address and rectify the pervasive discrimination and social stigma suffered by people of color and women. These measures strive in various ways to facilitate, encourage, or (rarely) compel the inclusion of these groups into the mainstream of American society. Such practices include aggressive recruitment and targeted advertising campaigns, remedial education and job training programs, vigilant enforcement of nondiscrimination laws, flexible hiring goals, recruitment targets, and promotion timetables, "weighting" applications from members of racial minority groups by assigning these applicants additional "points"(much as is done for veterans applying for certain government positions), and, in the extremely rare case of entrenched discrimination and the failure of voluntary measures, mandatory hiring and/or promotion quotas.

The basic premise of affirmative action is that given the longstanding and deeply rooted cultural stigma attached to factors such as dark skin color, racial minorities and others will continue to suffer social exclusion without concerted, conscious, and deliberate efforts to incorporate them into American public life.

One reason why affirmative action is such a divisive and uncomfortable topic is precisely because it seeks to address historic wrongs and continuing injustices. One simply cannot discuss or evaluate affirmative action without considering the reality of past and present racially based disadvantages. As the noted constitutional scholar Mary Frances Berry observed: "The reason we need *affirmative* action is because we've had so much *negative* action throughout American history."[53] As a nation, we are struggling to overcome the present consequences of a history of brutal bigotry and bruising exclusion that we have never fully acknowledged. An honest debate over affirmative action demands a hard look at racially based exclusionary practices and discriminatory behaviors that many are hesitant (to say the least) to face. Affirmative action, then, is a painful, public reminder of how our tragic and embarrassing past still lingers and haunts us in the present.

Affirmative action has at least a twofold purpose: (1) to compensate for the enduring effects of our history of publicly sponsored racial exclusion and segregation; and (2) to minimize the occurrence of present and future discrimination with the goal of creating a just and inclusive society.[54]

The struggle to eradicate discrimination is the context for the church's endorsement of affirmative action. The most recent statement of this teaching is in the second edition of the Pontifical Commission for Justice and Peace's document *The Church and Racism* issued in 2001. Here, the Holy See notes the need to overcome the "weight of history" that often impedes the progress of racial groups. The statement also calls attention to the increased interdependence that marks culturally diverse societies. These realities — the summons to eradicate racial divisions, the need to overcome the legacy of past discrimination, and the fact of growing cultural intermingling — lead the church to reaffirm its support for targeted programs of preferential redress. The document declares, "It cannot be denied that the weight of historical, social, and cultural precedents requires at times positive action by States.... It is not enough to recognize equality — it has to be created."[55]

As stated before, affirmative action is only one form of affirmative redress to heal racial wounds and injustice. There is no way to consider the wide varieties and forms of redress and healing that are possible or necessary. What must be stressed, though, is that without proactive, intentional, and conscious efforts to rectify social relationships, what often results is but a covering over of social tensions, not a fundamental change. Without a firm commitment to concrete action to right past and present wrongs and make whole those who have been harmed, verbal apologies or statements of regret over racial injustices are empty rhetoric, if not worse.

OTHER RESOURCES
IN THE FAITH TRADITION

Despite a corpus of official Catholic social teaching and a tradition of ethical reflection upon pressing social issues, a search of the theological literature on the topics of "race," "racial discrimination," and "race relations" yields little that is specifically concerned with racial reconciliation.[56] The Catholic perspective offers nothing comparable to either the genre or the amount of literature found in the evangelical tradition. The most notable fact concerning the Catholic theological contribution to racial reconciliation is its absence.[57]

If the essence of racial reconciliation in the United States is the critique and dismantling of the structured pattern of racial privilege and disadvantage, then Catholic theological ethics has the resources for making a substantial contribution. This faith tradition possesses an understanding of distributive justice that requires that social harms be apportioned in such a way as not to burden those members of the community least able to bear them. It provides a sophisticated understanding of social sin, which recognizes that sin becomes embodied in public life and social institutions. It also advocates an understanding of the Gospel that entails a stance of solidarity with and decisive commitment on behalf of the poor, dispossessed, and socially vulnerable. It is not, then, a lack of resources that prevents a Catholic presence and contribution to this discussion.

I believe that there are at least two kinds of factors that contribute to Catholic absence in this discourse. The first is theological. For example, despite the resources listed above, moral theologians observe that Catholic theological ethics has not fully overcome the influence of the practice of auricular confession upon its moral teaching and reflection. The moral historian John Mahoney has masterfully demonstrated the decisive impact of the discipline of private confession on Catholic moral praxis and reflection.[58] He argues that among its effects is a lingering privatized understanding of sin. While I agree with Mahoney, I maintain his inadequate appreciation of the communal dimensions of sacramental reconciliation, along with an overly privatized concept of sin, also hinders Catholic theological reflection on racial reconciliation.[59]

A second factor that hinders Catholic theological reflection on this issue is something Catholic ethicist Paul Wadell describes as a lack of hospitality toward the African American experience on the part of American Catholic moralists. Indeed, Wadell declares, "Hospitality is a precondition for justice and justice is a precondition for morality. American Catholic ethics can move to justice when it begins showing hospitality to the stories, experiences, and challenges of African Americans."[60] I can only concur. A lack of hospitality — a lack of regard, attention, or sensitivity — to the African American experience on the part of the Catholic moral guild is undoubtedly a significant factor in the lack of Catholic reflection upon racial reconciliation.

It would be a major oversight not to mention recent efforts in Catholic theology and ethics to rectify this pattern of omission and lack of hospitality.[61] Among many potential contributions, the linkage between reconciliation and the pursuit of justice and the need for a spirituality to undergird efforts at systemic reconciliation are especially noteworthy.

Lament and Compassion

As valuable as Yamamoto's insights are and despite my strong agreement with him, something seems to be missing from his proposals. While Yamamoto admits that the realities of recognition, responsibility, reconstruction, and reparation are dynamic and even messy processes, he still frames these as tactical practices or techniques. This runs the risk of feeding into our American tendency to believe that we can solve our social problems solely through rational analysis, hard work, and tenacious determination.

But such an overly practical and technical approach cannot contend with the deeply entrenched racial injustices in our nation and world. The insufficiency becomes particularly evident when we take seriously the preconscious and nonrational character of racism and its role as an identity marker. Racism engages us viscerally. This makes racial injustice, on its deepest levels, impervious to rational appeals and cognitive strategies. Moreover, through the selective sympathy and indifference it instills, racism numbs us to the reality of injustice and makes us calloused and hardened to its manifold harms. Logic alone seldom compels action in the face of indifference. As stand-alone tactical strategies, truth-telling and affirmative redress fall short of what is required and will often lead their advocates to a sense of futility, cynicism, resignation, and despair.

We cannot save ourselves solely through rational analysis, study, and planning. Another kind of response is also needed, one that transcends the limits of logic and reason. I believe that racial reconciliation and the justice it demands require a prior response, namely, a response of *lament*, which both stems from and leads to deep *compassion*.

Lament

Dorothee Sölle, in considering the challenge of piercing through the callus of indifference to the plight of those who suffer injustice, writes:

> If people are not to remain unchanged in suffering, if they are not to be blind and deaf to the pain of others, if they are to move from purely passive endurance to suffering that can humanize them in a productive way, then one of the things they need is a language.[62]

One such language present in our faith tradition is that of lament. Lament is a profound response to suffering, one that stems from acknowledging its harsh reality and entails "simply being truthful, avoiding denial (which could be so easy) and admitting the pain and horror of the suffering.... We express our pain in lament [by] crying out [which] allows us to grieve."[63]

Laments are cries of anguish and outrage, groans of deep pain and grief, utterances of profound protest and righteous indignation over injustice, wails of mourning and sorrow in the face of unbearable suffering. Lamentation is a cry of utter anguish and passionate protest at the state of the world and its brokenness.

Laments name the pain present, and they forthrightly acknowledge that life and relationships have gone terribly wrong. They are
uncivil, strident, harsh, and heart-rending. They are profound inter-
ruptions and claims to attention. Laments pierce the crusty calluses
of numbness, cynicism, indifference, and denial.

Such emotionally laden protests in the face of suffering and injustice are a principal part of Israel's prayer and of our faith heritage.
Walter Brueggemann points out that laments and cries of personal
and communal distress comprise fully one-third of the psalter. He
lists the following characteristics of biblical laments: the *complaint*
or "vexation," which is the cause for distress, a complaint that often
implicates God for this state of affairs; a *petition* for help and divine
intervention; the *reasons* why such divine assistance is warranted
(often through a reminder of God's own promises that seem to be
breached); and *a statement of resolution* and praise. Thus scriptural
laments are marked by a movement from protest and petition to
praise and hope. Brueggemann concludes that the Hebrews' laments
were exercises of "enormous *chutzpah*" and writes, "Israel did not
hesitate to give full voice to its fear, anger, and dismay, which are
palpably present in life and speech, and which contradict the settled
claims of faith."[64]

Denise Ackermann echoes these sentiments after her rediscovery
of this scriptural response to injustice and its harms:

> These ancient people simply refused to settle for things as
> they were. They believed that God could, should, and indeed
> would do something to change unbearable circumstances.
> Their lament was candid, intense, robust, and unafraid. They
> complained, mourned, wept, chanted dirges and cursed. They
> assailed the ears of God, believing they could wring the hand
> of God and insisting their petitions be taken so seriously that,
> in doing so, God is put at risk....I found a language that
> is honest, that does not shirk from naming the unnameable,
> that does not lie down in the face of suffering or walk away
> from God.[65]

Thus, in laments we find a "not readily explainable" paradox of protest and praise.[66] Lamentation is an expression of complaint, grief, and hope rooted in a "trust against trust" that God hears the cry of the afflicted and will respond compassionately to their need. Lamenting holds together both loss and hope in ways that defy easy rational understanding. Laments honestly, forthrightly, even brutally recognize wrenching circumstances, yet proclaim that in the midst of the pain there is another word to be heard from God — a message of compassion and deliverance.

To balance this analytical and abstract discussion of a profoundly interruptive experience, I now explore some concrete instances of lamentation in the African American experience. These laments vividly illustrate the dynamics of the Bible's ancient protests.

"Nobody Knows the Trouble I've Seen"

In the corpus of sacred song that we call the African American spirituals, one finds many expressions of unbearable grief and anguished protest so intense that they strain the limits of speech. Such songs include "Sometimes I Feel Like a Motherless Child" and "I Wish I'd Never Been Born." But among the most heartrending is "Nobody Knows the Trouble I've Seen."

> Nobody knows the trouble I've seen,
> Nobody knows my sorrow [or "but Jesus"];
> Nobody knows the trouble I've seen,
> Glory, halleluiah![67]

Scholars report that this wail of mourning and protest originated from the heart of an enslaved African "whose trials were almost more than he could bear. After wife and children had been sold away, he withdrew into his cabin and poured out his sorrow in this song." Later, even after emancipation, the putatively freed blacks used this song as the vehicle for their intense distress at a government's broken promise to provide the land necessary for economic self-sufficiency and thus effective liberty.[68] The singers declare that nobody but Jesus — only the Divine — can comprehend the depths of agony, affliction, and desperation this community bears because of the injustice visited upon it. This pain, so raw and existential, can scarcely be expressed even through this song's haunting cadence. Yet the injustice demands a forthright articulation.

However, note how the lament ends — in a way "not readily explainable" — on a note of praise: "Glory, hallelujah!" The song ceases to be only an expression of sorrow; the hope in an ultimate justice serves as a catalyst for risky and defiant action. The enslaved husband and father returns to his task, fortified by an inner strength and resolve that leave him uncrushed by his circumstances. The emancipated community, though betrayed, continues to seek means of survival and future redress. As John Lovell notes, "The mere creation or singing of such a song, from the standpoint of personal character, is a great victory over adversity."[69]

This spiritual, then, exemplifies a core characteristic of the lament genre: it expresses the reality and pain of evil and suffering, and yet is more than mere mourning or catharsis. The act of lamenting overcomes psychic numbness and stunned silence in the face of evil. Its wails, cries, and pleas tear asunder the veil of complacency and the shroud of immobilizing fear. Lament facilitates the emergence of something new, whether a changed consciousness or a renewed engagement with outer events.[70] It is indeed a paradox of protest and praise that leads to new life.

"A Litany at Atlanta"

In 1906, the city of Atlanta was torn apart by vicious white mob violence directed against an emerging black middle class. These attacks stemmed from white anxiety and resentment at African Americans who defied the restrictions of Jim Crow segregation and refused the narrow social and economic opportunities allowed under white supremacist laws and customs. Under the false pretext of avenging sexual assaults of white women by black men, thousands of white men and boys rampaged through Atlanta's streets over a two-day period, killing between twenty-five and forty blacks, injuring hundreds more, and destroying many black-owned businesses.[71]

In the aftermath of this violence, the noted activist and scholar W. E. B. Du Bois poetically expressed the community's pain, fury, and protest:

O Silent God, Thou whose voice afar in mist and mystery hath left our ears an-hungered in these fateful days —
    Hear us, good Lord! ...

A city lay in travail, God, our Lord, and from her loins sprang twin Murder and Black Hate. Red was the midnight; clang, crack and cry of death and fury filled the air and trembled underneath the stars when church spires pointed silently to Thee. And all this to sate the greed of greedy men who hide behind the veil of vengeance!
    Bend us Thine ear, O Lord! ...

Bewildered are we, and passion-tost, mad with the madness of a mobbed and mocked and murdered people; straining at the arm-posts of Thy Throne, we raise our shackled hands and charge Thee, God, by the bones of our stolen fathers, by the tears of our dead mothers, by the very blood of Thy crucified Christ: *What meanth this?* Tell us the Plan; give us the Sign!
    Keep not Thou silence, O God!

Sit no longer blind, Lord God, deaf to our prayer and dumb to our dumb suffering. Surely Thou too art not white, O Lord, a pale, bloodless, heartless thing?
    Ah! Christ of all the Pities!

Forgive the thought! Forgive these wild, blasphemous words. Thou art still the God of our black fathers. . . . But whisper — speak — call, great God, for Thy silence is white terror to our hearts! The way, O God, show us the way and point us to the path. . . . Tempt us not beyond our strength. . . . [72]

Du Bois presents us with a classic expression of lament in the biblical mode: a complaint against a brutal injustice that calls God to account and even questions a divine role in the tragedy, a petition for help in redressing the community's wounds and sorrow, and reasons that the Divine should respond heedfully ("Surely Thou too art not white, O Lord," in other words, you are not an ally of oppressors and the perpetrators of racial hatred). This lament, however, does not end with an articulated statement of praise or hope. Perhaps the very act of honest lamentation is itself an expression of trust that this outrage is not history's — or God's — final act.

Similar to the singers of the spirituals, this lament facilitates the emergence of a new thing. Du Bois does not succumb to numbing paralysis and continues his long career of challenging racial injustices and atrocities. Some young victim-witnesses to these events, including the jurist Walter White, will go on to become major advocates in the struggle against racial segregation.[73] As John Swinton observes, "Lament provides us with a language of outrage that speaks against the way things are, but always in hope that the way things are just now is not the way they always will be. Lament is thus profoundly hopeful."[74]

What, then, is the relevance of lament to the achievement of racial justice? The nonrational and unconscious dimensions of racism show us that this injustice cannot be defeated solely or even principally through intellectual responses. Lament, however, provides a language that can disrupt the apparent normalcy of a skewed racialized culture and identity. Its cry of pain, rage, sorrow, and grief in the midst of suffering interrupts the "way things are" and demands attention.

Lament has the power to challenge the entrenched cultural beliefs that legitimate racial privilege. Lament makes visible the masked injustice hidden beneath the deep rationalizations of social life. It engages a level of human consciousness deeper than logical reason; its harrowing cries of distress indisputably announce: "All is not well! Something is terribly wrong! Such things should not and must not be!" Laments thus propel us to new levels of truth-seeking as they raise profound and uncomfortable questions that cannot be easily answered with the existing cultural template. The standard accounts of social reality wither before a lament's strident account of agony.

As Denise Ackermann concisely notes: "When lamenting people assume the power to define reality and to proclaim that all is not well, things begin to change. . . . The lamenter's voices become subversive."[75] This nonrational activity of lament, I believe, is essential before truth-telling and affirmative redress can succeed in a culture of racialized privilege and indifference inhabited by a people "uneasy with injustice but unwilling to pay a significant price to eradicate it." Recovery of this practice and genre, so deeply rooted in our faith heritage, is an important tool in the arsenal of racial justice.[76]

Laments and the Privileged

There is another aspect of lament that is relevant and useful for the achievement of racial justice. It lies in the realization that others, in addition to the direct and immediate victims of injustice, can lament. The beneficiaries of injustice can also lament, grieve, and protest. The lament of the victims reveals the social truth to others, and an awareness dawns that social injustice is more rampant and virulent than one has been led to believe. As Ackermann observes, in speaking of the context of South African apartheid, "penitent people [can] lament what they have done because they see that their wrongdoing is the cause of grief and suffering and this fact grieves and saddens them."[77] The prior lament of the victims enables the privileged to engage in lament as well.

For the beneficiaries of white privilege, lament involves the difficult task of acknowledging their individual and communal complicity in past and present racial injustices. It entails a hard acknowledgment that one has benefited from another's burden and that one's social advantages have been purchased at a high cost to others. Here lament takes the form of a forthright confession of human wrongdoing in the light of God's mercy. It is a form of truth-telling and contrition that acknowledges *both* the harms that have been done to others *and* one's personal and communal culpability for them.

Pope John Paul gave the Catholic Church an example of lament over racial injustice, one yet to be appropriated by the U.S. faith community. At a prayer service in St. Peter's Basilica during the 2000 Jubilee Year, the pontiff prayed these words:

Lord our God, you created the human being, man and woman, in your image and likeness, and you willed the diversity of peoples within the unity of the human family. At times, however, the equality of your sons and daughters has not been acknowledged, and Christians have been guilty of attitudes of rejection and exclusion, consenting to acts of discrimination on the basis of racial and ethnic difference. Forgive us and grant us the grace to heal the wounds still present in your community on account of sin, so that we will all feel ourselves to be your sons and daughters.[78]

For Catholics in the United States, this lament needs to be made more specific and concrete. Lament in our context demands a searching confession of the "counter-witness and scandal"[79] on the part of many believers in the struggle for racial justice and equality. Notwithstanding the heroic witness of some, too frequently Catholics — rather than being agents of social change and cultural transformation — have conformed to the racial mores of our society and engaged in practices of racial denigration. As the U.S. bishops admitted in *Brothers and Sisters to Us,* "We have allowed conformity to social pressures to replace compliance with social justice."[80]

Catholic Christians have shared in and even abetted the racial fears and prejudices of American society

♦ through active participation in the evil of black chattel slavery;

♦ by permissive silence during the horrors of African American lynchings;

♦ by a lack of respect for the cultural traditions of this land's Native peoples;

+ by a refusal and/or hesitancy to welcome people of color into the priesthood, religious life, and positions of lay leadership;

+ by confusing the cultural values of white society with the truths of the Gospel in missionary activities;

+ through a hesitant or belated embrace of the movement for civil rights;

+ by hostility or rudeness toward persons of color when they sought membership in our parishes;

+ by ostracizing those who spoke and acted in prophetic ways for racial justice; and

+ by clinging to racial wounds and being closed to sincere requests for forgiveness.

In these and many other ways, Catholic Christians have acted in complicity with the endemic racism of our society.[81] Lament acknowledges these sins of the past and present with sorrow and humbly seeks forgiveness both from God and from those who have been harmed by the counterwitness of Catholics.[82]

Lament as contrition and sorrow for the wrongs that one has done or that have been done in one's name is not rooted in a political correctness, but in the deep awareness that as a faith community we have betrayed our own faith convictions thorough our entanglement with the sin of racism. We become aware that all people, no matter their racial designations, are injured by a racial ideology that damages and wounds us though in different ways. Yet we are also aware that our realization and confession is possible only by the mercy of God.[83]

The lament of the socially privileged is also a stance of hope that human wrongdoing is not God's final act in the drama of personal and social salvation. This hope permits truthful and direct acknowledgment of social estrangements and one's participation in them. Stirred by the laments of the more immediate victims, the beneficiaries of white privilege can also be moved to lament in anger and sorrow: "I no longer stand by my wrongdoing [or complicity]; I repent of it and side with you in condemning it."[84] Note how such a stance of lament also involves a change of social location and identity. Here, as with the victims, the expression of pain serves as a catalyst for risky and defiant action. For the beneficiaries of systemic injustice, lament is a stance on behalf of its victims. Here we see the beginnings of compassion and solidarity.

Compassion

Honest lament then gives rise to a deep sense of *compassion*. Given the fertile theological and ethical literature on compassion, the overview here can be briefer than the previous treatment of lament.[85] I first consider compassion as it is manifested in the life of Jesus, and then ponder its importance for the task of racial justice-making.

The Gospels relate how Jesus was often moved with compassion by the anguish and misery he encountered. The Greek word for compassion often used in this context, *splanchnizesthai,* connotes a visceral response of profound feeling and strong emotion; it emanates from one's bowels or guts.[86] Compassion, then, is the response stirred within one's deepest humanity when confronted with human agony or need.

The Gospels further relate how such compassion is the motive for many of Jesus' miracles and parables. Jesus raises the only son of a widowed mother out of compassion not only for her human grief, but also for the severe social vulnerability to which the death of her only male protector exposed her. The Samaritan comes to the aid of a sworn enemy because he was moved to compassion at the sight of injury and violation. An elderly father hastens to welcome his estranged son, being moved to compassion by his humiliation and outcast status.

In each of these situations, the Gospels say that compassion is the motive for moving beyond the social boundaries decreed by culture and custom. They describe compassion as something visceral, as an inner stirring and a movement of one's innards. This profound emotion and deep visceral reaction is the hallmark of authentic compassion. Compassion arises not through an avoidance of suffering, but from a deeper entering into it. Compassion is a gut-wrenching response to human suffering and anguish that propels one to act beyond the limits of what is considered reasonable and acceptable. As Maureen O'Connell rightly notes, "Compassion overrides social, cultural, racial, economic, and religious boundaries."[87]

Seen in this light, compassion is an essential dimension of racial reconciliation and justice-making. Caleb Rosado, a longtime racial activist, goes so far as to maintain that compassion is the counterpart of racism.[88] He develops this thought by distinguishing compassion from its often taken synonyms of sympathy and empathy. He describes sympathy as a *feeling* of sorrow for the plight of another, but one that is often from a stance of social distance or remove from the victim. It's a sense of pity at another's need, along with a response of "I'm-not-like-you." Sympathy remains at the level of mere emotion.

Empathy builds on this emotional response as there is not only sorrow but *identification* with the other in need. Empathy establishes a "bridge of identification" with the other, enters his or her emotional sphere, and identifies with the pain. One sees how this plight could be one's own. A popular way of saying this is, "There but for the grace of God go I." Rosado says that out of empathy arises a "weeping with those who weep."

Compassion is a response of a different level. Here there is not only sorrow for and identification with, but *action* to meet the other's need. Compassion acts to alleviate the suffering of another. Rosado further argues that authentic compassion tends toward a mutuality of action so that the victims are also empowered as agents in the process of change. He draws an explicit connection to the biblical understanding of compassion when he declares: "This is what the story of the Good Samaritan is all about — to see oneself in the experience of the Other and move into action to change the circumstances, and not just limit one's efforts to a mere sympathetic or empathetic response." Genuine compassion manifests itself in action for the sake of another's dignity, respect, and social worth.

Insofar as racism is characterized by a systemic indifference or social callousness based on skin color differences, compassion is its polar opposite. I believe that compassion is a decisive Christian attitude. Without it, the Jesus story is incoherent, and a life inspired by the Gospels is impossible. I also believe that without a prior stirring of compassion, without a deeply felt response to the agony of agony of racial crucifixions and the scandal of social ostracism, we will not be moved to justice and the repair of social divisions. We act justly, not because we are intellectually convinced, but because we are passionately moved. Compassion moves the will to justice.

COMPASSION AND INTENTIONAL CROSS-RACIAL SOLIDARITY

Compassion gives rise to solidarity, that key virtue in Catholic social thought that leads us to recognize our responsibility for one another and how we really are given to each other's care.[89] "Solidarity" has emerged as a pivotal concept in Catholic social thought, especially under the pontificate of Pope John Paul II. He viewed solidarity as that moral and social virtue that stems from a reflection upon both the fact of human interdependence and the tragic reality of social and economic divisions. Thus he defines solidarity as a *"firm and persevering determination* to commit oneself to the common good; that is to say to the good of all and of each individual, because we are *all* really responsible for *all.*"[90] He argues that solidarity is not a mere sentiment of vague feeling at another's plight; it is not, in other words, only sympathy or empathy for another's plight. Rather, John Paul teaches that solidarity is a commitment, a "firm and persevering determination" to act. Solidarity, then, is an expression of compassion. This commitment to the common good of all will lead individuals and communities to recognize one another as persons, and move them to overturn the "structures of sin" that embody the human vices of a "desire for profit" and "thirst for power."[91]

Solidarity is based upon the deep-seated conviction that the concerns of the despised other are intimately bound up with our own, that we are, in the words of Martin Luther King Jr., "bound together in a garment of mutual destiny." James H. Cone extends this argument, contending that solidarity is the means by which all — victims and beneficiaries of systemic injustice — realize their full humanity:

The truly free are identified with the humiliated because they know that their being is involved with the degradation of their sisters and brothers. They cannot stand to see them stripped of their humanity. This is so not because of pity or sympathy, but because their own existence is being limited by another's slavery.[92]

Thus solidarity is exercised in a society when, as John Paul declares, "its members recognize one another as persons." Since the poor, racial outcasts, and the culturally marginalized are those whose personhood is most often attacked, questioned, or reviled, the acid test of solidarity is our sense of connection with and commitment to the poor and excluded.

Solidarity entails a constant effort to build a human community where every social group participates equitably in social life and contributes its genius for the good of all. In view of the seismic racial and ethnic demographic transformations occurring in the United States, cultivating and promoting the cause of solidarity is a major challenge facing religious believers and institutions.

Yet racism is precisely a breach of human solidarity, manifested in an indifference to the plight of persons of color. As cited in the first chapter, Jesse Jackson opined in the aftermath of Katrina, "We have an amazing tolerance for black pain," and "There's a historical indifference to the pain of poor people and black people" in this country. Indeed, we have seen how authors speak of "racially selective sympathy and indifference," that is, the "unconscious failure to extend to a minority the same recognition of humanity, and hence the same sympathy and care, given as a matter of course to one's own group."[93]

Joe Feagin, a prolific scholar on the sociology of white racism, notes that socialization in a culture of racism blunts one's ability to feel the pain of the oppressed. He calls this "social alexithymia," that is, "the sustained inability to relate to and understand the suffering of those who are oppressed." He posits that such emotional blunting or callousness is essential for the maintenance of an unjust racialized society: "Essential to being an oppressor in a racist society is a significantly reduced ability, or an inability, to understand or relate to the emotions, such as recurring pain, of those targeted by oppression."[94]

This leads me to posit that the only way for cross-racial solidarity to occur is through the recovery or development of *compassion*. Compassion is thus both the ground and the fruit of authentic cross-racial solidarity. But what facilitates its accomplishment?

Feagin's research again is valuable and instructive. He has discovered that in developing authentic cross-racial identification and solidarity, white Americans typically pass through three different stages: sympathy, empathy, and what he calls autopathy:

> The initial stage, sympathy, is important but limited. It typically involves a willingness to set aside some racist stereotyping and hostility and the development of a friendly if variable interest in what is happening to the racialized other. ...Empathy is a much more advanced stage of development in that it requires a developed ability to routinely reject distancing stereotypes and a heightened and sustained capacity to see and feel some of the pain of those in the outgroup.[95]

Feagin admits that autopathy, the third stage of white development, has not been fully analyzed by the social sciences (perhaps because it requires responses that go beyond their horizons). This stage, which he also calls "transformative love," occurs when whites intentionally place themselves, "if only partially, into the racist world of the oppressed and thereby not only receive racist hostility from whites but also personally feel some of the pain that comes from being enmeshed in the racist conditions central to the lives of the oppressed others."[96]

Here the beneficiaries of white privilege and advantage not only grieve the suffering of others through vicarious experience, but themselves endure some of the same racial rejection and exclusion. Feagin notes that this is often the experience of whites who are the close friends, partners, parents, or other close relatives of blacks who are the direct targets of racism. This goes beyond being a "white ally" as that term is sometimes understood. Here white people, out of a commitment to share life with the other — indeed, to share the life of another — "intentionally place themselves in the discriminatory settings of loved ones and thus endure some of the hostility and pain of those settings."[97]

Such transformative love or interracial solidarity, what I have been calling compassion, has the power to profoundly affect the racial attitudes — and even the very identity — of white Americans. Feagin and O'Brien provide an illuminating testimony of such racial alteration:

> Well, you know, I don't consider myself totally white.... Physically, I'm white, I know.... But my wife and my love is a black woman and my son is this little golden boy. He's over there [points to photo].... I don't really permit myself to think of myself as just white, you know. Now, maybe that, part of that's out of an abhorrence to what the whites have done ... to the Native Americans and the African Americans, and how intolerant as a group we've been. But I remember years ago being at a party with my wife, in a local city.... And on the ride home, and it was a party that was all white people, sort of yuppies, and it was a polite, nice party. But there was no music, no real liveliness to the party at all and if you're, if you're around people of color they usually have music on, you know, a lot of, a lot of warmth.... And when we were riding home, I said, "Geez, we were the only black people there," and that was just, you know, sort of a spontaneous comment. And she started laughing, you know.[98]

Another insightful account of the significance of transformative love and solidarity is provided by Walt Harrington, a white man married to a black woman and the father of two biracial children. Harrington was shocked into an awareness of the depth of racism through a casual racist joke uttered in his presence. Moved by this incident, he undertook a year-long journey to discover "black America." At the end of his journey, he writes:

> But what I discovered while sitting in the dentist's chair more than a year ago, what I learned from the dentist who stopped

by and casually told a racist joke about a black man who was stupid, still remains the greatest insight I have to share: *The idiot was talking about my kids!* ...

This kind of understanding changes everything. Only when I *became* black by proxy — through my son, through my daughter — could I see the racism I have been willing to tolerate. Becoming black, even for a fraction of an instant, created an urgency for justice that I couldn't feel as only a white man, no matter how good-hearted. It is absolute proof of our continued racism that no white person in his or her right mind would yet volunteer to trade places, *become* black, in America today.[99]

What is truly remarkable in these testimonies is how deep interracial friendship and love can shatter the false personal identity built upon the racialized "set of meanings and values" that informs American society. Each one spoke of "becoming black," that is, of a new way of being white and experiencing social reality. Such a person is truly "born again" and lives out of a different identity and social consciousness. Such loving and committed relationships give one the visceral outrage, courage, strength, and motivation to break free from the "rewards of conformity" that keep most whites complacent with white privilege.[100] Transformative love, or compassion, empowers them for authentic solidarity. This makes them effective agents of racial reconciliation who are willing to speak the truth and endure the demands of affirmative redress that are essential for real social transformation. Without the cultivation of such solidarity — rooted in lament, compassion, and transformative love — truth-telling and affirmative redress result in superficial palliatives that leave the deep roots of injustice undisturbed.

CHURCH PRACTICES THAT FACILITATE RACIAL SOLIDARITY

With this understanding of the task and possibility of authentic reconciliation and solidarity, let us briefly reflect on some practices of the church that can facilitate the development of authentic racial identity. Recall the observations with which this chapter began, namely, that the Christian faith has a valuable contribution to make to racial justice-making by providing an alternative identity grounded in a counter set of meanings and values. I will consider three church practices for supporting such identity formation: conversion, baptism, and the celebration of the Eucharist.

Conversion

Theologian Bernard Lonergan's understanding of the conversion experience is helpful for this discussion. By conversion he means a fundamental shift in one's paradigm of understanding, interpreting, and acting upon reality. It entails taking on an entirely new field of vision, that is, entering into a totally new horizon of reference and understanding that dramatically expands the scope of one's interests and range of knowledge.[101] Using the metaphor of sight, Lonergan says of a conversion experience: "It is as if one's eyes were opened and one's former world faded and fell away,"[102] so that "what hitherto was unnoticed becomes vivid and present...what had been of no concern becomes a matter of high import."[103] Conversion implies a radical transformation of the subject and his or her relationships with self, others, and God.

Lonergan's perspective on conversion gives Christian believers a context for articulating the religious significance of racial compassion and for appreciating the challenge of cross-racial solidarity in a culture of endemic racism. Such solidarity demands nothing less than a conversion, that is, a fundamental break with the mental categories and group allegiances that give us meaning and identity. Racial conversion is a radical experience of personal and social redefinition. It is both the outcome of an experience of "transformative love" and that which makes such love possible. Racial solidarity is a *paschal* experience, one that entails a dying of a false sense of self and a renunciation of racial privilege so as to rise to a new identity and a status that is God-given. It is a dying to sin and alienation and being reborn with a new orientation or way of being in society.

This understanding of conversion also points to a contribution that the church can make. Conversion demands the successful negotiation of a time of passage and transition, of a period of crisis and intense change.[104] Yet this crisis is not always successfully resolved. The experience of conversion — involving as it does the crumbling and surrender of the old and familiar when at times not even the outline of the new can be discerned — is often an experience of tension, fragmentation, fear, panic, and anxiety. These reactions can lead one to abort the conversion process.

The Christian community can help facilitate the process of conversion. Through its rituals and symbols of belief, "it names and offers the assurance of meaning to an experience which threatens to overwhelm the person"; it renders the experience intelligible and less terrifying and thus enables the individual to complete the journey to newness of life.[105] It offers a faith-based narrative that makes the process of racial conversion — the journey through indifference, complicity, sympathy, empathy, and solidarity — comprehensible and worthwhile.

By providing the strength and courage for facing difficult truths, the church can help manage the crisis of personal conversion and hence facilitate attaining the promise and hope of new life. The faith community thus serves as a kind of incubator for new life. Through its rites and sacred story it offers the assurance of new life and identity on the other side of loss and transition. In this way, it can sustain the journey undertaken to a fuller and more authentic racial identity, one purged from the set of meanings and values that justify racial supremacy and white privilege.

Baptism

The Christian practice and understanding of baptism radically relativizes all human social status and cultural identities. In the letter to the Galatians Paul declares: "For all of you who were baptized into Christ have clothed yourselves with Christ. There is neither Jew nor Greek, there is neither slave nor free person, there is not male and female; for you are all one in Christ Jesus" (3:27–28). What a powerful declaration not only of the unity of the human community in Christ, but, more importantly, of the stripping away of the ultimate significance of human demarcations of social rank and privilege. Baptism does not result in a monochrome faith community; rather, the social significance of skin color is redefined and indeed undermined. The social meanings of skin tone cannot — and must not — compromise the fundamental equality of the baptized gained through Christ.

This radical equality conferred in baptism is one that is intuitively grasped, and resisted, by Christians. It was the reason, for example, that Christian slavemasters were reluctant to have their slaves baptized; they had a well-founded concern over owning a fellow believer. This means that one of the most powerful contributions the Christian community can make toward the goal of racial justice is to celebrate the sacrament of baptism regularly, publicly, and well. For when the community reverently washes the body, lathers it in oil, and lovingly swaddles it in new garments, it communicates a belief about the reverence of life *regardless of color* on a level that cannot be addressed by legislation or social policy (as necessary as these are). Such baptismal practices and catechesis instill within the preconsciousness of believers a new understanding of social identity that is at odds with and subversive to the dominant racial cultural narratives.

Let me make this concrete by an appeal to the Rite of Baptism itself. In the Catholic baptismal ritual, the child or adult is wrapped in a white garment. As the parents and/or godparents clothe the newly baptized, the priest says: "You have become a new creation, and have clothed yourself in Christ. See in this white garment the outward sign of your Christian dignity. With your family and friends to help you by word and example, bring that dignity unstained into the everlasting life of heaven." You have become a new creation, clothed in Christ! Notice the awesome charge of these words.

In baptism, Christ effects in us a "spiritual revolution," an inner transformation of our ways of thinking, valuing, and deciding, which turns upside down our "default" value systems. Our baptismal charge is no longer to think and act as "everybody else," that is, according to the racialized ethos that defines American (especially "white") identity. We are to be a "new creation," a "new being," radically remade in the image of Christ.

Our baptismal call is to see life in a new way and to become more and more who we are. For we have been transformed and changed. Our challenge is this: will we be who we say we are, new beings clothed in Christ, living by a different standard of hospitality for the racially other as a fellow new being in Christ? Will our life be marked by the renunciation of racial evil as contrary to the inner life within us? Baptism rightly understood and practiced cannot but affect our social valuing, our political decisions, and the way we understand our fundamental identities and our relationship to one another and the society in which we live.

Eucharist

The social egalitarianism at the heart of the Lord's Supper is well attested to in our foundational New Testament accounts (for example, 1 Cor. 11). One of the core practices of the Christian community is its ritual remembrance of Jesus at a meal, and Jesus' earthly meals were characterized by a shockingly inclusive table fellowship. What are the social implications of Jesus' practice of scandalously inclusive table fellowship with the religious outcasts, sexual deviants, and socially scorned of his time?[106]

Every time we gather in the eucharistic assembly, we remember a Jesus whose meals are foreign and peculiar to the ways of the world. The eucharistic action thus carries subversive memories. In the words of the liturgical scholar Nathan Mitchell:

> Normally, a table's prime function is to establish social rank-
> ing and hierarchy (by what one eats, how one eats, with
> whom one eats). Normally, a meal is about social identifica-
> tion, status, and power. . . . But Jesus' table habits challenged
> this system of social relationships modeled on meals and man-
> ners. It wasn't that Jesus ate with objectionable persons —
> outcasts and sinners — but that he ate with anyone, indiscrim-
> inately! Hence, his reputation: He has no honor! He has no
> shame! . . . *The table companionship practiced by Jesus thus*

recreated the world, redrew all of society's maps and flow charts. Instead of symbolizing social rank and order, it blurred the distinctions between hosts and guests, need and plenty.[107]

In other words, Jesus' meal ministry and his practice of table fellowship seems a deliberate strategy by which he symbolized and made real his vision of radical human equality before God. This stands in fierce opposition to and judgment upon any culture — secular or religious — that excludes or denigrates certain classes or races of human beings. All must find a welcome place at the faith community's table, if that table is truly a reflection of that of Jesus.

Jesus' table fellowship thus stretches our social imaginations, and challenges the boundaries we give to our inclusion and acceptance. Does our worship facilitate an encounter with Jesus' scandalous and dangerous memory? If so, would it not so expand our awareness so as to leave us disturbed in the face of white privilege? If not, then can there be any wonder that Catholic worship too often fosters complacency and inertia in the face of social injustice? Authentic worship cannot leave one at peace with social injustice, for it immerses us in a larger reality that bursts the limits of our social imagination, limits that are necessary for our complacency with the status quo.

The worthy celebration of the Eucharist, the primordial sacrament of unity, cannot but challenge the existence of white privilege and form in believers a counteridentity more amenable to attitudes of compassion and risky acts of racial solidarity. Such celebrations enable an encounter with the Divine Mystery that stretches our imaginations, expands our awareness, disturbs our complacency, nourishes our hearts, and sustains our hope.

CONCLUDING REFLECTION:
A CONFESSION OF FAITH

I have focused upon the nonrational aspects of racism, those deeply ingrained and often preconscious patterns of meaning and value that undergird the more visible systems of racial privilege, advantage, and benefit. Racism engages us at a visceral level, on the level of personal meaning and group identity; therefore, adequate responses to it must also engage us viscerally. This is not at all to disparage systemic strategies of truth-telling and affirmative redress. These are vital and essential for challenging the nexus between skin color and structured white privilege. They are necessary, yet insufficient.

My contention is that the Christian tradition and the Catholic faith have many resources that can ground renewed and more adequate engagement in the task of racial reconciliation and justice-making. Among these are the practice of lament, the attitude of compassion, the charge of solidarity, and its understandings of conversion, baptism, and Eucharist. These practices are informed by a different set of meanings and values, one that grounds an alternate way of life. They shape a cultural identity informed by another narrative, one that empowers people to undertake risky acts of racial transformation.

In other words, faith communities are called to be communities of conscience, that is, places where the truth is spoken about how our culture has both formed and malformed our personal identities to the detriment of our public life together. Situating our ethical strivings for racial justice in a counternarrative — in an alternative set of meaning and value — is an indispensable contribution that a religious faith makes to the goal of achieving a more racially just society.

As Catholic Christians, then, we espouse certain fundamental beliefs about God, the human family, and social justice — an alternate set of meanings and values that inform a nonracist way of life:

1. *We believe in one Creator God and the common origin of the human family.* Because human beings have a common Creator, the human race has an essential unity that is prior to any distinctions of race, nationality, or ethnicity. All humankind is created in the image and likeness of God (Gen. 1:26). We further believe that God has endowed all men and women with an equal and inviolable dignity,

value, and worth. In the words of Pope Benedict XVI, "Before God, all men and women have the same dignity, whatever their nation, culture, or religion."[108] Our response to this intrinsic human dignity is to defend it from all forms of attack and to create the social conditions in which all human persons may flourish.

Racism fractures the unity of the human family, violates the human rights of individuals and groups, and mocks the God-given equal dignity of human beings. It is absolutely incompatible with authentic faith in God.

2. *We believe that the diversity of the human family is a divine blessing and mirrors the inner life of God.* In the story of Pentecost, we read how the various peoples of the earth were able to hear God's word proclaimed "each in their own language" (Acts 2:11). The Holy Spirit's descent upon the church did not cancel or annul differences of race, language, or culture. Instead the Spirit's presence caused these differences not to be an obstacle to the unity of the human family. Instead, the Spirit enriches the church and the human family with a variety of gifts.[109] Indeed, because the church is "catholic" — that is, inclusive and universal — the diversity of peoples, languages, cultures, and colors among us must not only be tolerated, but also cherished and celebrated.

Furthermore, we believe the diversity of the human family reflects the interior life of the Triune God. Christians believe in a Trinitarian God, a community of persons who exist in a communion of life and love. In God, the Divine Persons relate to one another in neither domination nor subordination.[110] In God, there is distinction without separation, unity without uniformity, difference without division. Since we are created in the image of this God, God's own life becomes the model for human social life.[111] The variety of languages, cultures, and colors in the human family, then, is a mirror of the Trinitarian God whose essence is a loving embrace of difference.[112]

3. *We believe in the solidarity of the human family, which leads to the conviction that we are responsible for each other's welfare.*[113] Just as the Divine Persons of the Blessed Trinity are united in love,

so the human family is bound together by that social form of charity that is called solidarity.[114] Solidarity moves us to have a concern for those who are different from us and to see them as fully sharing in our humanity — indeed, as neighbors and friends. As Pope John Paul taught, "Solidarity helps us to see the 'other' — whether a person, people, or nation — not just as some kind of instrument...but as our 'neighbor,' a 'helper' (Gen. 2:18–20), to be made a sharer on a par with ourselves in the banquet of life to which all are equally invited by God."[115]

4. *We believe that the poor and the marginalized have a privileged claim upon the consciences of believers and the public concern of the state.* Often called an "option for the poor," Pope John Paul describes this as "a call to have a special openness with the small and the weak, those that suffer and weep, those that are humiliated and left on the margin of society, so as to help them win their dignity as human persons and children of God."[116] As the U.S. bishops observed in their pastoral letter *Economic Justice for All,* though the majority of the poor in our nation are white, "the rates of poverty are highest among those who have borne the brunt of racial prejudice and discrimination."[117] Because racism both exacerbates the poverty of those who are poor and results in economic disadvantage even for those who are not, a preferential concern for the poor and socially vulnerable requires a proactive struggle against the social evil of racism.

5. Finally, *we believe that racial reconciliation is a divine gift and promise, partially realized here on earth and of certain fulfillment in a time known only to God.* This facet of reconciliation is well articulated in the Catholic Church's liturgy. In the second "Eucharistic Prayer for Reconciliation" we pray: "In that new world, where the fullness of your peace will be revealed, gather people of every race, language, and way of life to share in the one eternal banquet with Jesus Christ the Lord." *"In that new world...."* Implicit in this prayer is a recognition that all of our human efforts at reconciling estranged racial groups will prove inadequate, incomplete, and lacking. To put it bluntly, we cannot save ourselves. Thus we confess that reconciliation is, ultimately, God's doing. It stems from

God's initiative and is brought to completion in the fullness of time known by God alone. Our challenge is that of grounding our halting yet resolute efforts of the present in the assurance of a divinely given future. In this way, the Catholic Christian community can become that "alternative community" that anticipates in limited, partial, yet ever less imperfect ways the broadly inclusive messianic banquet to come.

Chapter Four

"A Dream Deferred"

MEDITATIONS ON AFRICAN AMERICAN
UNDERSTANDINGS OF JUSTICE AND HOPE

What happens to a dream deferred?

Does it dry up
like a raisin in the sun?
Or fester like a sore —
And then run?
Does it stink like rotten meat?
Or crust and sugar over —
like a syrupy sweet?

Maybe it just sags
like a heavy load.

Or does it explode?[1]

I HAVE LONG FELT dissatisfied while attending lectures or partici-
pating in discussions about justice in the academy. The typical
treatments of justice that one finds in the standard accounts and
classic texts usually leave me cold. This is not solely because such
discussions make no reference to my cultural experience. My dissatisfaction stems from the fact that the standard accounts and usual
discussions render justice abstract and sterile.[2] They do not at all
reflect the richness, vibrancy, and urgency that so affected me in

my youth as I listened to my parents, family, and friends when they gathered around the kitchen table discussing and debating current events that impacted black people. In contrast, the standard accounts of justice I encountered in the academy usually celebrate their dispassionate tone as the mark of a desired intellectual detachment. Indeed, in these settings passionate discourse is often dimly viewed as a "red flag" that an unwarranted bias has infiltrated one's reasoning and compromised one's objectivity in the pursuit of truth.

As I pondered this disconnect between my academic training and my cultural experience, an intuition began to take root, namely, that justice is a pathos, a desire, a longing, a yearning... indeed a *passion*... before it is a concept or a definition. In the African American experience, justice is something visceral; it is an ache, a groan, an inner fire. This visceral or "gut" characteristic of justice is seldom reflected in the standard accounts upheld by accepted academic discourse. Yet as I continued to ponder this disconnect over the years, I have begun to believe that it is the standard accounts that are lacking and deficient.

Thus what motivates the following "meditations" on the African American understanding and pursuit of justice is the conviction that there is an implicit presumption behind or beneath the professional discussions and popular debates about justice in the African American experience. This presupposition has not, to my knowledge, been explicitly articulated. Yet this tacit understanding of justice not only guides, permeates, and animates this community's discourse, that is to say, what one can isolate and dissect analytically for the purposes of intellectual discussion. I believe that this tacit understanding also functions as a "dream," as a vision, as a horizon of possibility, as a passionate hope that energizes and sustains risky justice praxis. I further believe that this "dream" or vision of justice has a transgenerational quality, that it has been passed on through successive generations of the African peoples in the diaspora of the United States and endures despite severe and persistent obstacles to its realization.

I begin by presenting a synthesis of how the African American tradition of religious ethics understands the "fundamental norm" that guides its ethical strivings. After this, I will attempt to go underneath or behind this synthesis and excavate the tacit vision that is presupposed in this norm. This movement is primarily constructive or even archeological as it seeks to bring to conscious awareness an animating vision that, to my knowledge, is largely unstated and simply assumed in African American ethical discourse. From this excavation, I will advance an understanding of justice and relate how it finds expression in some classic pieces of African American literature. I then conclude with a reflection on the need for hope in the pursuit of justice — an especially important consideration in light of its almost perpetual deferment in the experience of African Americans.

My purpose in undertaking this exploration is to show what attentiveness to the African American experience can offer Catholic moral discourse and understanding. Rather than simply applying the insights of the Catholic ethical tradition (for example, its trifold understanding of justice as commutative, social, and distributive) to the quest for racial justice, I seek to offer the gift of an African American understanding of justice — a sensibility and perspective informed by centuries of cultural struggle — to the faith tradition of my belonging. How does the struggle for the unambiguous recognition of our humanity, which I argued is constitutive of the set of meanings and values that inform African American culture, affect our perception and pursuit of justice? That is this chapter's major question.

THE FUNDAMENTAL PRINCIPLE OR NORM: UNIVERSAL INCLUSION

Peter J. Paris, a noted African American social ethicist, provides a cogent presentation of the fundamental moral conviction that characterizes the ethical reflection of black Americans:

> The tradition that has always been normative for the black churches and the black community is not the so-called Western Christian tradition per se, although this tradition is an important source for blacks. More accurately, the normative tradition is that tradition governed by the principle of nonracism which we call the black Christian tradition. *The*

fundamental principle of the black Christian tradition is depicted most adequately in the biblical doctrine of the parenthood of God and the kinship of all peoples.... The doctrine of human equality under God is ... the final authority for all matters pertaining to faith, thought, and practice.[3]

In other words, the constitutive, essential, and distinctive characteristic of African American religious ethics is an emphatic insistence upon and unreserved commitment to the principle of the freedom and equality of *all* persons under God. It is difficult, if not impossible, to overstate the importance of this norm in the black religious experience. Paris maintains that this doctrine is "the essence of the black Christian tradition"[4] and thus declares, "In short, its function in the black experience is categorical, that is, it is unconditional, absolute, and universally applicable."[5]

A survey of the works of other leading black religious ethicists also reveals the essential character of this primary commitment to the equal dignity of all human beings under God. It is the signal feature of the ethical thought of retired Harvard ethicist Preston Williams. In an authoritative article, Williams writes: "The Afro-American moral perspective makes central the belief in the common origin and humanity of individuals and thus their sacredness and equality."[6] The corpus of Williams's writings demonstrates his commitment to this principle as fundamental to his own perspective. Indeed, it is the central norm for his vision of social life and critique of social policies:

> Black response to enslavement, oppression, disenfranchisement, discrimination, and other forms of racist social structure has traditionally been a call toward inclusive and open community structures. In general Black response to white racism has not involved a *quid pro quo* retaliation toward past and present injustice.... [In the words of Dr. Williams]: "Suffice it to say that most black visions of a racially and socially just community stem from the desire on the part of blacks to be counted as equal, fully person, and citizen, in the human family *and to have all others similarly counted.*"[7]

The noted black intellectual Cornel West demonstrates how this principle of universal inclusion is so absolute and fundamental that it even functions as a prophetic critique of the African American community itself and its praxis and discourses about justice. West's writings show that he is rooted in the inclusive tradition of the black community. He embraces what he calls a "moral universalism," that is, "an all-inclusive moral vision of freedom and justice for all."[8] In light of this, he develops an unsparing critique of what he calls "the pervasive patriarchy and homophobia in the black community." West insists that the African American pursuit of social justice must have an ethical foundation, it must stem from and reflect an unwavering commitment to the dignity of *all* peoples, especially a recognition of "the equality of black men and women [and] the humanity of black gays and lesbians."[9] What West does, then, is advocate not only a nonracist appropriation of Christian faith and practice, but an antisexist and nonhomophobic realization as well. West insists that there can be no compromise regarding who is meant by or included in "all" — and thus engages in principled criticism of any who would tolerate such a compromise, including the African American community itself and its leadership.[10]

Finally, the contributions of black womanist scholars and black feminist ethicists advance this inclusive vision in profound and essential ways. Drawing on the experience of black women, they have critiqued the preoccupation of early black theology with the experience of black men and white feminism's racial blindness and complicity. In doing so, they are offering the Christian tradition one of the most comprehensive visions of inclusion and equality I know of, one that in the words of historian Robin Kelley "recognizes the deep interconnectedness of struggles around race, gender, sexuality, culture, class, and spirituality."[11] These African American women offer a vision of universal inclusion that both builds upon the fundamental convictions of African American Christianity and also challenges its own sinful practices of exclusion and marginalization.[12]

Thus what is expressed time and again in the black ethical perspective is an insight well articulated by Martin Luther King Jr.,

"Injustice anywhere is a threat to justice everywhere."[13] The works of other contemporary black ethicists build upon and expand this insight, especially through their self-critical challenges to the limits that their people, or any human community, would place upon the range of their moral concern or the scope of their commitment to universal inclusion.

In sum, the foremost, bedrock principle of African American ethical reflection and sensibility is an existential and core commitment to a conviction that other Christian bodies may espouse in a merely rhetorical manner: the equal dignity of all peoples in the sight of God. For black Christians, this is not an abstract idea but a "normative condition" and "the most fundamental requirement" of faith.[14] In the words of the African Methodist bishop C. M. Tanner, written at the beginning of twentieth century:

> We preach, stand for and practice the truth that all men the white, the red, the yellow, the brown, the black, are all and are to the same extent, our brothers. We claim that there is but one race in the sight of God, the human race, and the blackest and the whitest are brothers. This we strive to hold, not as a mere high sounding, general statement, but as a great truth of which we seek to make practical application at every opportunity that presents itself.[15]

THE UNSTATED VISION: THE "WELCOME TABLE" AND THE "BELOVED COMMUNITY"

> Feel the Fire
> Motivating you and me
> Motivating justice;
> Stirring in your heart,
> Feel the blood
> Coursing through your veins.
> Feel the Fire!![16]

Yet from whence comes this fundamental norm? What is it in the African American sensibility that requires an inclusive notion of justice and demands concern with issues other than racism? Logically, this following section should be the first, as the norm is the expression or embodiment of a prior vision. It was necessary, however, to examine the fundamental norm of the black Christian tradition in order to demonstrate how, or even if, the vision I propose is indeed faithful to this reality.

The importance of articulating the vision or "fire" that inspires the pursuit of inclusive justice in the black experience is necessary for several reasons. Perhaps the most important is this: No one gives one's life for the sake of an abstract concept. No one risks humiliation, ostracization, vilification, persecution, and other forms of opposition for an intellectual idea or sterile definition. The reality that so many persons of African descent in the United States have been and continue to be willing to pay such high prices in the pursuit of justice suggests that its meaning in African American life cannot be fully expressed or captured through rational deliberation alone. As Kirk-Duggan's poem suggests, justice is a "fire" — a passion — before it is a discursive articulation.

Therefore we must delve into the realm of the "meta-rational" to truly appreciate what justice in this cultural tradition entails. We must speak in terms of "vision," "image," "metaphor" — and yes, dreams. For visions function nonrationally, beyond the bounds of reason. Vision, image, and metaphor express more than discursive media can convey. They have a surplus of meaning that is always unfolding and never definitively comprehended. Metaphors and images have a dynamic character; they appeal to the imagination and inspire creative thought and action. Visions, metaphors, and images have a dynamism that pulls those captivated by them to unknown and unforeseen places; thus they are fertile ground for risk-taking behaviors and daring acts of resistance for the sake of justice.

Second, discerning the impulse that gives rise to the conviction of universal inclusion is useful for determining the similarities and differences between this cultural tradition's understanding of justice and others that might have similar rhetorical phrasings. Many other ethical traditions, including the Catholic social teaching tradition, espouse a commitment to the equal dignity of the human person (see *Gaudium et Spes*, 29). Excavating the vision that underlines or gives rise to the African American commitment to this belief may help us to understand the deeper differences that could be masked by the use of similar rhetorical expressions.

Third, the effort of articulating an animating vision helps us to address questions such as: What are we striving for? What do we stand for? What is the goal of the struggle for justice? What are we trying to achieve or bring about in the praxis of justice? What does justice look like? What does it *feel* like?[17] Such questions take us beyond abstract intellectualizing and move us into the realm of animating visions, guiding ideals, and sustaining dreams. For as Robin Kelley rightly notes, without dreams and visions, "we don't know what to build, only what to knock down."[18]

Finally, unearthing the animating vision of African American justice brings us to the heart of African American culture. Recall how I argued that "struggle" is a pervasive theme and constitutive component of black culture, specifically, the struggle to be recognized and treated as a fully equal human being. This exploration of its justice vision helps us to understand more profoundly the set of meanings and values that informs this way of life, that is, the "soul" that animates the art, music, literature, and religion of African Americans.

Thus in this section I articulate the animating vision of justice that lies behind the African American commitment to universal inclusion by examining two images or metaphors: the "welcome table" and the "Beloved Community."

The Welcome Table

The metaphor of the "welcome table" was articulated by the enslaved bards and poets who composed the songs known to us as the black (or Negro) spirituals. One of the spirituals that uses this image goes as follows:

> I'm gonna sit at the welcome table,
> I'm gonna sit at the welcome table one of these days,
>   hallelujah.
> I'm gonna sit at the welcome table,
> I'm gonna sit at the welcome table, one of these days.
>
> I'm gonna walk the streets of glory....
> I'm gonna tell God how you treat me....
>
> I'm gonna feast on the milk and honey....
> I'm gonna drink at the crystal fountain....
> We'll give thanks at the welcome table....[19]

The "welcome table" is a potent image in the African American cultural tradition. Its enduring influence and authority are evidenced by the fact that this song, first composed by the enslaved captives from Africa, was "resurrected" and sung with new lyrics by those struggling for justice during the civil rights movement of the 1960s:

> I'm gonna be a registered voter....
> I'm gonna get my civil rights....
>
> I'm gonna sit at Woolworth's lunch counter....[20]

What can we discover from these various redactions of this song? First, the image of the "welcome table" is the polar opposite of exclusion and neglect. This is significant, for it advocates a revision — and hence, a thinly veiled critique — of the social conditions routinely endured by the enslaved Africans and their descendants. By stating that they will sit at the "welcome table," the singers articulate their conviction that their present condition of political exclusion and social degradation is not the way things ought to be. The very existence of the song is a subversive critique of the social conventions that make members of the human community despised, stigmatized, and ostracized.

Another way of saying this is that the song conveys a profound conviction regarding the kind of community that ought to be normative for human life. This metaphor expresses hospitality and embrace, but not a hospitality and embrace of just any and all. Hospitality and welcome should be extended precisely to those whom it is socially and culturally permissible to exclude and oppress. Thus African American religious ethics is impassioned about the pursuit of justice, especially for those who are excluded from practical membership in the human community.

Also note that this is a hospitality that is lacking now, yet that one day will be realized in the Kingdom (at least in the enslaved bards' version). But this is not a vision solely of a future consummation; this hospitable society is partly a reality that can be brought about through the efforts of the singers themselves.

This leads to another facet of this image. The singers chant this song in the social contexts of the extreme exclusion of slavery and Jim Crow discrimination. They know that they are not welcome, and so they declare that they will *make* themselves welcome! "I'm *gonna* sit at the welcome table." The singers articulate their agency even in the face of inhumane conditions. As Kirk-Duggan relates, "The singers would make themselves welcome whether someone extended an invitation or not."[21] The metaphor of the welcome table thus contains a "fire" that gives rise to concrete acts of risky resistance in order to enact the vision conveyed in song. Thus the "welcome table" metaphor expresses a conviction of inherent dignity, worth, and agency that is independent of the self-serving ideological assessments of African American identity on the part of the dominant white culture.

Finally, the image of the welcome table conveys an understanding of justice that is concrete, direct, and immediate. Justice is described as being able to eat sufficient and nourishing food, sit at a lunch counter and obtain courteous service, exercise the right to vote, and enjoy civil rights without harassment and danger. Justice is described as being recognized with respect, treated with dignity, welcomed as an equal in social and cultural life, and regarded as fit to be invited to the table. Perhaps this is the richest "definition" of justice inherent in the image of the "welcome table": *Justice is that state wherein the despised and outcast are respected and treated as worthy to dine as honored guests at the table.* This understanding of justice in the African American tradition is well expressed by the poet Langston Hughes in a classic poem whose narrator speaks of both exclusion from and making himself present at the "table" of U.S. social life:

> I, too, sing America.
>
> I am the darker brother.
> They send me to eat in the kitchen
> When company comes,
> But I laugh,
> And eat well,
> And grow strong.
>
> Tomorrow,
> I'll be at the table
> When company comes.
> Nobody'll dare
> Say to me:
> "Eat in the kitchen,"
> Then.
>
> Besides,
> They'll see how beautiful I am
> And be ashamed —
>
> I, too, am America.[22]

The Beloved Community

Another protean metaphor in African American culture that gives rise to the understanding of justice codified in the norm of universal inclusion is that of the "Beloved Community." This image receives its best articulation in the black experience in the thought of Martin Luther King Jr. For King, the "Beloved Community" was the normative ethical vision that guided his movement and "the organizing principle of all his thought and activity."[23] A short definition of the Beloved Community is that it is "an inclusive and interracial society characterized by freedom and justice for all."[24] The mature

King used another metaphor for the Beloved Community, speaking of "the great world house" where people relate across their differences according to the norms of love and justice:

> We have inherited a large house, a great "world house," in which we have to live together — black and white, Easterner and Westerner, Gentile and Jew, Catholic and Protestant, Moslem and Hindu — a family unduly separated in ideas, cultures, and interests, who, because we can never live again apart, must learn somehow to live with each other in peace.[25]

Hence, by framing his praxis for justice against the horizon of the Beloved Community, King was expressing an all-encompassing concern. The vision that guided his thought and action was the realization of an inclusive human community where all are accepted whatever their differences, which is to say, a human community where social differences are neither a cause for fear nor an occasion for grudging toleration, but rather a source of celebration. This is seen in his insistence that genuine integration entailed more than a "romantic mixing of colors"; it demanded "a real sharing of power and responsibility."[26] The Beloved Community, then, is evidenced by the embrace of the other as a full participant in social, economic, and political life.

The expansive scope of King's justice vision is further evidenced by his repeated articulation, in the final years of his life, that the three greatest threats to the realization of the Beloved Community were the evils of racism, poverty, and war. What especially distinguishes King's analysis, however, was his contention that these social realities, though distinct, were not isolated from one another. Instead, he contended that they were "interwoven into a single garment," so deeply linked and conjoined that an effective struggle against any one of these threats necessarily required a conscious and proactive engagement against the others as well.[27]

The insight that King arrived at in the last years of his life was that the struggle against racism — what he would later call "white supremacy" — could not be complete or effective without a movement against poverty. For civil rights were hallow and almost meaningless in the absence of economic opportunity or in the presence of economic exploitation. Moreover, he came to the realization that the nation would never commit the funds, energy, and attention needed for the eradication of poverty so long as these resources were siphoned off into the pursuit of war and the quest for military dominance. In his own words: "I knew that America would never invest the necessary funds or energies in the rehabilitation of its poor so long as adventures like Vietnam continued to draw men and skills and money like some demonic, destructive suction tube. So I was increasingly compelled to see the war as an enemy of the poor and to attack it as such."[28]

This is not the place for a fuller exposition of this important aspect of King's thinking. What has been said suffices to show how King's metaphor of the Beloved Community is an able carrier of the expansive justice vision that runs deep within the African American cultural tradition and that gives rises to the fundamental norm of universal inclusion. In the words of the King Center website:

> Dr. King's Beloved Community is a global vision, in which *all* people can share in the wealth of the earth. In the Beloved Community, poverty, hunger and homelessness will not be tolerated because international standards of decency will not allow it. Racism and all forms of discrimination, bigotry, and prejudice will be replaced by an all-inclusive spirit of sisterhood and brotherhood. In the Beloved Community, international disputes will be resolved by peaceful conflict-resolution and reconciliation of adversaries, instead of military power.[29]

It is tempting to dismiss King's Beloved Community as a lofty utopian ideal that not only bears little semblance of reality, but also has almost no chance of realization. It is tempting to regard King as a naive idealist and his dream as a noble but flawed delusion. The intense opposition that the civil rights movement endured, and his premature death by an assassin's bullet, testify to the resistance encountered and the demands entailed in realizing this vision. And herein lies the significance of the vision of the Beloved Community, the image of the welcome table, and indeed the importance of "vision" in the quest for and theorizing about justice.

King's life — and the lives of many other African American agents for justice — testify to the power and meaning of "vision." Visions illumine possibilities that are overlooked, paths not taken, potentials that lie dormant, and capacities not yet developed. Visions spring from and fuel the nonrational centers of the human person from which come the courage, fortitude, and determination needed to engage and persevere in protracted struggles against injustice. Only "vision" — understood here as a passion or pathos — can lead to and ground effective justice praxis. Unlike a mere "dream," a vision has the power to transform even recalcitrant realities. This is the rationale for my deep intuitive conviction that we will never get our theorizing about justice right, nor truly understand African American praxis for justice, without some account of the power of vision, in particular, the visions of the welcome table and the Beloved Community.

THEORETICAL IMPLICATIONS OF THIS VISION

In a very cursory fashion I want to point out a significant consequence of this expansive vision of universal inclusion for African American theorizing about justice. Typically, African American religious ethicists do not dwell upon the abstract question, "What is justice?" Rather, more pointed questions are raised: *Whose* justice? Justice *for whom?* What is it about prevailing notions of justice that make them either supportive of or complacent with the existence of racial and other forms of oppression? In other words, what one finds in this cultural tradition, and the ethical reflection that springs from it, is an ideological critique of the dominant culture's concept and practice of justice.[30]

This leads to a "hunch" that time does not allow me to explore fully. The impulse toward universal inclusion suggests that African

American religious ethics will give privileged attention to what classical Christian and Catholic social thought considers under the heading of "distributive justice." Distributive justice refers to the obligation, especially on the part of the state, to ensure a proportionate share in the benefits and burdens of social life among those who are members of a society. More formally, distributive justice can be defined as "that form of justice which imposes an obligation to share burdens and benefits in accordance with the proportionate equality demanded by the common good."[31] The basis for this obligation lies in the community's obligation to its members in light of their membership in the community and their contribution to its common welfare:

> Distributive justice affects the strict right of the members of the community. It affects things which are due to the members because they belong to the community, and because the community has an obligation towards them. Hence the community has to make a just distribution of advantages and burdens, for its members can claim that what is there for all, or what has been achieved by all, will not be withheld from them, and that they will not be called upon to shoulder more than their due share of the burdens.[32]

It is commonly acknowledged that the burdens and benefits of social life are to be distributed on the basis of merit, suitability, and need; in fact, these have been deemed "the only valid criteria."[33] Moreover, "need" can be the just basis for special consideration and attention, justifying a preferential lessening of social burdens or sharing in social benefits. In the words of one authority, "One of the most important obligations of distributive justice consists in the building and carrying out of a social policy and social institutions *to protect social groups which suffer from the malfunctioning of the social system.*"[34] The U.S. Catholic bishops go so far as to state: "Distributive justice requires that the allocation of income, wealth, and power in society be evaluated in light of its effects on persons whose basic material needs are unmet."[35] At any rate, what is absolutely excluded and prohibited is a preferential allocation of benefits and avoidance of harms on account of greater social rank, standing, or privilege — the primary offense against distributive justice.[36]

Further research is needed to test whether my hunch concerning the privileged place of distributive justice in African American ethics is in fact the case. Yet there is no doubt that there is a certain resonance or congruence between the African American passion for universal inclusion and the distributive justice's concern for the vulnerable as articulated in Catholic social thought.

THE IMPORTANCE OF HOPE
IN THE PURSUIT OF JUSTICE

The question posed by the opening poem of this essay — What happens to a dream deferred? — leads to a final consideration of an African American understanding of justice. For the experience of this people shows that the promise of justice is all too often "a dream deferred." As Barack Obama has observed: "The street corners of ghettoes around the country are gathering places for young men and women without hope, without miracles, and without a sense of destiny other than life on the edge — the edge of the law, the edge of the economy, the edge of family structures and communities."[37] These populations are enclaves of *transgenerational suffering and even despair,* for many black and brown youth in our communities deeply believe that "things are not going to get any better." Theirs is a sentiment well-expressed by Gustavo Gutiérrez: "The poor and marginalized have a deep-rooted conviction that no one is interested in their lives and misfortunes."[38] Or, as a guide expressed to me, in answer to why such squalid famine camps exist in parts of Africa: "No one gives a damn about Africa."

Thus a praxis of justice rooted in the black cultural experience must also be a praxis of hope. The pursuit of justice must be guided by a vision capable of inspiring a hope that can sustain a people in the face of the always difficult, often elusive, and perhaps permanent quest for full recognition as human beings and definitive acceptance at the welcome table.

The cultural products — the poetry and spirituals — that we have considered bear witness to a tense hope that characterizes the African American pursuit of justice. Few have expressed this distinctive hope better than W. E. B. Du Bois, who in commenting on the black spirituals notes:

> Through all the sorrow of the Sorrow Songs, there breathes a hope — a faith in the ultimate justice of things. The minor cadences of despair change often to triumph and calm confidence. Sometimes it is faith in life, sometimes a faith in death, sometimes an assurance of boundless justice in some fair world beyond. But whichever it is, the meaning is always clear: that sometime, somehow, men will judge men by their souls and not by their skins. Is such a hope justified? Do the Sorrow Songs sing true?[39]

James Cone builds on this insight. He relates that in the black spirituals, "heaven" is an image used to express this guiding and sustaining hope in the midst of a hostile social milieu:

> In the black spirituals, the image of heaven served functionally to liberate the black mind from the existing values of white society, enabling black slaves to think their own thoughts and do their own things. For [Harriet] Tubman and [Frederick] Douglass, heaven meant the risk of escape to the North and Canada; for Nat Turner, it was a vision from above that broke into the minds of believers, giving them the courage and the power to take up arms against slave masters and mistresses. And for others, heaven was a perspective on the present, a spiritual, a song about "another world...not made with hands"...[enabling blacks] to transcend the enslavement of the present and to live as if the future had already come.[40]

Put another way, "heaven" offered a vision of a future social order that inspired and guided revolutionary reflection and action with regard to existing social arrangements. Far from being illusory, escapist, or otherworldly, "heaven" is an example of utopian thinking characterized by a profound concern with and anchoring in the present — indeed by a *subversive* relationship with regard to present historical reality.

This is why I speak of hope in the African American experience as that *inner orientation of the human spirit that motivates and sustains one to work for a nonguaranteed future in the face of formidable obstacles.* Hence hope is the expectation of a new future that is neither a simple rearranging of the old furniture nor a continuation of former ways in different configurations. Hope is the belief that things can — and will — be radically other than how they are now. Hope is the expectation of a new beginning that is as yet but dimly perceived. Hope is the calm confidence that the Beloved Community and the welcome table are visions worthy of trust, and worth giving one's life for their realization.

Though he speaks from a different cultural context, I find Vaclav Havel's description of "hope" helpful, illuminating, and consistent with the thrust of black sensibilities:

[Hope is] a state of mind, not a state of the world. Either we have hope within us or we don't; it is a dimension of the soul, and it's not essentially dependent on some particular observation of the world or estimate of the situation. Hope is not prognostication. *It is an orientation of the spirit, an orientation of the heart;* it transcends the world that is immediately experienced, and is anchored somewhere beyond its horizons....

Hope, in this deep and powerful sense, is not the same as joy that things are going well, or willingness to invest in enterprises that are obviously headed for early success, but, rather, an ability to work for something because it is good, not just because it stands a chance to succeed.... Hope is definitely not the same thing as optimism. It is not the conviction that something will turn out well, but the certainty that something makes sense, regardless of how it turns out.[41]

I believe that it is ethically important to distinguish responsible from irresponsible hopes.[42] It seems that three conditions are necessary for responsible hope:

◆ Hope demands a *genuine ambiguity*, where there is at least some possibility — however remote — for substantial change in a situation, though no absolute certitude of it.[43]

◆ Hope presupposes a situation in which *human activity can make a difference* concerning the realization of the desired outcome. If human actions are determined, or if human activity can in no way affect an outcome or social situation, then there can be no hope.[44]

◆ Inherent in the past and present situation is the *genuine possibility* of what is hoped for; that is, the desired future must be rooted somehow in the reality of the past and/or present. Another way of stating this is that hope is not illusory or escapist; there must be "seeds" or "intimations" in the past or present for one's future hope.[45]

Yet we also must honor how Du Bois ends his reflection on hope on a questioning note. His concluding questions — "Is such a hope justified? Do the Sorrow Songs sing true?" — are why I stated that the hope for justice is a "tense" hope, partly because genuine hope is very different from the facile optimism so pervasive in American culture. Optimism is the belief that good *always* triumphs over evil, and sooner rather than later. It is a belief in relatively quick and painless solutions. It is fundamentally a denial of the tragic intransigence of evil.

Hope, on the other hand, is a stance that good *ultimately* — but not always — triumphs over evil . . . and in the process, more than a few good people will pay a high and awful price. Authentic hope is neither illusory nor escapist. It looks squarely at the intransigence of evil; acknowledges the tragedy of loss and defeat; yet refuses to accept that evil, tragedy, and defeat will have the final say in human affairs. As Cone observes:

Hope, in the black spirituals, is not a denial of history. *Black hope accepts history, but believes that the historical is in motion, moving toward a divine fulfillment.* It is the belief that things can be radically otherwise than they are: that reality is not fixed, but moving in the direction of human liberation.[46]

To put this another way, the distinctive characteristic of hope in the black experience is that it is a "blues" hope, that is, a hope that conveys "a kind of disillusionment without defeat."[47] In his treatment of what he calls "the blues aesthetic," cultural activist Kalamu ya Salaam maintains that among its core elements are a sense of "brutal honesty clothed in metaphorical grace," rooted in a "faith in the ultimate triumph of justice."[48] A blues hope, then, has a "profound recognition" of the dire social and economic situation with which African Americans must contend, yet refuses to accept this situation as all-encompassing, without weakness, or fully determinative of their situation. Or, as James Cone expresses it: "The blues are an expression of fortitude in the face of broken existence. . . . [The] blues are that stoic feeling that recognizes the painfulness of the present but refuses to surrender. . . . The blue mood means sorrow, frustration, despair, and black people's attempt to take these existential realities upon themselves and not lose their sanity."[49] Such a "blues hope" is the only kind of hope that is adequate to the cultural experience of blacks in the United States.

Because of its refusal to accept as final the empirical evidence of tragedy, because hope in some measure always demands a leap beyond the obvious, it follows that hope is not capable of fully rational articulation or explanation, much less ironclad "proof." Responsible hope is not, and cannot be, *ir*-rational; but it is often meta-rational or transrational, for it is a fundamental orientation of the human spirit. Hope, then, cannot be "proved," but only "witnessed to." Humans cannot be compelled to hope; we have to be *inspired*. Thus hope is adequately explained, expressed, and conveyed only by those media that can touch or express the nonrational centers of the human person: for example, compelling narratives, inspirational testimony, song/music, dance, art, poetry, drama, symbol, and myth.

Religious hope places human hope in an ultimate perspective by rooting it in the transcendent, the Divine. Religious hope addresses the question: Why should we risk failure and death for a justice we will never see and might well never come? In a paradoxical way, religious hope "assures" the future by grounding it in the reality and promises of God. For example, from a Christian stance, one can avow, "When one is doing the work of justice, one cannot fail, for one is doing the work of God. Human activity can delay, but cannot deny, the fruition of God's reign." Therefore, one can risk and endure "ultimate" failure — especially death — because from a religious perspective, temporal failures, though real, are neither final, decisive, or ultimate.

This is why I have focused on the importance of vision, image, metaphor, and dreams — the transrational element — in this "meditation" upon justice in the African American experience. I do not mean to slight or demean an appreciation for rational discourse and intellectual rigor. But the abstract and "hypothetical"[50] speculation all too characteristic of standard Western accounts of justice is simply inadequate to the task of sustaining — or even giving an adequate account of — this community's historic and passionate pursuit of its realization.

But what is true of the African American experience also reflects a universal dynamic in humanity. We simply cannot undertake and sustain justice praxis in the absence of passion. The African American experience, then, points to a fundamental flaw in our discourse and theorizing about justice. The challenge to Christian ethicists and theologians is to become more aware of and articulate about the nature of justice as a "meta-rational" passion and to move hope from the margins of our concern to the center. Our task is to take seriously the transrational character of hope and the nonrational dimensions of justice. Scholarly attention to the nonrational character of justice — that is, to justice as a passionate drive — and to the phenomenon of hope will not, in and of themselves, bring about a society of justice and inclusion. But it is certain that without hope, justice will not — indeed cannot — prevail.

Chapter Five

The Vocation of the
Black Catholic Theologian
and the Struggle of the
Black Catholic Community

SPEAKING TRUTH TO – AND FROM –
TWO TRADITIONS

W HEN I FIRST BEGAN to think about this book project, I
thought of an earlier work, *The Catholic Viewpoint on Race
Relations*, written by a leading voice of the U.S. Catholic interracial
apostolate in the middle of the twentieth century, John LaFarge, S.J.[1]
As you can imagine, my outlook on the matter differs significantly
from what was presented at that time. This is not only because of
the span of more than four decades of momentous social change, for
LaFarge lived in an America where Jim Crow segregation reigned
and the prospect of an African American president was sheer fan-
tasy, if not lunacy. The difference in our views stems also from my
experience of negotiating the obstacles and overcoming the barriers present in a church and society formed by a racialized set of
meanings and values. It seems self-evident that there are important
insights and perspectives that can be gained only through direct
encounters with this moral evil.

This chapter seeks to articulate that experience of being black, Catholic, and theologian both to help the reader better understand what has gone before and to help the church better understand the "new thing" of black Catholic theology that is in its midst. I am somewhat reluctant to do so. The risk of self-revelation in an age of public confession via so-called "reality" television programming, Internet "blogs," and YouTube postings is that one's voice becomes no more significant than the general cultural chatter — and thus devalued and with little claim to attention. In short, who cares?

Yet this risk must be taken, if for no other reason than that a work examining Catholic theological and ethical engagement with racial injustice would be incomplete without some account of how the Catholic presence — and absence — impacts those members who most endure its burdens. How does the "black experience," that is, the experience of contending with the crushing ordinariness of daily assaults upon one's talent, beauty, character, and intelligence, qualify theological work so that it makes a distinctive contribution to the church's understanding of faith and what it requires? What unique insight does this cultural experience provide to the craft of theological scholarship? Why should this experience matter to the rest of the church? And on a more personal level, but more existentially relevant especially for the black Catholic faithful: Given the history and continuing reality of the Catholic Church's complicity in white racial privilege, why would a black man choose not only to belong to it, but also to serve it as a scholar and minister? To write a work on Catholic engagement with race and avoid such questions would indulge in the same abstraction and lack of "passion"of which I am so critical.

My aim is not to speak a complete word concerning this vocation and its contribution, but rather to contribute to the ongoing conversation among black Catholic scholars and ministers. What I offer is undoubtedly a personal reflection, but not a private one. My concern is to situate the vocation of the black Catholic theologian within the context of both African American intellectual life and Catholic theology. Hence, this chapter's subtitle: "Speaking Truth to — and from — Two Traditions."

After first reflecting on the vocation or self-understanding of the black scholar, I will then turn to that of the Catholic theologian, and finally the vocation of the black Catholic theologian. Then I will take up the challenges and struggles as well as the joys of the black Catholic theological enterprise and being a black Catholic scholar and theologian.

Let me briefly describe what I mean by "vocation." For me, vocation means living in response to something that is beyond and deeper than myself. Denise Ackermann captures much of what I intend when she writes that vocation entails "working in a field that feels right, that you enjoy, that is accompanied by a sense of service in obedience to something outside of oneself."[2] Vocation, then, is more than simply a career; it is more than an endeavor pursued for notoriety, fame, self-satisfaction, or material comfort. To speak from a faith perspective, vocation is a loving response to the Mystery that has taken hold of and possesses us. Moreover, I believe that vocation is always contextual, that is, this "summons" is rooted in and influenced by a particular time, place, and culture. We pursue our life's "calling" in response to the needs and concerns of a specific time. Our response to the summons from within and beyond is always conditioned and shaped by the social and cultural circumstances in which we live. Thus, the vocation of the black Catholic theologian represents a life lived in response to a charge experienced as coming from within and beyond the self, as specified by the exigencies or demands of a particular culture and people.

THE VOCATION OF THE BLACK SCHOLAR

In his magisterial study of African American intellectual life, William Banks defines an intellectual as one who is "reflective and critical, who act[s] self-consciously to transmit, modify, and create ideas and culture."[3] In a seminal article (one that inspired this chapter's title), Vincent Harding further specifies the unique vocation and tasks of black scholars in the U.S. context. His understanding rests upon the pivotal assertion that black scholars do not and cannot "exist in splendid isolation from the situation of the larger black community."[4] The black scholar's "essential social, political, and spiritual context," he provocatively argues, "is the colonized situation of the mass of the black community in America."[5] Because of this "colonized situation," he argues that black people in the United States constitute what he calls a "community-in-struggle,"[6] that is, a people engaged in an elusive and ongoing quest for self-definition, self-determination, and the recognition of their authentic humanity. Therefore, the black scholar, as a member of this "community-in-struggle" must "transmit, modify, and create ideas and culture" in a way that furthers the efforts of this community in its quest for justice and well-being.

Echoing the African American poet Mari Evans, Harding believes that a distinctive vocation of the black scholar is that of "speaking the truth" on behalf of a community-in-struggle. A selection from Mari Evans's poem provides the charge that inspires Harding:

> Speak the truth to the people
> Talk sense to the people
> Free them with reason
> Free them with honesty
> Free them with Love and Courage and Care
>   for their Being...
>
> Speak the truth to the people
> To identify the enemy is to free the mind
> Free the mind of the people
> Speak to the mind of the people
> Speak Truth[7]

Harding maintains that fidelity to this vocation requires the black scholar not only to speak the truth, or even to live the truth, but indeed to come to be *possessed* by the truth. He declares, "It is obviously not enough to speak the truth to our people. We must somehow find ways, stumbling ways, to live the truth — to run the risk of being possessed by our struggle for justice and hope."[8]

Harding further specifies the agenda or summons of black scholarship by positing that the following questions guide responsible
scholars:

How can a victimized, oppressed people begin to see its
true identity as more than that of victims and sufferers,
and begin to grasp the vast potentialities of their humanity?
How can we move from talk of "making it" in the system to the work of total transformation of the system?...
What do liberation, independence, authentic black humanity,
self-determination...mean in the world of the [twenty-first
century]? What is the nature of the society we seek?[9]

I do not believe that Harding intends these questions to be either
exhaustive or exclusive. Rather, they illustrate his central thesis: If
"struggle" is a constitutive and fundamental dimension of the black
experience in the United States,[10] then authentic black scholars must
be truly identified with and participants in this "community-in-
struggle." In common with other intellectuals, black scholars pursue
and speak the truth they have discovered (or believe they have discovered). But black scholarship is not pursued in cultural isolation
or for mere self-interested curiosity. The black scholar's "speaking
the truth" is an activity engaged in, on behalf of, and in solidarity
with a community-in-struggle.[11]

There is much that is rewarding, demanding, and challenging in
Harding's meditation. I lift up three considerations.

First, I present Harding's reflections because I believe that black
Catholic theologians are part of the broader tradition of African
American intellectual life. Harding thus reminds us how our self-
understanding and the pursuit of our theological vocations are
shaped not only by our religious faith and church membership, but
also by the African American intellectual tradition and the debates
within it concerning the purpose of black scholarship.[12]

Second, it is critical to note how the black scholar's passion —
that is, passionately voicing truth on behalf of the "community-in-
struggle" — neither demands a stance of blind, uncritical apology
for black people, nor does it entail a lack of intellectual rigor and

discipline. Harding, in fact, states that the black scholar not only must speak the truth about white America, but also must speak truths about those pathological and self-destructive forces within the black community that impede its struggle for justice and self-determination.[13] Moreover, liberation theologians have maintained that the tasks of disciplined intellectual reflection and passionate advocacy on behalf of the oppressed are not mutually exclusive. As James Cone argues:

> There can be no creative black theology without a disciplined mind, without a solid knowledge of black, third-world, and white theological traditions as they are related to sociology, psychology, philosophy, and history. *But how this knowledge is to be used should be decided by our love for the poor.* Love demands that we participate in their liberation struggles, fighting against the forces of oppression.[14]

Third, while I agree with Harding regarding the organic relationship of black scholars to a specific "community-in-struggle," I also believe that black Catholic theologians do and ought to recognize that persons of African descent in America are not the only "community-in-struggle." We have, in the words of Peter Paris, a charge to contribute to the well-being of both "our communities-of-belonging and to the world at large."[15] For example, black Catholic theologians have been attentive to and in dialogue with our Latino and Asian colleagues. Moreover, many of us are engaged in other justice concerns besides racism; for example, the struggle for environmental justice, the role of women in church and society, and the civil rights of gay and lesbian persons lay a claim to our theological concern. Most of us resonate with Audre Lorde's insight that for the black community there cannot be a single-issue justice struggle because most black folk do not live single-issue lives.[16]

Thus I believe that the black Catholic theologian is called to be what Cornel West calls "a race-transcending prophet," by which he means "someone who never forgets about the significance of race but refuses to be confined to race.... [Someone] concerned about the development of each human being regardless of race, creed, gender, [sexual orientation,] and nationality.... [One] who moves beyond the confines of race without ever forgetting the impact of racism on Black people in this society."[17] Elsewhere West describes this "race-transcending prophet" as one who "puts forward a vision of fundamental social change for all who suffer from socially induced misery."[18] While rooted in our particular "community-of-struggle," black Catholic scholars are also aware of and concerned about other "communities-of-struggle." Thus we can conclude that the responsible black Catholic scholar today has a vocational commitment to "fusing the life of the mind with the struggle for justice and human dignity."[19]

In summary, in common with other African American intellectuals, black Catholic theologians are called to be people who take the life of the mind seriously, and link the life of the mind to spiritual, political, and cultural struggle. There is a constitutive ethical dimension to this vocation: "The mission of the African American scholar is a moral mission, because its final aim is the realization of racial justice in the nation's thought and practice. Apart from the realization of that aim, African peoples will surely perish on this continent and elsewhere."[20]

THE VOCATION OF
THE CATHOLIC THEOLOGIAN

It is difficult to give a concise yet comprehensive definition of a Catholic theologian. I find it helpful to conceive of the theologian as "a thinker for the church."[21] That is, the theologian is a fellow believer or disciple in the faith who offers the faith community the gifts and fruits of his or her education, that is, an in-depth knowledge and familiarity with the Scriptures, the traditions of our faith, and the community's doctrines, customs, and practices to help the community come to deeper and truer insight into the meaning, challenges, and privileges of discipleship in the Lord Jesus.

One of the tasks of the theologian, then, is to listen to the stories of the contemporary community and the world in which we live, and then to put them into dialogue with the larger tradition of the faith witnesses who have preceded us. Thus theologians are charged with helping the faith community articulate the relevance of its faith to contemporary human experience and help uncover the faith dimension of human experience. In doing so, theologians help the community to clarify the convictions of faith, the demands of love, and the reasons for its hope in the God of Jesus Christ.

Thus the theologian is charged with developing a critical reflection upon the faith of the believing community. To this end, the theologian is engaged in the quest to provide serious, disciplined reflection on questions such as:

♦ What is the purpose of human existence?

♦ Who is God?

♦ What does God desire or intend for creation, including humankind?

♦ How do we know what God wants?

♦ Why should we do what God wants?

♦ How do we cooperate with the unfolding of God's intentions for creation?

♦ What is the fitting human response to the experience of sacred mystery encountered in human existence?

And in light of the importance of tradition for Catholic faith and practice, the theologian must ponder the further questions: How have our forebears in faith answered such questions, and what is the relevance or significance of those responses for contemporary believers?

Catholics are heirs to a complex and complicated religious tradition, one that is marked both by shadow and glory, inspirational witness and horrifying callousness, heroic sanctity and barbarous cruelty, pathetic failure and extraordinary grace, maddening plurality and frightening ambiguity. The factual pluralism and moral ambiguity of the Catholic heritage are evident in matters as mundane as the postures prescribed for our liturgical celebrations, and as weighty as Catholic attitudes and practices concerning slavery, divorce, warfare, indigenous peoples, the Jews, and the papacy. It is difficult to find a single matter on which the Catholic tradition has held a univocal and invariant point of view, that is, a position maintained "always, everywhere, and for everyone." One of the responsibilities of Catholic theologians, then, is to hold the various strands of the Catholic tradition in critical tension, fruitful dialogue, and mutual correction.

Black Catholic theologians are not only formed by our cultural community's struggle for justice and equality. We also belong and contribute to the long and expansive Catholic tradition of "faith seeking understanding." Our particular task, I believe, is resonant with Mark Jordan's self-description as a "Talmudic Catholic." He writes, "I choose to inherit Catholic traditions, which means that I have the responsibility to think through them about their contradictions and to wonder with them about who gets to count as part of the tradition."[22] Thinking about the Catholic tradition's pluralism, ambiguity, and contradictions through serious, responsible, careful, and disciplined scholarship while also being attentive to the dynamics of exclusion, silence, and repression of certain voices in that tradition strikes me as an essential dimension of the vocation of Catholic theologians today, and especially so for Catholic scholars of African descent.

THE VOCATION OF
THE BLACK CATHOLIC THEOLOGIAN

To be a black Catholic theologian, then, is not to be an "either/or," or a bifurcated reality. Rather, we are "both/and"; in the classic phrasing that has become a rallying cry of the contemporary black Catholic movement, we are both "authentically black and truly Catholic." Nor are we simply a "hybrid," as in cars that sometimes run on batteries and at other times burn gas. At our best, we do not take off our "black" hat in order to put on the "Catholic" one. Our vocation is shaped by the reality of simultaneous truths

and multiple identities, being indivisibly members of the theological academy, the black "community-in-struggle," and the Catholic
faith communion.

Therefore if the essence of the black scholar's vocation is that of
"speaking the truth" for the sake of a "community-in-struggle," and
that of the Catholic theologian to help the faith community come to
a less and less imperfect understanding of its response to the Divine,
then the vocation of the black Catholic theologian can be phrased
as "passionate participation in reasoned inquiry on behalf of God's
oppressed and despised people."[23] Whatever else can be said of the
Gospel of Jesus Christ, it is certainly "good news" for the poor, the
oppressed, the outcast, the despised, and the disdained. Theology
worthy of the name "Christian" must give privileged attention to
the tears and moans, the groans and the hopes, the hidden struggles
and quiet desperation of those forced to the margins of our society
and church. Dealing with what Shawn Copeland has termed "the
virulent residue" of slavery and its "protracted and pervasive influence" upon the social order and religious experience of the United
States is a cognitive, moral, and existential imperative for black
Catholic scholars.[24]

Black Catholic theological scholarship, then, must originate from
a stance of engagement and commitment. It cannot maintain a posture of dispassionate objectivity or academic distance, for theology
and intellectual inquiry are matters of life and death for our people.
Yet despite its passion on behalf of the victims of systemic injustice,
and I would argue precisely because of this bias, this theological
scholarship must also be rigorous, disciplined, and painstaking. The
complexity and urgency of our situation as black believers in the
United States does not permit us the luxury of indulging in superficial analyses, simplistic interpretations, irresponsible solutions, or
intellectual laziness.

I suggest the following questions as being among those that convey the vocation and tasks of black Catholic theological scholarship:

◆ What does it mean to exercise the theological vocation, that is, to
think through the faith community's complex and complicated

faith tradition, in the midst of a church both historically and (still) practically committed to white racial privilege?

◆ How do black Catholics "sing the Lord's song in a foreign land" (Ps. 137:4)? That is, what does it mean to affirm the real experience of God found in a church that is sometimes hostile, often indifferent, and seldom fully affirming of one's humanity?

◆ What does it mean to "speak the truth" to both church and society, on behalf of all who suffer social oppression, out of a Catholic tradition that is tainted by complicity in and collusion with the social evil of racism?

◆ What in the Catholic tradition is "good news" for the oppressed of whatever "community-of-struggle"?

◆ What in Catholicism resonates with the passions and concerns of persons of African descent, especially those living in North America? What in Catholicism, particularly as it has been lived in the United States, resonates with the heartaches, groans, and cries of black peoples?

◆ How does the "virulent residue" of slavery and segregation, such as the continuing stigmata of black inferiority, challenge the integrity of the Catholic faith, the mission of the church, and the identity of its theologians?

◆ What are the distinctive tasks of "speaking the truth" for the sake of and in solidarity with a particular subset of the "community-in-struggle," namely, Catholics of African descent in the United States?

These questions are not meant to be all-inclusive or exhaustive. Nor do they have easy or obvious answers. Given the newness of black Catholic scholarship, it is too soon to attempt comprehensive or definitive answers to such questions. Moreover, I am not implying that my black Catholic colleagues would totally agree with my questions, the ways that I have phrased them, or the answers I would give to them at this time. However, I do believe that questions such as these get us to the heart of the theological vocation of those

162 The Vocation of the Black Catholic Theologian

who are both black and Catholic. For such questions acknowledge both the theological task we have in common with all Catholic theologians and our solidarity with a community that is still seeking an unambiguous recognition and acceptance of their God-given humanity.[25]

Thus the vocation of the black Catholic theologian is to think through the complexities and "ideological deformations"[26] of this faith tradition. Our charge is not only to speak out of our black Catholic experience and culture, but also to speak of the contemporary reality of black Catholic existence. We undertake this task not merely out of self-interest or self-satisfaction, but for the sake of the integrity and credibility of Catholic faith and witness. Our ultimate goal is to help transform the Catholic Christian community into a less imperfect witness to the broad, expansive, and inclusive "welcome table" that is the reign of God. Our distinctive vocational challenge is to think through and struggle with the contradictions, paradoxes, and potentials of the Catholic faith, and then prophetically challenge this faith community's propensity to sinful attitudes and practices of exclusion.

After this reflection on the vocation, mission, and identity of the black Catholic theologian, I will now consider some of the professional challenges, existential struggles, and personal joys of this vocation.

THE CHALLENGES OF THE BLACK CATHOLIC THEOLOGICAL VOCATION

The Paucity of Our Numbers

Currently, there are about twenty Catholics of African descent in the United States who possess a doctoral degree in the traditional sacred sciences (scripture, systematics, and moral theology).[27] This group is augmented by seven who possess a doctorate in history with a focus on religious studies; and four who possess a doctorate in canon (church) law.[28] There are also a little more than a dozen who possess a doctorate of ministry in various pastoral disciplines.[29]

We also include in the membership of the Black Catholic Theological Symposium[30] a number of Catholic scholars who possess doctoral degrees in ancillary disciplines essential for a comprehensive understanding of the black experience.[31] A closer examination of the number of those who possess terminal degrees in the traditional theological disciplines, however, reveals that some are no longer active scholars; in addition, many are not African Americans but are from the continent of Africa or the Caribbean Islands, with related but distinctive formative histories and concerns. Thus there are only about a dozen African American Catholic theologians who are current active members of the theological guild.

Among the most pressing challenges posed by the scarcity of our numbers is that there are so few to shoulder the work of developing a nascent black Catholic theology. Such tasks include: contributing to professional journals; conducting seminal research and scholarship; convening special consultations and sessions for the theological guild; leadership of and teaching in the Institute for Black Catholic Studies;[32] sponsoring and coordinating the Black Catholic Theological Symposium; mentoring future black Catholic theologians, scholars, and ministers; and networking with other colleagues, especially our Latino and Asian colleagues and other African American religious scholars. All of this is vitally important and necessary, yet there are only a few who can do the job.

Another challenge posed by our numbers is the strain of being what one of us has called the "lonely only" at the institutions at which we serve or at most gatherings that we attend. Because we are usually the lone "raisin in the oatmeal," we often are called upon to be the expert on all other "raisins" and "raisin" matters. At times, this leads to others seeing us as competent to speak *only* on issues of race, racism, and black theology, neglecting our expertise in so-called "mainstream" theological concerns. Because we are often the sole faculty member of color, or one of a handful, in our departments or institutions, we also face the challenge of balancing traditional academic scholarship with the hats we must wear as mentor, role model, advocate, political advisor, personal counselor, and "cultural invigorator" at our institutions. This leads not only to loneliness and exhaustion, but also to a sense of being misunderstood and unappreciated (especially during evaluation and/or tenure processes, as our "adjunct roles" count for little in promotion and salary considerations). One could also mention the lack of a community of discourse and dialogue and the stresses that accompany creating a new field of intellectual inquiry; these challenges are also exacerbated by the fewness of our numbers.

Before leaving this issue, I want to briefly advert to the crucial question of *why?* Why are there so few? There are two factors to highlight. As detailed previously, the Catholic Church has not been proactive in developing leadership from among the black Catholic community. Indeed, some have declared that this community has the worst record among mainstream Christian bodies in supporting and utilizing black leadership talent.[33] A second factor, related to the first, is the lack of black ordained ministers and vowed men and women religious in Catholic life. Many professionally trained white theologians active today received their education under the auspices of diocesan or religious sponsorship. For example, the first wave of Catholic women theologians active today received their theological formation under the sponsorship of their religious communities. This pathway, for the most part, was not available to African Americans (until very recently). There are fewer than 225 African American priests in the United States (less than one-third of 1 percent of the total) and about 500 African American women religious (less than one-half of 1 percent of the total). The reasons for this are directly related to the historic exclusion and discrimination directed against blacks by diocesan seminaries and religious communities. That there are so few black Catholic religious and theologians, then, is in no small degree a legacy of the racial exclusion suffered by this "community-in-struggle" at the hands of their coreligionists.

The Pressing Needs of the Black Catholic Community and the Challenge of Community Leadership

I stressed above the organic relationship between black intellectual activity and the black intellectual's membership in a specific stigmatized community of belonging. This close solidarity raises unique challenges when one considers black Catholic scholars and the struggles of the black Catholic community. Because of our close connection with the black Catholic community, the smallness of its numbers, and the reality that there are so few who can provide the theological expertise this community needs and desires, black Catholic theologians find ourselves involved in the so-called "pastoral" life of the faith community to a far greater extent than most of our white colleagues.

We are speakers at days of reflection for black Catholics across the nation; presenters at and resources for the National Black Catholic Congress by drafting its documents and providing expert guidance and commentary; theological consultants for various committees of the United States Conference of Catholic Bishops, especially on issues that pertain to African American life; keynote presenters at national black Catholic pastoral convocations (for example, Lyke Conferences and "Pastoring in Black Parishes"); speakers at King Day and Black History Month commemorations — and this merely scratches the surface of our various involvements.

I state these things not in complaint, but for understanding. One of the challenges of being an organic part of a community is that it requires participation in activities that many in the academy deem outside the professional purview of intellectual endeavors. Some, indeed, deride such involvements as inimical to serious scholarship. Yet black Catholic theologians contend that this involvement is essential to our vocation, born of both desire and necessity.

By *desire,* for we have been nurtured by this community and are sustained by it. Our fellow black Catholics are there for us when, sadly, few others are. We value our organic connection to this community of faith. And we are there by *necessity,* not only because there are few others who have both the training and willingness to be of theological service to this community. But even more important, because such a presence is an essential contribution to our more intellectual endeavors. Indeed, we consider such activism on behalf of the black Catholic community a constitutive part of our "scholarly" work, so much so that many of us would rather describe ourselves as "scholar-activists" (as opposed to the "teacher-scholar" designation typical in today's colleges and universities). For example, many of the central ideas, concepts, and lines of argument in this book were developed in response to "pastoral" invitations and then refined, critiqued, and verified in "pastoral" venues.[34] Such an organic relationship with the community is essential if the black Catholic experience is to be a real font and locus for theology, and not merely a nominal appeal or abstract notion.

Being a "Minority within a Minority": A Double Invisibility or Marginalization

Black Catholics number only about 8 percent of the U.S. black Christian population and less than 4 percent of the U.S. Catholic population. It is not unusual for black Catholic scholars to find ourselves either the only black in many Catholic settings, and the only Catholic among gatherings of black scholars. Because of this "minority within a minority" status, our perspective and contributions are often overlooked or slighted by both groups.

We are absent and invisible in the discourse of black theology and discussions of black faith in America. Symptomatic of this is that in major works on black liberation theology and African American religious thought, one finds scant reference to black Catholic scholarship.[35] Indeed, in a work (hailed as "seminal") detailing the African American religious experience, there is no mention of black Catholicism.[36]

We often are rendered invisible in Catholic theological discourse as well. At times, my colleagues and I have the distinct impression that our white Catholic peers dialogue more often with black Protestant theologians than with their black Catholic colleagues.[37] There have been recent noteworthy efforts to redress this matter, specifically the annual Black Catholic Theology consultation at the conventions of the Catholic Theological Society of America (CTSA); the special issue of *Theological Studies* (December 2000) exploring the reception of black theology in Catholic theology;[38] two seminal works on white privilege and Catholic theology; and the elections of Shawn Copeland (2003–2004) and myself (2009–2010) to the presidency of the CTSA. These are laudable and significant accomplishments, but there remains a long way to go.

THE STRUGGLES OF BEING A BLACK CATHOLIC THEOLOGIAN

Depression and Despair

Perhaps the struggle is best conveyed through the following haunting questions: "Why do I keep doing what I am doing for a church that would be more comforted by my absence and silence? A church that would be happier if I just walked away? A church that probably would not even miss my presence or contributions? All of this effort, and for what?" Such questions are usually out of place in serious academic works, but must be mentioned here for the sake of honesty and credibility. I confess to feeling at times like those disciples who labored all night and had nothing to show for their efforts (Luke 5:1–11). Or, in the words of the black spiritual, "Sometimes I feel like a motherless child . . . a long ways from home" in the Catholic Church. It is the sense of being overwhelmed by the everyday experience of belonging to a faith community that deems my cultural experience, indeed, my black body, as exotic, foreign, threatening, or irrelevant.

Such questions and feelings usually emerge when I am physically, emotionally, and spiritually exhausted, and there are weeks to go before the calendar has a space for rejuvenating rest and reflection, or when I have moved beyond simple tiredness to being weary to the depths of my soul and overwhelmed by the challenges of keeping my sanity in a white culture and its institutions. I have experienced such despair as a true "dark night" of sense, will, and spirit in which all I have to cling to is the naked faith that being a theologian in the Catholic Church is what God has called me to do.[39] The will to persevere stems from a core conviction that I am called to the Catholic community because that community needs me and my voice if it is to be "catholic" in reality and not simply in rhetoric. That is what has and continues to sustain me in the darkness: the bone-deep and existential certainty that despite the evidence to the contrary, this vocation is God's will and God's work. I struggle on through the despair occasioned by rejection and irrelevance, clinging to the hope often expressed in black religious circles that "the grace of God will not lead me where the grace of God cannot keep me."

The Temptation to "Fit in"
and Be "Like Everybody Else"

The harsh reality is that we (meaning Americans of any race) are rewarded for conducting ourselves in accordance with the racialized set of meanings and values that informs the dominant institutions of American life. Those who describe, much less challenge, the reality of white privilege and entitlement often pay a price. Superficial politeness, ostracism, refusal of tenure, trivialization of one's research, or denial of promotion are among the dangers that confront the middle-class academic. Much less severe than brutal lynchings and death threats, yet real enough.

Thus the temptation is to become hostage to a desire for white acceptance and approval, to "go along to get along" by not raising the pointed question, making the pertinent (though imprudent) observation, or conducting the needed research. This struggle often manifests itself in the posture that declares, "I'm not a black scholar, but a scholar who happens to be black."

Such a stance, though understandable, is terribly misguided, for in a racialized culture, one's skin color is never wholly irrelevant or entirely escapable. Yet the temptation to seek white validation and approval is an endemic one that confronts all persons of color at some time and in one form or another. How can it be otherwise, given the human desire for being valued in the sight of those who determine the standards for acceptance, achievement, and accomplishment?

Fear and/or Cowardice

The theological vocation, as lived by many scholars, does not confront one with a decision to defy conventional understandings of faith or human experience. The black Catholic theological calling, however, of necessity entails a struggle against fear: fear of being misunderstood; of making a false start in developing a new voice and perspective; of self-revelation; of self-doubt ("Who am I to say what I do, and why would this be of interest to anyone?"); of self-censorship; of retaliation both personal and professional ("Why do I have to be the one to speak?"); of ecclesiastical penalty and censure; of ecclesial alienation and estrangement ("If I really examine this question, how can I remain a Catholic?").

Of course, some of these struggles are not unique to black Catholic theologians. Yet for us they take on a different hue, given the inherent mission of black religious scholarship as a prophetic analysis and critique of the devaluing of dark-skinned persons in Western societies. In such a cultural milieu, black Catholic thought entails thinking and acting against the grain; hence, the temptation to succumb to fear and give in to cowardice must be named and forthrightly addressed.

THE JOYS OF BEING
A BLACK CATHOLIC THEOLOGIAN

The Sacred Trust of Being an Esteemed Part of the Black Catholic Community

One of the highlights of the annual gatherings of the Black Catholic Theological Symposium is the evening spent with the black Catholic community of the city in which we meet. By conscious intention, we gather simply to listen to the community and to hear their concerns. There is no set agenda; we are not there to lecture or teach. We are present to listen and receive the voices and experiences we try to articulate in our scholarship.

I never fail to be moved by these meetings with "the folk." At a meeting with the black Catholics in Spokane, the community turned out in force on a damp, rainy Saturday night. One of the "elders" who attended just sat still for most of the meeting, quietly listening and intensely staring. Near the end of the gathering, he spoke with quiet dignity: "I have never, in all my years as a Catholic, heard of a black Catholic theologian. So I was determined to come tonight, to see what a black Catholic theologian looked like." I cannot convey the sense of pride that this faith community has in us and who we are, even without knowing us. (Indeed, the fact that a community shows up en masse on an inclement Saturday night to see "ivory tower intellectuals" speaks volumes about who we are *not*). It is a pride rooted in the recognition and appreciation that there are those who work to validate their "uncommon faithfulness"[40] and affirm their faith commitments.

A similar experience took place in Milwaukee as we concluded our annual gathering at Sunday Mass at a local black Catholic parish (another tradition of our Symposium). We were introduced to the congregation at the beginning of the Mass; the presider concluded his remarks by saying: "These are your theologians." The church erupted in sustained and thunderous applause. And many of us theologians wept, awed and humbled by this communal acclaim, affirmation, and ratification of our vocational commitment, struggle, and choice. This is the joy of being a black Catholic theologian.

Yet there is more to be said. At the Spokane gathering, many spoke movingly of the anger and frustration they felt in being a member of the Catholic Church, and of the dogged determination and quiet fidelity of their faith. One of the women in particular spoke haltingly and painfully of her struggle to pass on the Catholic faith to her daughter, who refused to come to church because of how white "believers" pointedly ignored and ostracized her. At one point, she could not continue her story as she was overcome with tears. Moved by such pathos, I leaned over to my colleague, Shawn Copeland, and said, "We have been given a sacred trust. We are entrusted with the tears of our people. They trust us to speak the truth about their tears and give voice to their pain."

Someone expressed a similar sentiment at a gathering of black Catholic men in Brooklyn: "We are faithful, but alienated; faithful, but excluded; faithful, but hurt; faithful, but our culture is not welcome." This, then, is one of the deepest joys of my theological vocation: being entrusted with the tears, pathos, struggle, and the uncommon, unnoticed heroic fidelity, of my fellow believers. Many of my white colleagues do not understand this experience, and cannot share this joy.

The Joy of Being in Struggle and Creating Something New

The noted cultural activist and critic bell hooks, in reflecting upon African American intellectual life observes:

> We also need to remember that there is a joy in the struggle. . . . We must teach young Black folks to understand that struggle is process, that one moves from circumstances of difficulty and pain to awareness, joy, fulfillment. That the struggle to be critically conscious can be that movement which takes you to another level, that lifts you up, that makes you feel better. You feel good, you feel your life has meaning and purpose.[41]

There is a sense of profound joy and delight in giving oneself to a cause or mission that is greater than oneself, that aims in small yet real ways to make a difference in how social and ecclesial life is understood and lived. This is joy, not in the sense of an ephemeral happiness or fleeting pleasure, but rather of deep satisfaction that what one is doing is fundamentally worthwhile. Such joy can be pervasive even while feeling tired and spent after a day of intense labor, teaching, lecturing, and writing. Amid the tiredness there is the inner satisfaction of having spent one's energies on a cause that is meaningful, purposeful, and attuned with the promptings of the Spirit.

The Joy of Collaboration

Here I speak of the joy of sharing my theological vocation with wonderful fellow travelers and companions, namely, my colleagues in black Catholic theology. These are people of deep faith, conviction, and spirituality. We have our differences of temperament, outlook, opinion, and perspective. Yet there are among us deep bonds of respect and admiration as each of us tries, in our own fragmentary and partial ways, to contribute to the evolution of this project we call "black Catholic theology." The sessions of the Symposium and the informal discussions at the Institute for Black Catholic Studies are places where our work receives the honest critique and critical commentary needed for genuine intellectual development. In these settings, our work suffers neither uncritical rejection nor fawning (though well-intentioned) acclaim. The most junior among us is free to question the more senior. Again, to speak of the joys of collaboration amid the mutual exchange of ideas and insights seems out of place in a serious intellectual work. Yet the existential support (also known as laughter, fun, and camaraderie) occasioned by these gatherings of intellect and faith are critical for sustaining a commitment to the ongoing quest of being agents for justice and wholeness on behalf of God's despised and disdained people.

THE SIGNIFICANCE OF THE BLACK CATHOLIC THEOLOGICAL VOCATION

Why is the vocation of the black Catholic theologian relevant or of interest to the Catholic faith community and its ongoing quest for a deeper understanding of its faith? Why should it be of concern to the craft of U.S. Catholic theology?

Our vocation should be a concern for at least two reasons. One stems from the meaning of "catholic." Unless we celebrate black Catholic scholarship and nurture more Catholic scholars of African descent, then we will have neither a truly "catholic" nor a genuinely "American" theology. For a "white" church and a "white" theology, that is to say, a church and theology in (unconscious) complicity with white privilege and entitlement, is not and cannot be a carrier of a "catholic" and truly universal faith.

Moreover, the black experience is a pivotal and constitutive part of the American experience. We cannot understand who we are as Catholics and as U.S. citizens if the fortunes and misfortunes, the joys and tragedies, the sorrows and exaltations of black peoples are not heard and understood. Despite the overwhelming denials and silences of our curricula, African Americans are central to this country's fortunes and prospects. Nor has there ever been a U.S. Catholicism in which there have not been black witnesses of Catholic sanctity and faith.[42] But these voices cannot be adequately heard unless there is a critical mass of trained theological scholars who are part of this community and can speak from within this cultural experience.

The second reason this particular, and at times peculiar, vocation should be a concern for Catholic theology is that the calling of the black Catholic scholar provides an alternative model and/or needed corrective for understanding the role of the Catholic theologian in the church and society. Our specific vocation reminds all Catholic religious scholars that the measure of our calling cannot rest in the acclaim of the academy, the achievement of tenure, the holding of a named chair, an increase in salary, or any of the other typical and usual ways of measuring "success" in our guild. *Success as a theologian — as a Catholic theologian — must include above all else the qualities of constant fidelity to a call in the midst of persistent difficulties; humble service to a people spurned and despised; a willingness to speak unpopular, uncomfortable, yet necessary truths; and a commitment to the life of the mind for the sake of social and ecclesial transformation.* Each religious scholar is called to do these things in his or her own fashion. But without some understanding and appropriation of this aspect of the theological vocation, then Catholic theology risks becoming merely a self-serving career and an unworthy witness to the Crucified and Risen One whose message it is our privileged duty to study, share, and speak.

To conclude on a personal note: My grandmother was a major influence both in my life of faith and in nurturing my budding sense of scholarship. I was the first person in my extended family to attend and graduate from college, and my grandmother took special delight in that occasion. She dressed in her "Sunday best" for the commencement ceremony; she would not fail to witness this special event in our family's history. She glowed with pride after the ceremony as I showed her my degree. She took the folder in her hands, stared at it with a little awe, and she said: "Look at that! This sure is something." Then turning to me, with love and pride and affection and wisdom, she asked: "Now, who are you going to help with it? Who are you going to use it for?"

My grandmother was a poor woman and could not afford to give me a material gift, yet her words were precious beyond measure. My family rejoiced in my accomplishment, which was the fulfillment of our family's dream. All were genuinely happy that my degree would open opportunities for me that none of them ever enjoyed. That, too, was their hope, that I would "do better" than they had. Of course, my grandmother also shared their wishes and hopes for me. Yet she was a wise woman. She knew that the comforts of privilege and opportunity can be seductive, and even corrosive, if pursued as ends in themselves. My grandmother was also a woman of simple faith, who took her Bible seriously, especially that line, "To whom much is given, much will be required." So her questions were a haunting challenge, and yet the most loving gift she could give: How would I use the privileges and opportunities that my education opens for me? Whom do I use them for?

"Who are you going to help with it? Who are you going to use it for?" These, I submit, are *the* vocational questions, not only for black Catholic theologians, but for us all.

Epilogue

E ARLIER IN THIS WORK, I discussed Martin Luther King's idea of the "Beloved Community," that ideal human community where human differences are not a cause for suspicion, animosity, or hierarchy. As this work comes to a close, I think of another Kingian concept, namely, the distinction he made early in his career between "desegregation" and "integration."

King viewed desegregation as primarily negative, in that it "eliminates discrimination" and the obvious barriers that people of color encounter in public accommodations, education, housing, and employment. Desegregation, King notes, can be accomplished or ordered by legislation and legal initiatives.[1] However, a desegregated society is not yet an integrated society. Legal desegregation in itself can only create "a society where people are physically desegregated and spiritually segregated, where elbows are together and hearts are apart. It gives us social togetherness and spiritual apartness."[2] A community that is only legally desegregated, King observed, is still all too often marked by suspicion, anger, resentment, tokenism,[3] grudging toleration, and wary coexistence.

In contrast, King viewed integration as more than merely living together, side by side, in tolerant coexistence. Integration, King notes, is "the positive acceptance of desegregation," evidenced in the welcome embrace of the other as a full participant in social, economic, and political life.[4] Toward the end of his life, King declared: "Integration is meaningless without the sharing of power. When I speak of integration, I don't mean a romantic mixing of colors. I mean a real sharing of power and responsibility."[5] Integration

175

requires not only changes in laws and public policies — as necessary as these are. It also demands "a change in attitudes, the loving acceptance of individuals and groups."[6]

Integration not only demands proactive social policies as well as changed economic structures. It also requires that we confront what King called the "nonrational psychological barriers" to human unity. He delineated these fears as "fear of loss of preferred economic privilege; altered social relations; intermarriage; and adjustment to new situations." King's words are even more relevant today: "A vigorous enforcement of civil rights will bring an end to segregated public facilities, but it cannot bring an end to fears, prejudice, pride, and irrationality, which are the barriers to a truly integrated society."[7]

King's words are an apt description of contemporary race relations in the United States. We are a desegregated nation; we are not yet truly integrated. We have slain the demons of officially sanctioned segregation and savagely brutal injustice. Yet genuine and effective equality is still lacking for far too many of our citizens. As a nation, we are still plagued with wary coexistence, latent suspicions, subtle exclusions, covert tensions, and barely concealed resentments — all rooted in an often unacknowledged but entrenched network of racial privilege and dominance. The next frontier of racial justice is the task of dismantling the edifice of white privilege, which demands confronting and naming the "nonrational" set of meanings and values — the white cultural identity and symbol system — that sustains it.

This is where the Catholic Church, and indeed every religious community of goodwill, can make an invaluable contribution. For we have an alternative symbol system of ritual and belief that is the basis for an alternative identity, one that is not dependent upon racial dominance and subordination.

Let me make this clear by way of example. All Saints Catholic Church is a racially mixed, predominately African American parish in Milwaukee. It is my home parish where I grew up, and I regularly have the privilege of leading the community in its Sunday worship. It has a renowned Gospel choir, and the parish's 10:30 Mass attracts a variety of visitors from all parts of the archdiocese. These are often students from our Catholic high schools, or confirmation candidates and their parents, who attend in order to fulfill a "requirement" to witness another form of Catholic worship. And they are almost always whites from suburban and rural parishes who are attending a "Gospel Mass" for the first time.

I confess to feeling a little resentment and impatience with this practice, regarding it as a kind of "liturgical tourism" or "cultural voyeurism," until I decided to make this a real teaching moment. So at the conclusion of the Mass before dismissing the congregation, I ask our visitors what they noticed was different about this Mass as compared to those in their home parishes. After some hesitation, they will comment about the music, the clapping, the "more interesting homily,... " and the length of the service! I then prod them about what else is different. After a silence, I tell them to look around. And then I mention the obvious: "There are black people in the assembly. And I know you don't find that in your parishes."

Then I visually point out the diversity of the host community. I have all the elders stand. Then those with newborn infants. Then those who come from the continent of Africa (as there are a number of African Catholics who make the parish their home). Then those who are Latino (it always seems to surprise our guests that there are Latinos in a predominately African American parish). Then those who are African Americans. Then those who are in interracial marriages (as many have found a welcome there). Then those who have a biracial cultural heritage. Then those whose ancestors come from Europe. Finally, I ask all who are baptized to rise. The whole community applauds as it stands in unison.

I then turn to our visitors and give them a dismissal in words like these: "This is the real reason you are here. You aren't hear to listen to a Gospel choir, or to have a fun time by clapping and singing in a different rhythm. You are here because this is a dress rehearsal for the Kingdom, because in the Reign of God everyone will not look like you, pray like you, sing like you, or think like you. You are here to celebrate a new identity, your true identity, one that is not based on race or color. Here, at last, you see *all* of your sisters and brothers. And if we are *truly* "brothers and sisters," then it's

up to you to build a world when you leave here where this isn't just
an empty phrase, but a living reality. We are here to practice for
the Kingdom, and you are now sent forth to make that Kingdom
more real by living differently from what you have experienced."
At times, I lead the community in a prayer over our visitors, and
then the choir sings a concluding anthem, "We Are One."

Preparing for the Kingdom and being witnesses to the in-breaking
of the Reign of God: this is the mission of the church. Catholics
possess an alternate symbol system, one grounded in baptism and
the common table, that speaks the truth of the intrinsic equal dignity
of the human community regardless of race, color, gender, or any
other human characteristic. We have a wisdom and insight that our
nation and world desperately need as we grapple with the problem
of creating authentic solidarity in the midst of the ruptures and
fractures of divided and torn communities.

But we cannot offer what we do not ourselves genuinely believe.
Too often, the Catholic faith community is "catholic" in rhetoric
and aspiration alone. Becoming genuinely "universal" in our welcome will entail dying to the "empty promises" of racial and social
privilege. It means a willingness to sing in another language, to pray
in a different idiom, to redefine our parish boundaries, to welcome
darker faces into church leadership, and to imagine new configurations and possibilities of being "church" not dependent on the
racialized values and idolatrous identities of our nation.

This will entail loss, grief, and letting go. As King noted, a
racially just society demands overcoming our fears, the relinquish-
ing of privilege, and cultivating a new way of being Americans and
Catholics. The pain of this dislocation is real. It is a paschal journey
through death to new life.

I am reminded of a consultation I had with a group of vowed
religious men who were experiencing tensions as younger Latinos
were becoming more numerous in their community. One of the
older members lamented, "We aren't a community of O'Briens and
O'Malleys anymore. Now it's Sanchez and Fernandez." I responded
only a little facetiously, "And don't forget Jesús!"

Don't forget Jesus! On the other side of dying to privilege is the promise of new life. That's the story of Jesus. That is the new narrative that can sustain us in the movement from false identities founded on spurious racial advantage to genuine selves who live in the freedom of the children of God.

In an age of "sound-bites," allow me to restate the message of this book in the following succinct statements:

+ The Catholic Church of the twenty-first century will be shaped by, and must respond to, a seismic shift in the demographics of U.S. society and in its own membership.

+ It cannot adequately respond to these shifts unless it attends, in a way that it has not done heretofore, to the ongoing struggle for racial equality.

+ Therefore, if the Catholic Church is to be viable, meaningful, and relevant in twenty-first century U.S. society, it must become a proactive force for racial justice.

+ The Catholic Church cannot be a proactive force for racial justice unless its teaching, catechesis, and practices forthrightly address the reality of white privilege and embrace an understanding of racism beyond its personal and intentional manifestations.

+ Catholic reflection, witness, and action for racial justice will be neither credible nor effective unless this faith community and its leadership cultivates intentional racial solidarity with, and "transformative love" for, black Catholics and other Catholics of color.

In a work published after his death, King gave a final testimony to the struggles and promise of creating a genuinely integrated society:

There is no easy way to create a world where men and women can live together, where each has his own job and house and where all children receive as much education as their minds can absorb. But if such a world is created in our lifetime, it will be done in the United States by Negroes and white people of goodwill. . . . It will be done by rejecting the racism, the materialism and violence that has characterized Western civilization and especially by working toward a world of brotherhood, cooperation, and peace.[8]

In other words, social life is made by human beings. The society we live in is the outcome of human choices and decisions. This means that human beings can change things. There is nothing necessary or fated about racial hierarchies or white racial privilege. They are the result of human agency; it does not have to be so. What humans break, divide, and separate, we can — with God's help — also heal, unite, and restore.

What is now does not have to be. Therein lies the hope. And the challenge.

Notes

Preface

1. Bryan N. Massingale, "James Cone and Recent Catholic Episcopal Teaching on Racism," *Theological Studies* 61 (2000): 700.

2. I want to explain the reason for what may appear to be a strange circumlocution in speaking of groups "designated" as "black" and "white." Contrary to popular understanding, the meaning of these terms, and especially the matter of who is included within them, is far from clear and obvious. In fact, the legal and social definitions of these racial categories have been contested throughout our history. Consider the following questions: Why was Homer Plessy refused admission to the "whites only" train car in the 1890s, even though he was seven-eighths white . . . and not known to be "of color" until he revealed this fact? Why are Halle Berry, Derek Jeter, and Tiger Woods considered black, despite their mixed-race parentage, yet others of mixed race such as Dean Cain, Keanu Reeves, and Mark-Paul Gosselaar are often considered white? One could also point to numerous court cases where people have sued for the right to be classified as "white." My point is that racial classifications and group membership are *social and political constructs*, not biological realities. People are "designated" as black or white (or Latino or Asian or American Indian) for social and political reasons. I will return to this point in chapter 1.

3. Joe R. Feagin, *Systemic Racism: A Theory of Oppression* (New York: Routledge, 2006), xi.

4. The work of Eduardo Bonilla-Silva is important here. He argues that the United States is evolving toward a tripartite racial system of "whites," "honorary whites" (such as light-skinned Latinos, Japanese Americans, and Middle Eastern Americans), and "collective blacks" (for example, blacks, dark-skinned Latinos, and some Asian groups). Note how skin color remains the critical variable for one's place in the group hierarchy, and how "honorary white" status is tenuous as it "is dependent upon whites' wishes and practices." Thus even in a more pluralistic racial order,

181

"black" and "white" remain the critical frames of reference. See the discussion in his *Racism without Racists: Color-Blind Racism and the Persistence of Racial Inequality in the United States,* 2nd ed. (New York: Rowman and Littlefield, 2006), 177–205.

5. These insights became clear to me while conducting a workshop for Catholic leaders of religious orders in the United States. After a discussion of "white privilege," someone commented publicly: "Okay, I get it. I see that I am privileged. But why would I want to change a system that benefits me?" I was reminded of an observation attributed to Martin Luther King Jr. to the effect that privileged groups seldom surrender their status voluntarily. The unwillingness of many whites to address their privileged status is also evidenced in a recent invitation to keynote a local diocese's "Celebration of Diversity." I was told I could discuss "racism" as long as I didn't focus on "white privilege." Such restrictions, unfortunately, are increasingly common.

1: What Is Racism?

1. The discussion of these terms is indebted to reflections found in Bishop Dale J. Melczek's *Created in God's Image: A Pastoral Letter on the Sin of Racism and a Call to Conversion* (Gary, Ind.: Diocesan Chancery, 2003), 22. Available at *www.dcgary.org/bishop/CreatedInGodsImage.pdf.* In significant ways, however, the explanations presented here expand that discussion.

2. U.S. Census Bureau, 2000 Census of Population, Public Law 94–171, Redistricting Data File, available at *http://quickfacts.census.gov/qfd/meta/long_68184.htm;* emphasis added.

3. These concerns are eloquently expressed by Bishop Edward K. Braxton, "There Are No 'Minority' Americans," *America,* June 3–10, 2000, 6–8.

4. See *Dred Scott v. Sanford* (1857).

5. Kevin Johnson, "Scope of Obama's Secret Service Protection Proves Daunting," *USA Today,* December 14, 2008. Online at *www.usatoday.com/news/washington/2008-12-14-obamasecurity_N.htm.* Accessed on September 9, 2009.

6. The above incidents were reported by the Associated Press and are documented by NPR, "Obama Election Spurs Race Crimes around Country" (November 16, 2008). See online at *www.npr.org/templates/story/story.php?storyID=97055760&sc=emaf.* Accessed November 16, 2008.

7. ABC News, "Newt Gingrich on Twitter: Sonia Sotomayor 'Racist,' Should Withdraw" (May 27, 2009). See online at *http://abcnews.go.com/Politics/SoniaSotomayor/story?id=7685284&page=1.* Accessed August 30,

2009. This source also documents similar comments made by conservative activists Rush Limbaugh and Ann Coulter.

8. Southern Poverty Law Center, *The Second Wave: Return of the Militias* (Montgomery, Ala.: Southern Poverty Law Center, 2009), 4.

9. Cited by David S. Broder, "A Price to Pay for the Town Hall Rage," *Washington Post,* August 13, 2009.

10. HBO Documentary Films, *Prom Night in Mississippi,* (2009). Summary online at *www.promnightinmississippi.com/.*

11. Michael O. Emerson and Christian Smith, *Divided by Faith: Evangelical Religion and the Problem of Race in America* (New York: Oxford University Press, 2000), 7.

12. Ibid.

13. Doug Simpson (Associated Press), "Jesse Jackson Lashes Out at Bush over Katrina Response," available at *www.wwltv.com/local/stories/wwl090205jackson.1c68e297.html.* Accessed September 9, 2009.

14. Remark made by Democratic strategist Paul Begala on CNN, *Anderson Cooper 360,* Fall 2008.

15. I discuss this at length in my essay "Signs of the Times: The Changing Faces and Voices of "America," *New Theology Review* 14 (November 2001): 80–83.

16. National Research Council, *America Becoming: Racial Trends and Their Consequences,* vol. 1, ed. Neil J. Smelser, William Julius Wilson, and Faith Mitchell (Washington, D.C.: National Academies Press, 2001), 1.

17. For a discussion of the "birthers," those who refuse to believe that Obama is a native-born U.S. citizen, see Larry Keller, *The Second Wave,* Intelligence Report, Fall 2009 (Montgomery, Ala.: Southern Poverty Law Center, 2009), 8. Some news reports suggest that 28 percent of Republican voters subscribe to this false belief, with another 30 percent of the party reporting that they are "not sure." See Daily Kos, "Birthers Are Mostly Republican and Southern" (July 31, 2009). Available online at *www.dailykos.com/storyonly/2009/7/31/760087/-Birthers-Are-Mostly-Republican-and-Southern.* Accessed August 13, 2009.

18. "[Today] differential treatment of blacks infrequently takes the form of blatant hostility and overt discrimination. Differential treatment is most likely to occur when it allows someone to avoid close interracial contact; it prevents the establishment of interracial relations of equal status or black dominance, especially in employment and housing; *and it is possible to find a nonracial explanation for differential treatment"* (National Research Council, *A Common Destiny: Blacks and American Society* [Washington, D.C.: National Academies Press, 1990], 49).

19. For example, consider the following reflections offered on the meaning of "whiteness": "And if white folks remind each other about

being white, too often the reminder is about threats by outsiders — non-whites — who steal white entitlements like good jobs, a fine education, nice neighborhoods, and the good life" (Bonnie Kae Grover, "Growing Up White in America?" in *Critical White Studies: Looking behind the Mirror,* ed. Richard Delgado and Jean Stefancic [Philadelphia: Temple University Press, 1997], 34).

20. Klor de Alva, as quoted in Cornel West, *The Cornel West Reader* (New York: Basic Books, 1999), 511.

21. See the Southern Poverty Law Center, *The Second Wave,* which notes the rise of right-wing demagoguery — even among elected officials and in mainstream media outlets — as our society moves toward greater social equality (8–9). The report names Glenn Beck, Lou Dobbs, and some elected officials as evidencing this reality. The dynamics of race-based demagoguery and extremism in times of social upheaval are described in the classic work by the social psychologist Gordon W. Allport in *The Nature of Prejudice,* 25th anniv. ed. (Reading, Mass.: Addison-Wesley Publishing, 1979), 410–24.

22. Devah Pager, *Marked: Race, Crime and Finding Work in an Era of Mass Incarceration* (Chicago: University of Chicago Press, 2007).

23. See Allport, *The Nature of Prejudice,* 3–16, for a discussion of the distinction between prejudice (negative attitudes, beliefs, and generalizations) and discrimination (the expression of prejudice in behavior).

24. Cited by Gerald A. Arbuckle, "Dress and Worship: Liturgies for the Culturally Dispossessed," *Worship* 59 (1985): 429.

25. Bernard Lonergan, *A Second Collection,* ed. William F. J. Ryan and Bernard J. Terrell (Philadelphia: Westminster Press, 1974), 232.

26. Ibid., 102.

27. Bernard Lonergan, *Method in Theology* (New York: Seabury Press, 1979), 32.

28. M. Shawn Copeland, "Theology as Intellectually Vital Inquiry: A Black Theological Interrogation," *CTSA Proceedings* 46 (1991): 52, at n. 7.

29. Lonergan, *A Second Collection,* 102.

30. Indebted to Clifford Geertz, as cited by Arbuckle. See also "A Baseline Definition of Culture," online at *www.wsu.edu/gened/learn-modules/top_culture/culture-definition.html.* Accessed September 9, 2009.

31. Lonergan, *A Second Collection,* 233; emphases added.

32. Lonergan, *Method in Theology,* 57.

33. Please note that I am limiting my treatment to African *American* culture. This is because the cultural experiences and stances of black African and Caribbean peoples can differ significantly from that of black Americans. Having said this, it is important to acknowledge that much of what I say about African American culture will be shared by any black person of

African descent living in the United States. The reason for this will become obvious.

34. Henry H. Mitchell, *Black Preaching* (New York: Harper and Row, 1979), 36; modified for gender inclusion.

35. Audre Lorde, *Sister Outsider* (Freedom, Calif.: Crossing Press, 1984), 42.

36. James Cone, *The Spiritual and the Blues: An Interpretation* (New York: Seabury Press, 1972), 24, 25.

37. Roy L. Brooks, *Rethinking the American Race Problem* (Berkeley: University of California Press, 1990), 180; emphases added.

38. "How Whites See Themselves," in *Critical White Studies: Looking behind the Mirror,* ed. Richard Delgado and Jean Stefancic (Philadelphia: Temple University Press, 1997), 1. See also the work of Joe R. Feagin and Hernan Vera, who similarly observe: "Relatively few whites think reflectively about their whiteness except when it is forced on them by encounters with or challenges from black Americans" (*White Racism: The Basics* [New York: Routledge, 1995], 139).

39. Feagin and Vera, *White Racism: The Basics,* 139.

40. Grover, "Growing Up *White* in America?" 34.

41. Derrick Bell, *Faces at the Bottom of the Well: The Permanence of Racism* (New York: Basic Books, 1992), 8–9.

42. Also, many African Americans noted with irony and anger that the first English word many immigrants learned was "nigger." (See the discussion in David R. Roediger, ed., *Black on White: Black Writers on What It Means to Be White* [New York: Schocken Books, 1998], 19). Mastery of, and assimilation into, the racial subordination of American society was essential to the success of American immigrants. For example, Greeks had the consolation of being considered as only "half-niggers." On this point, see James R. Barrett and David Roediger, "How White People Became White," in *Critical White Studies: Looking behind the Mirror,* ed. Richard Delgado and Jean Stefancic (Philadelphia: Temple University Press, 1997), 402–6.

The process by which ethnic immigrants became "white" often has been remarked upon by African American activists and scholars. For example, James Baldwin points out that becoming white was the "price of the ticket" to acceptance in America (see his essay, "The Price of the Ticket" in his *The Price of the Ticket: Collected Nonfiction 1948–1985* [New York: St. Martin's Press, 1985], xx). Also Malcolm X noted with indignation that civil rights bills were not needed to bring Germans, Russians, and Polish people — the former enemies of the United States — into the mainstream of American life denied to black folk native to this land (Malcolm X, *By Any Means Necessary* [New York: Pathfinders Press, 1970], 80–81).

43. Ruth Frankenberg, *White Women, Race Matters: The Social Construction of Whiteness* (Minneapolis: University of Minnesota Press, 1993), 1, 6.

44. Gary L. Chamberlain, "A Model to Confront Racism," *Theology Today* 32 (January 1976): 355; emphases in the original.

45. Ibid.

46. Grover, "Growing Up *White* in America?" 34.

47. Charles R. Lawrence III, "The Id, the Ego, and Equal Protection: Reckoning with Unconscious Racism," *Stanford Law Review* 39 (January 1987): 317–88, at 322.

48. Ibid., 323; emphases added.

49. Ibid., 343; emphasis added.

50. Cited in the *Milwaukee Journal Sentinel*, "Book Illustrates Discriminatory Practices in Hiring," November 28, 2007, 1D, 2D.

51. "Brian," as found on *http://politicalticker.blogs.cnn.com/2008/09/22/race-could-play-big-role-in-election-poll-suggests/*. Accessed on September 22, 2008.

52. Lawrence, "The Id, the Ego, and Equal Protection," 323. It should be noted that by "collective unconscious" Lawrence means "the collection of widely shared individual memories, beliefs, and understandings that exist in the mind at a non-reporting level. This non-reporting mental activity is widely shared because individuals who live within the same culture share common developmental experiences." He is not using this term as it is understood in Jungian psychology (see n. 26 of his work).

53. Angela Davis, untitled remarks at American University College of Law; online at *www.wcl.american.edu/humright/center/presentations.pdf*. Accessed December 13, 2005.

54. Lawrence, "The Id, the Ego, and Equal Protection," 338–39.

55. CBS News, "Race an Issue in Katrina Response," available online at *www.cbsnews.com/stories/2005/09/03/katrina/main814623.shtml*. Accessed September 9, 2009.

56. Remarks Attributed to Sheriff Jack Strain, "Sheriff Jack Strain Is Sticking to His Guns," *New Orleans Time Picayune*, July 16, 2006. Available online at *www.nola.com/news/t-p/frontpage/index.ssf?/base/news-6/1153036129164970.xml&coll=1*. Accessed September 9, 2009.

57. Noting the propensity of police officers to use deadly force more often in situations involving black people, one researcher notes: "Either police officers are bigots who intentionally target racial minorities... or they are completely unbiased and color-blind. Racial stereotypes operate at a subconscious level to influence the police officer's decision to use deadly force. The police officer may not consciously decide to use deadly force because of the suspect's race, but the suspect's race nonetheless influences

the officer. Racial stereotypes thus may alter the officer's perception of danger, threat, and resistance to authority.... Police officers may also see danger more readily when dealing with a person of color" (Cynthia Ann Lee, "But I Thought He Had a Gun: Race and Police Use of Deadly Force," *Hastings Race and Poverty Law School Journal* [2004]).

58. Lawrence, "The Id, the Ego, and Equal Protection," at n. 135.

59. Doug Simpson (Associated Press), "Jesse Jackson Lashes Out at Bush over Katrina Response," available at *www.wwltv.com/local/stories/wwl090205jackson.1c68e297.html*. Accessed September 9, 2009.

60. Decrying the "obvious and inexcusable disparity in responding to the needs of victims," the president of the National Baptist Convention offered the following examples: (1) "Tulane University. Hospital personnel and patients were helicoptered out first; meanwhile Charity Hospital staff and patients waited and watched in full view. (2) A major hotel's 'guests' were given escorted exodus from the area of disaster while others — city residents — could get no assistance. These hotel evacuees received antibiotics from adjacent stores to protect themselves from the health hazards of wading through polluted water. However, native citizens received no health care on the whole" (statement of Dr. William J. Shaw, President, National Baptist Convention, USA, Regarding NBCUSA Responses and Reflections in the Wake of Hurricane Katrina," September 7, 2005).

61. Lawrence, "The Id, the Ego, and Equal Protection," 330; emphasis added.

62. Lonergan, *A Second Collection,* 233.

63. Ibid., 102.

64. National Research Council, *A Common Destiny: Blacks and American Society* (Washington, D.C.: National Academies Press, 1989), 138.

65. Ibid., 5.

66. Ibid., 49 and 155.

67. Martin Luther King Jr., *Where Do We Go from Here: Chaos or Community?* (Boston: Beacon Press, 1967), 8 and 11; emphases added.

68. The literature that treats racism as a system of white systemic privilege, advantage, and dominance is vast. The seminal essay on white privilege is by Peggy McIntosh, "White Privilege and Male Privilege: A Personal Account of Coming to See Correspondences through Work in Women's Studies." This essay, and other important works, can be found in Richard Delgado and Jean Stefancic, eds., *Critical White Studies: Looking behind the Mirror* (Philadelphia: Temple University Press, 1997). The work of Ruth Frankenberg is also helpful; see her *White Women, Race Matters: The Social Construction of Whiteness* (Minneapolis: University of Minnesota Press, 1993). A very useful introduction suitable for college instruction is by Allan Johnson, *Privilege, Power, and Difference,* 2nd ed.

(New York: McGraw-Hill, 2005). A very illuminating study comes from Joe Feagin and Eileen O'Brien, *White Men on Race: Power, Privilege, and the Shaping of Cultural Consciousness* (Boston: Beacon Press, 2003). For valuable treatments on white privilege from a Catholic perspective, see Laurie M. Cassidy and Alexander Mikulich, eds., *Interrupting White Privilege: Catholic Theologians Break the Silence* (Maryknoll, N.Y.: Orbis Books, 2007); and Catholic Charities USA, *Poverty and Racism: Overlapping Threats to the Common Good* (Alexandria, Va.: Catholic Charities, 2007).

69. National Research Council, *A Common Destiny*, 49; emphases added.

70. George Kelsey, *Racism and the Christian Understanding of Man* (New York: Scribner's, 1965), 9.

71. Bishop Dale J. Melczek, "Created in God's Image: The Sin of Racism and a Call to Conversion," *Origins* 33 (September 25, 2003): 268.

72. Ibid., also published as *Created in God's Image: A Pastoral Letter on the Sin of Racism and a Call to Conversion* (Gary, Ind.: Diocesan Chancery, 2003). Online at *www.dcgary.org/bishop/CreatedInGodsImage .pdf.*

73. McIntosh, "White Privilege," 291.

74. Among the studies that survey the evolution and creation of white privilege and economic advantage, see Ira Katznelson, *When Affirmative Action Was White: An Untold History of Racial Inequality in Twentieth-Century America* (New York: W. W. Norton, 2005); Joe R. Feagin, *Racist America: Roots, Realities, and Future Reparations* (New York: Routledge, 2000); and David R. Roediger, *Working toward Whiteness* (New York: Basic Books, 2005).

75. Joe R. Feagin, *Systemic Racism: A Theory of Oppression* (New York: Routledge, 2006), 13.

76. See U.S. Department of State, "Indian Treaties and the Removal Act of 1830," *www.state.gov/r/pa/ho/time/dwe/16338.htm.* Accessed September 9, 2009; and PBS, "Indian Removal 1814–1858," *www.pbs.org/wgbh/ aia/part4/4p2959.html.* Accessed September 9, 2009.

77. See John Hope Franklin and Alfred A. Moss, *From Slavery to Freedom: A History of African Americans*, 9th ed. (New York: Knopf, 2000).

78. "Not All Caucasians Are White: The Supreme Court Rejects Citizenship for Asian Indians," *http://historymatters.gmu.edu/d/5076.* Accessed September 9, 2009. See also Ronald Takaki, *Strangers from a Different Shore: A History of Asian Americans* (New York: Back Bay Books, 1989).

79. The discussion of this and the following two items is indebted to Katznelson's study, *When Affirmative Action Was White*, 53–79 and 113–41.

80. See also my observations on the current thinking of James Cone in Bryan N. Massingale, "James Cone and Recent Catholic Episcopal Teaching on Racism," *Theological Studies* 61 (December 2000): 716.

81. David T. Wellman, *Portraits of White Racism* (New York: Cambridge University Press, 1993), xi, 4.

2: An Analysis of Catholic Social Teaching on Racism

1. I analyze these statements in Bryan N. Massingale, "James Cone and Recent Catholic Episcopal Teaching on Racism," *Theological Studies* 61 (December 2000): 700–730.

2. James H. Cone, *Risks of Faith: The Emergence of a Black Theology of Liberation, 1968–1998* (Boston: Beacon Press, 2000), 133.

3. This figure is obtained from a review of several USCCB websites, including those for African American and Hispanic Catholics. See *www.usccb.org*.

4. M. Shawn Copeland, "Guest Editorial," *Theological Studies* 61 (December 2000): 605.

5. *"What We Have Seen and Heard": A Pastoral Letter on Evangelization from the Black Bishops of the United States* (Cincinnati: St. Anthony Messenger Press, 1984), 20.

6. Pope John Paul II, "Homily in the Trans World Dome," *Origins* 28 (February 11, 1999): 601; emphasis added.

7. See the seminal study of Cyprian Davis, *The History of Black Catholics in the United States* (New York: Crossroad, 1995), and Stephen J. Ochs, *Desegregating the Altar: The Josephites and the Struggle for Black Priests, 1971–1960* (Baton Rouge: Louisiana State University Press, 1993).

8. Davis, *The History of Black Catholics in the United States*, 217–19.

9. John LaFarge, *The Catholic Viewpoint on Race Relations* (Garden City, N.Y.: Hanover House, 1956), 61.

10. Ibid., 62–63.

11. Ibid., 73.

12. Ibid., 71.

13. Ibid., 66–67.

14. The complete text of this document can be found in John LaFarge, *The Catholic Viewpoint on Race Relations*, rev. ed. (New York: Hanover House, 1960), 186–92. All references to this document are taken from this work; page numbers are indicated parenthetically in the text.

15. The above comparisons were drawn from a representative sampling of the statements of major national assemblies as presented in Thomas F.

Pettigrew and Ernest Q. Campbell, *Christians in Racial Crisis* (Washington, D.C.: Public Affairs Press, 1959), 137–70.

16. John F. Cronin, "Religion and Race," *America,* June 23–30, 1984. See also the M.A. thesis of Rory T. Conley, *"All Are One in Christ:* Patrick Cardinal O'Boyle, the Church of Washington and the Struggle for Racial Justice, 1948–1973," Catholic University of America, 1992, 99–100.

17. William Osborne,*The Segregated Covenant: Race Relations and American Catholics* (New York: Herder & Herder, 1967), 14.

18. Ibid., 13–18.

19. Ibid., 234.

20. The complete text of this document can be found in *The Pope Speaks* 13 (Spring 1968): 175–79. All references to this document are taken from this work and page numbers are indicated parenthetically in the text.

21. Extensive selections of the Kerner Report can be found in Leon Friedman, ed., *The Civil Rights Reader* (New York: Walker & Company, 1986), 346–57.

22. Joseph A. Francis, "The Debilitating Virus of Racism," *Origins* 11 (1982): 743.

23. The complete text of this statement can be found in Gayraud S. Wilmore and James H. Cone, eds., *Black Theology: A Documentary History, 1966–1979* (Maryknoll, N.Y.: Orbis Books, 1979), 322–24.

24. *National Catholic Reporter,* April 24, 1968, 1.

25. *National Catholic Reporter,* May 1, 1968, 3.

26. *Newsweek,* May 6, 1968, 66.

27. Davis, *History of Black Catholics in the United States.*

28. The complete text of this document can be found in *Origins* 9 (1979): 381–89. All references to this document are taken from this work and page numbers are indicated parenthetically in the text.

29. *U.S. News & World Report,* November 19, 1979, 59. Note the striking parallels to our own times, as noted in chapter 1.

30. Joseph Davis, "Black Catholics and the Bicentennial," *Origins* 5 (1975): 413. See also the testimony of Sr. Jamie Phelps, "Black Catholics/ Strangers in a Strange Land," *Origins* 5 (1975): 417–19.

31. The entire text can be found in *Origins* 6 (1976): 333–37.

32. Eugene Marino, "Black and Catholic," *America* 142 (1980): 273.

33. Here we need to note the pioneering efforts of Father Clarence Rivers and Bishop James Lyke, who spearheaded the development of the black Catholic hymnal, *Lead Me, Guide Me.*

34. Edward Braxton, "The Key Role of Black Catholic Laity," *Origins* 14 (1984): 39.

35. Joseph Francis, "Pastoral on Racism Called Church's Best-Kept Secret," *Origins* 14 (1984): 393.

36. Bishops' Committee on Black Catholics, *For the Love of One Another: A Special Message on the Occasion of the Tenth Anniversary of* Brothers and Sisters to Us (Washington, D.C.: United States Catholic Conference of Bishops, 1989); emphasis added.

37. *We Walk by Faith and Not by Sight: The Church's Response to Racism in the Years Following* Brothers and Sisters to Us: *A Research Report Commemorating the 25th Anniversary of* Brothers and Sisters to Us (Washington, D.C.: United States Conference of Catholic Bishops, 2004). An executive summary of this report is available at the Conference's Committee on African American Catholics website, *www.usccb.org/saac*.

38. Massingale, "James Cone and Recent Catholic Teaching on Racism," 704–12.

39. Ibid.

40. For example, there is no extended critique of media representations or depictions of African Americans that reflect deeply embedded cultural myths about black sexuality. For an example of extended critique of cultural representations of blackness and their role in the maintenance of white social dominance, see bell hooks, *Black Looks: Race and Representation* (Boston: South End Press, 1992). For a description of the cultural myths surrounding black sexuality and their contemporary impact upon public policy, see Kelly Brown Douglas, *Sexuality and the Black Church: A Womanist Perspective* (Maryknoll, N.Y.: Orbis Books, 1999).

41. S.v. "Parenesis" in *The Westminster Dictionary of Christian Ethics*, ed. James F. Childress and John Macquarrie (Philadelphia: Westminster Press, 1986), 448.

42. Cardinal Anthony Bevilacqua, "Healing Racism through Faith and Truth," *Origins* 27 (January 22, 1998).

43. Cardinal Francis George, *Dwell in My Love: A Pastoral Letter on Racism* (Chicago: Archdiocese of Chicago, April 4, 2001). I am working from the booklet produced by the Archdiocese of Chicago. This document can also be found online at *www.dwellinmylove.org*. Bishop Dale Melczek, "Created in God's Image: The Sin of Racism and a Call to Conversion," *Origins* 33 (September 25, 2003): 264–72. I am working from this version. This document is also available online at *www.dcgary.org/bishop/CreatedInGodsImage.pdf*. Archbishop Alfred Hughes, *"Made in the Image of God": A Pastoral Letter on Racial Harmony* (December 2006). Online at *www.arch-no.org/12.15_pastoral_final .pdf*.

44. Hughes, *"Made in the Image of God,"* 6; George, *Dwell in My Love*, 13; Melczek, "Created in God's Image," 266.

45. George, *Dwell in My Love*, 13; Hughes, *"Made in the Image of God,"* 12.

46. Hughes, *"Made in the Image of God,"* 11; Melczek, "Created in God's Image," 265; George, *Dwell in My Love,* 9, 12.

47. Indeed, one finds even among the well-intentioned a profound discomfort, even anxiety, in the face of creative and independent black initiatives for racial justice. For example, the moralist John Ford worried that encouraging such activity on the part of blacks would lead to violence. And the Catholic racial pioneer John LaFarge espoused a distrust of black racial activism. On these points see Bryan Massingale, "The African American Experience and U.S. Roman Catholic Ethics: Strangers and Aliens No Longer?" in *Black and Catholic: The Challenge and Gift of Black Folk,* ed. Jamie Phelps (Milwaukee: Marquette University Press, 1997); and David W. Southern, *John LaFarge and the Limits of Catholic Interracialism 1911–1963* (Baton Rouge: Louisiana State University Press, 1996), 360–62.

48. It should be noted that this hesitancy is probably due not only to the personal prejudices of American Catholic moralists, but also to the Catholic Church's commitment to an "organic model of society" in its social thought. Such an "organic" understanding of society leads to a stress upon harmony and social stability, especially if reform or justice efforts compromise social order or peace.

49. Because of its commitment to a natural law methodology, Catholic social thought demonstrates an overconfidence in the ability of human reason to know the good and motivate others to do the good.

50. Bernard J. F. Lonergan, *Insight: A Study of Human Understanding* (New York: Philosophical Library, 1970), xi, 191–206.

51. St. Thomas Aquinas, *Summa Theologica,* I-II, q. 71, a. 2; q. 73, a. 1.

52. See Osborne, *The Segregated Covenant.* Osborne describes his book as "the story of the slow and unsteady implementation of the bishops' [1958] declaration" (14).

53. Bishops' Committee on Black Catholics, *For Love of One Another: A Special Message on the Tenth Anniversary of* Brothers and Sisters to Us (September 1989).

54. Lyrics printed in John Lovell Jr., *Black Song: The Forge and the Flame* (New York: Paragon House Publishers, 1972), 298–99.

55. Bishop Braxton, "Evangelization: Crossing the Cultural Divide," *Origins* 27 (October 2, 1998): 275.

56. See the following historical studies for support of this contention: Davis, *The History of Black Catholics in the United States;* Stephen J. Ochs, *Desegregating the Altar: The Josephites and the Struggle for Black Priests 1871–1960* (Baton Rouge: Louisiana State University Press, 1990); and John T. McGreevy, *Parish Boundaries: The Catholic Encounter with Race*

in the Twentieth Century Urban North (Chicago: University of Chicago Press, 1996).

57. Why is this important? As explained previously, EWTN is the "media presence" of the Catholic Church and, for many, the public voice of U.S. Catholicism. That such a statement could be aired on a network renowned for its orthodoxy, that it was not officially repudiated or challenged, and that it could be made without fear of official rebuke or sanction not only illustrate how standing against racism is not a major component of Catholic identity or orthodoxy. It also shows how cultural expressions other than European ones are not considered really "Catholic" — or even "sacred!" — by influential elites in this church.

3: Toward a More Adequate Catholic Engagement

1. Gunnar Myrdal, *An American Dilemma: The Negro Problem and Modern Democracy* (New York: Harper & Row, 1962), 100; cited in Gary L. Chamberlain, "A Model to Combat Racism," *Theology Today* 32 (January 1976): 363.

2. Chamberlain, "A Model to Combat Racism," 356.

3. John Paul II, *Tertio millennio adveniente*, 33.

4. Charles Marsh, "The Beloved Community: An American Search," in *Religion, Race, and Justice in a Changing America* (New York: Century Foundation Press, 1999), 63; emphasis added.

5. So avows Christian ethicist Donald W. Shriver Jr., who calls anti-black racism "the oldest American civic injustice" in his *An Ethic for Enemies: Forgiveness in Politics* (New York: Oxford University Press, 1995), 171.

6. Philip S. Keane, *Christian Ethics and Imagination* (Mahwah, N.J.: Paulist Press, 1984), 81.

7. Harlon L. Dalton, *Racial Healing: Confronting the Fear between Blacks and Whites* (New York: Anchor Books, 1995), 213.

8. Ibid., 215.

9. In one place, Dalton opines that Beigia is like a world populated only with generic "birds," rather than starlings and cardinals (ibid., 218).

10. Ibid., 219.

11. Ibid.

12. I note that Dalton's text and the racial distribution he considers were based upon the then existing demographics of U.S. society. His point, however, remains relevant and instructive.

13. "Corps of Clerks Lacking in Diversity," *USA Today*, March 13, 1998, 12A.

14. Dalton, *Racial Healing*, 221.

15. Caleb Rosado makes a similar point in his essay "The Undergirding Factor Is POWER: Toward an Understanding of Prejudice and Racism" (1997). Online at *www.rosado.net/pdf/Under_factor_Power_article.pdf.*

16. Dalton expresses similar views to the one I advocate: "The fact that people come in different colors is not a problem, nor are racial differences necessarily a bad thing. . . . What needs changing is the negative value our society places on racial difference, and its use of race as a basis for maintaining a social hierarchy" (*Racial Healing*, 220).

17. J. Christopher Soper, *Evangelical Christianity in the United States and Great Britain: Religious Beliefs, Political Choices* (New York: New York University Press, 1994), 3.

18. See the following books: Raleigh Washington and Glenn Kehrein, *Breaking Down Walls: A Model for Reconciliation in an Age of Racial Strife* (Chicago: Moody Press, 1993); Spencer Perkins and Chris Rice, *More Than Equals: Racial Healing for the Sake of the Gospel* (Downers Grove, Ill.: InterVarsity Press, 1993); John Perkins and Thomas A. Tarrants, III, *He's My Brother: A Black Activist and a Former Klansman Tell Their Stories* (Grand Rapids, Mich.: Chosen Books, 1994); William Pannell, *The Coming Race Wars? A Cry for Reconciliation* (Grand Rapids, Mich.: Zondervan, 1993); George A. Yancey, *Beyond Black and White: Reflections on Racial Reconciliation* (Grand Rapids, Mich.: Baker Books, 1996); and Dennis L. Okholm, ed., *The Gospel in Black and White: Theological Resources for Racial Reconciliation* (Downers Grove, Ill.: InterVarsity Press, 1997). An overview of evangelicals and race relations is provided by Edward Gilbreath, "Catching Up with a Dream: Evangelicals and Race 30 Years after the Death of Martin Luther King Jr.," *Christianity Today*, March 2, 1998, 21–29.

19. See especially the works by Washington and Kehrein, Perkins and Rice, and Perkins and Tarrants. I note and puzzle over the absence of women's presence in this genre.

20. Here take note of the title of Pannell's book, *The Coming Race Wars?*

21. Perkins and Tarrants, *He's My Brother*, 171–73; emphasis in the original.

22. See Perkins and Rice, *More Than Equals*, 216–27; and especially Perkins and Tarrants, *He's My Brother*, 212–14.

23. Washington and Kehrein, *Breaking Down Walls*, 204; emphasis in the original. See also Yancey, *Beyond Black and White*, 35–39.

24. Washington and Kehrein, *Breaking Down Walls*, 107, 187.

25. Ibid., 187. See also Perkins and Rice, *More Than Equals*, 18; and Perkins and Tarrants, *He's My Brother*, 159.

26. Perkins and Rice, *More Than Equals*, 18–19.

27. Washington and Kehrein, *Breaking Down Walls,* 113–220.

28. Perkins and Rice, *More Than Equals,* 17.

29. Soper, *Evangelical Christianity in the United States and Great Britain,* 38–40.

30. That this suspicion about King still holds among many evangelicals is evidenced in Gilbreath's article, "Catching Up with a Dream." Moreover, one finds in the writings of evangelicals a tendency to draw a contrast, if not opposition, between "social gospel" and "personal biblical faith." On this, see Jay Kesler's remarks in the foreword to Pannell, *The Coming Race Wars?* 11.

31. There are evangelical exceptions to this lack of concern for the institutional and systemic dimensions of racism. The evangelical communities of reflection associated with the periodicals *Sojourners* and *The Other Side* are two very prominent examples. (Only *Sojourners* is still in publication as of this writing.) It must be pointed out, however, that these communities and their publications are outside of the mainstream of evangelical thought. On this point, see Pannell, *The Coming Race Wars?* 113.

32. See Spencer and Rice, *More Than Equals.*

33. On the enduring existence and significance of residential discrimination and segregation, see Douglas S. Massey and Nancy A. Denton, *American Apartheid: Segregation and the Making of the Underclass* (Cambridge, Mass.: Harvard University Press, 1993).

34. Eric K. Yamamoto, *Interracial Justice: Conflict and Resolution in Post-Civil Rights America* (New York: New York University Press, 1999), 8. He in turn cites his indebtedness for this insight to Elizabeth Martinez, "Beyond Black and White: The Racisms of Our Time," *Social Justice* 22 (1991): 20.

35. Hence the failure of so many calls for local, regional, and national "dialogues on race." Racism is not based simply upon misunderstandings or ignorance, even though these are part of the picture. Racial injustice at its core is about the distribution of goods, advantages, and benefits; it is a matter of personal and group identity. It stems from "the set of meanings and values that inform the way of life" of Western societies in general, and United States society in particular. Dialogue alone is an insufficient and inadequate tool to deal with the roots of racism. At best, it may set the stage or provide a foundation for deeper engagement with the real issues. At worst, it is a palliative salve that gives a superficial feeling of well-being ("Aren't we good for doing that?"), which excuses future action and deeper reflection (the "What more do they want?" syndrome).

36. Yamamoto, *Interracial Justice,* 9–10, 172. It should be noted that while Yamamoto's principal concern in this work is the estrangements that exist among communities of color in the U.S., he states that his

project is applicable to healing divisions "between whites and nonwhites" as well (175).

37. Ibid., 172–209.

38. The literature dealing with the various "truth and reconciliation" processes, and the South African experience in particular, is vast. A good overview of the South African process is provided by Russell Daye, *Political Forgiveness: Lessons from South Africa* (Maryknoll, N.Y.: Orbis Books, 2004).

39. Yamamoto, *Interracial Justice,* 160.

40. John Paul II, "Address to the Tribunal of the Roman Rota" (February 4, 1980), 1. Available online at *www.vatican.va.*

41. International Theological Commission, "Introduction," *Memory and Reconciliation: The Church and the Faults of the Past,* 1999. Available online at *www.vatican.va.*

42. Pontifical Council for Justice and Peace, "Contribution to World Conference against Racism, Racial Discrimination, Xenophobia and Related Intolerance" (Durban, August 31–September 7, 2001), 9.

43. Yamamoto, *Interracial Justice,* 180–81.

44. I am not taking a position on the ongoing debates over whether there should be an official apology to African Americans for the practice of slavery. As will become clear, I believe that this debate, focused as it is upon events of the past, is often misplaced. I further note that insofar as slavery is a common foundational experience in the Western hemisphere, dealing with its legacy is a challenge with implications far beyond the U.S. experience.

45. Yamamoto, *Interracial Justice,* 182–83. This author in turn is indebted to Dalton, *Racial Healing,* for critical insights.

46. Dalton, *Racial Healing,* 156–57.

47. Jack Miles (white editor at the *Los Angeles Times*), quoted in Shriver, *An Ethic for Enemies,* 214; emphasis added.

48. A further implication of this line of thought is that anti-black prejudice and discrimination cannot be adequately addressed by generic approaches or general appeals to "diversity" and "multicultural sensitivity." In fact, many suspect that appeals to "multiculturalism" often are subtle ways of avoiding a forthright engagement with the issue of race. On this matter, James H. Cone is particularly relevant: "White ethicists, from Reinhold Niebuhr to James Gustafson, reflect the racism current in the society as a whole. Here racism appears in the form of *invisibility* [emphasis in original]. White theologians and ethicists simply ignore black people *by suggesting that the problem of racism and oppression is only one social expression of a larger ethical concern*" [emphasis added] (James H. Cone, *God of the Oppressed* [Maryknoll, N.Y.: Orbis Books, 1997], 184).

49. This insight is indebted to Yamamoto, *Interracial Justice,* passim.

50. Among others, see Henry Davis, S.J., *Moral and Pastoral Theology,* 7th ed., vol. 2 (New York: Sheed & Ward, 1958), 314–53, at 316.

51. Pontifical Council for Justice and Peace, "Contribution to World Conference against Racism," 12.

52. National Conference of Catholic Bishops, *Economic Justice for All: Catholic Social Teaching and the U.S. Economy* (Washington, D.C.: USCCB, 1986), 73.

53. Cited in Bryan N. Massingale, "Catholics Should Stand Firm on Affirmative Action," *Salt of the Earth* 16 (September–October 1996): 10–15.

54. For a more complete discussion of affirmative action and Catholic social reflection, see Bryan N. Massingale, "Equality Control: A Catholic View on Affirmative Action," *U.S. Catholic* 68 (September 2003): 29–31.

55. Pontifical Council for Justice and Peace, "Contribution to World Conference against Racism," 19.

56. See, for example, the CD-ROMs *Religious Periodical Index* and the *Catholic Periodical Index.*

57. This is a reflection of the overall pattern of "omission, silence, neglect, and indifference" concerning racial justice that I have argued marks American Catholic moral theology. See my essay "The African American Experience and U.S. Roman Catholic Ethics: 'Strangers and Aliens No Longer?'" in *Black and Catholic: The Challenge and Gift of Black Folk,* ed. Jamie Phelps (Milwaukee: Marquette University Press, 1997), 79–101.

58. John Mahoney, *The Making of Moral Theology: A Study of the Roman Catholic Tradition* (New York: Oxford University Press, 1987), 1–36.

59. On efforts to develop the communal dimensions of the Sacrament of Penance, see Peter E. Fink, ed., *Alternative Futures for Worship: Reconciliation* (Collegeville, Minn.: Liturgical Press, 1987).

60. Paul Wadell, "Response to Bryan Massingale," in Phelps, *Black and Catholic,* 102–6.

61. See the writings of theologians who attempt to be in conscious dialogue concerning racism and the black experience such as Laurie Cassidy and Alex Mikulich, eds., *Interrupting White Privilege: Catholic Theologians Interrupt the Silence* (Maryknoll, N.Y.: Orbis Books, 2007); Jon Nilson, *Hearing Past the Pain: Why White Catholic Theologians Need Black Theology* (Mahwah, N.J.: Paulist Press, 2007); Dawn M. Nothwehr, *That They May Be One: Catholic Social Teaching on Racism, Tribalism, and Xenophobia* (Maryknoll, N.Y.: Orbis Books, 2008); Michelle A. Gonzalez, *Created in God's Image: An Introduction to Feminist Theological Anthropology* (Maryknoll, N.Y.: Orbis Books, 2007); Miguel H. Díaz, *On*

Being Human: U.S. Hispanic and Rahnerian Perspectives (Maryknoll, N.Y.: Orbis Books, 2001); Daniel C. Maguire, *A Case for Affirmative Action* (Wapwallopen, Pa.: Shepherd Press, 1991); Barabara Hilkert Andolsen, *Daughters of Jefferson, Daughter of Bootblacks: Racism and American Feminism* (Macon, Ga.: Mercer University Press, 1986); Robert Schreiter, *Reconciliation* (Maryknoll, N.Y.: Orbis Books, 1992); and Gregory Baum and Harold Wells, eds., *The Reconciliation of Peoples: Challenge to the Churches* (Maryknoll, N.Y.: Orbis Books, 1997).

62. Cited in Denise M. Ackermann, *After the Locusts: Letters from a Landscape of Faith* (Grand Rapids, Mich.: Wm. B. Eerdmans, 2003), 108.

63. Kenneth R. Overberg, *Ethics and AIDS: Compassion and Justice in a Global Crisis* (Lanham, Md.: Rowman & Littlefield, 2006), 152.

64. Walter Brueggemann, *An Introduction to the Old Testament: The Canon and Christian Imagination* (Louisville: Westminster John Knox, 2003), 280–91.

65. Ackermann, *After the Locusts,* 112.

66. Brueggemann, *Introduction to the Old Testament,* 282.

67. Bruno Chenu, *The Trouble I've Seen: The Big Book of Negro Spirituals,* trans. Eugene V. Leplante (Valley Forge, Pa.: Judson Press, 2003), 265.

68. John Lovell Jr., *Black Song: The Forge and the Flame* (New York: Paragon House Publishers, 1972), 122, 497; Richard Newman, *Go Down, Moses: Celebrating the African-American Spiritual* (New York: Roundtable Press, 1998), 46.

69. Lovell, *Black Song,* 122.

70. In *Introduction to the Old Testament,* Brueggemann describes the impact of the dynamic encounter in biblical laments (283–84): "The 'Thou' *answers* the plea of the 'I' and that answer signals a change in the opening situation. . . . The encounter between the 'I' and the 'Thou' is the signal for a change not merely in inner realm of consciousness but in the realm of outer events."

71. For a concise account of these events, see "Atlanta Race Riot of 1906," *New Georgia Encyclopedia.* Online at *www.georgiaencyclopedia .org/.* Accessed July 12, 2009.

72. W. E. B. Du Bois, "A Litany at Atlanta," in *Black Voices: An Anthology of Afro-American Literature,* ed. Abraham Chapman (New York: Penguin Books, 1968), 360–63; emphasis in the original.

73. "Atlanta Race Riot of 1906."

74. John Swinton, *Raging with Compassion: Pastoral Responses to the Problem of Evil* (Grand Rapids, Mich.: Wm. B. Eerdmans, 2007), 105.

75. Ackermann, *After the Locusts,* 116.

76. Brueggemann briefly ponders the question of why the practice of lament has seemingly disappeared from Christian worship. He attributes this to the church's longstanding "propensity" for "cultural accommodation" and/or the influence of modern stoicism. He concludes that recovering the psalms of lament is a "major enterprise" for the church (*Introduction to the Old Testatment,* 289–90). Similarly, see Ackermann's plea for a church that "laments suffering and loss." For when the language of lament has no place, "justice questions cannot be asked and eventually become invisible and illegitimate" (*After the Locusts,* 122–24).

77. Ackermann, *After the Locusts,* 117.

78. *L'Osservatore Romano,* Eng. ed. (March 22, 2000), 4; cited in Pontifical Council for Justice and Peace, "Contribution to World Conference against Racism, Racial Discrimination, Xenophobia and Related Intolerance," 7.

79. John Paul II, *Tertio Millennio Adveniente,* 33.

80. USCCB, *Brothers and Sisters to Us,* 8.

81. The record of Catholic complicity in U.S. racism can be found in the following studies: Cyprian Davis, *The History of Black Catholics in the United States* (New York: Crossroad Publications, 1990); Stephen J. Ochs, *Desegregating the Altar: The Josephites and the Struggle for Black Priests 1871–1960* (Baton Rouge: Louisiana State University Press, 1990); and John T. McGreevy, *Parish Boundaries: The Catholic Encounter with the Twentieth Century Urban North* (Chicago: University of Chicago Press, 1996).

82. The International Theological Commission states that even though we may not be personally responsible for the sins of the past, because of "the bond which unites us to one another in the Mystical Body, all of us . . . bear the burden of the errors and faults of those who have gone before us." Thus Pope John Paul implores that "the Church . . . should kneel before God and implore forgiveness for the past and present sins of her sons and daughters" ("Introduction," *Memory and Reconciliation*).

83. *The Rite of Penance,* 6b.

84. Ackermann, *After the Locusts,* 118.

85. This discussion of compassion is an expansion of my earlier treatment in "Healing a Divided World," *Origins* 37 (August 16, 2007). A very fine overview of compassion in theological ethics and its importance for contemporary moral life is provided by Maureen H. O'Connell, *Compassion: Loving Our Neighbor in an Age of Globalization* (Maryknoll, N.Y.: Orbis Books, 2009).

86. See O'Connell, *Compassion,* 68; also Joseph A. Fitzmyer, *The Gospel According to Luke I–IX* (New York: Doubleday, 1981), 658–59.

87. O'Connell, *Compassion,* 70.

88. The following presentation is indebted to Caleb Rosado's essay "The Undergirding Factor Is POWER: Toward an Understanding of Prejudice and Racism" (1997). Available online at *www.rosado.net.*
89. John Paul II, *Sollicitudo Rei Socialis,* 39.
90. Ibid., 38.
91. Ibid.
92. James H. Cone, *A Black Theology of Liberation,* 20th anniv. ed. (Maryknoll, N.Y.: Orbis Books, 1990, orig. ed., 1970), 95.
93. Charles R. Lawrence III, "The Id, the Ego, and Equal Protection: Reckoning with Unconscious Racism," *Stanford Law Review* 39 (January 1987): 317–88, at n. 135.
94. Joe R. Feagin, *Systemic Racism: A Theory of Oppression* (New York: Routledge, 2006), 27–28, 275.
95. Joe R. Feagin, *Racist America: Roots, Current Realities, and Future Reparations* (New York: Routledge, 2000), 254. Feagin revisits this research in a later work, Joe Feagin and Eileen O'Brien, *White Men on Race: Power, Privilege, and the Shaping of the Cultural Consciousness* (Boston: Beacon Press, 2003), 64–65.
96. Feagin, *Racist America,* 254–55; verbs modified for plural forms.
97. Feagin and O'Brien, *White Men on Race,* 65.
98. Ibid., 63–64.
99. Walt Harrington, *Crossings: A White Man's Journey into Black America* (New York: HarperCollins, 1992), 447.
100. Feagin and O'Brien, *White Men on Race,* 236.
101. Bernard Lonergan, *Method in Theology,* 2nd ed. (Toronto: University of Toronto Press [1973], 1990), 237.
102. Ibid., 130.
103. Walter Conn, *Conversion: Perspectives on Personal and Social Transformation* (New York: Alba House, 1978), 13.
104. Mark Searle, "The Journey of Conversion," *Worship* 54 (January 1980): 36.
105. Ibid., 47.
106. For an insightful treatment of this question, see Jan Michael Joncas, "Tasting the Kingdom of God: The Meal Ministry of Jesus and Its Implications for Contemporary Life and Worship," *Worship* 74 (July 2000): 329–65, at 350. See also Santos Yao, "The Table Fellowship of Jesus with the Marginalized: A Radical Inclusiveness," *Journal of Asian Mission* 3 (2001): 25–41.
107. Cited in Joncas, "Tasting the Kingdom of God," 350.
108. Pope Benedict XVI, "Visit to the Synagogue of Cologne" (2005).
109. *The Sacramentary,* "Preface for Christian Unity," 76.
110. Ibid., 43.

111. Pontifical Council for Justice and Peace, *Compendium of the Social Doctrine of the Church* (Washington, D.C.: United States Catholic Conference, 2004), 34.

112. The ethical implications of the doctrine of the Trinity need to be further developed. If we are indeed created in the image of God, and if God is constitutively one yet diverse, this cannot but have profound ramifications for an understanding of racial reconciliation. Some work on the relationship between Trinitarian confession and racial justice does exist; yet it remains true that Trinitarian doctrine and anthropology play a minor role in Catholic social ethical reflection. For example, see Michael Battle, *Reconciliation: The Ubuntu Theology of Desmond Tutu* (Cleveland: Pilgrim Press, 1997), 54–69; and Gary W. Deddo, "Persons in Racial Reconciliation: The Contributions of a Trinitarian Theological Anthropology," in *The Gospel in Black and White: Theological Resources for Racial Reconciliation*, ed. Dennis L. Okholm (Downers Grove, Ill.: InterVarsity Press, 1997).

113. Pope John Paul II, *Sollicitudo Rei Socialis*, 38. Here the pope teaches, "[Solidarity] is not a feeling of vague compassion or shallow distress at the misfortune of so many people. . . . It is a *firm and persevering determination* to commit oneself to the common good . . . because we are *all* really responsible for *all*" (emphases in the original).

114. "The principle of solidarity, also articulated in terms of 'friendship' or 'social charity,' is a direct demand of human and Christian brotherhood" (*The Catechism of the Catholic Church*, 1939).

115. Pope John Paul II, *Sollicitudo Rei Socialis*, 39.

116. Pope John Paul II, "Address to Bishops of Brazil," *Origins* 10 (July 31, 1980): 135; cited in United States Conference of Catholic Bishops, *Economic Justice for All*, 87.

117. *Economic Justice for All*, 181.

4: "A Dream Deferred"

1. Langston Hughes, "Harlem," *Selected Poems of Langston Hughes* (New York: Alfred A. Knopf, 1988), 268.

2. See, for example, the aspiration of the influential moral philosopher John Rawls: "What I have attempted to do is to generalize and carry to a higher order of abstraction the traditional theory of the social contract as represented by Locke, Rousseau, and Kant." The abstraction to which he aspires leads to his positing of a "hypothetical original state" as his starting point: "The guiding idea is that the principles of justice for the basic structures of society are the object of the original agreement. . . . They specify the kind of social cooperation that can be entered into and the form of government that can be established." Yet such a starting point glosses

over and cannot adequately respond to the concrete reality of oppression and social evil. His starting point, in light of the black experience of racial exclusion and degradation, is "hypothetical" to the point of absurdity. See John Rawls, *A Theory of Justice* (Oxford: Oxford University Press, 1971), viii; 11.

3. Peter J. Paris, *The Social Teaching of the Black Churches* (Philadelphia: Fortress Press, 1985), 10, 14; emphasis added.

4. Ibid., 11.

5. Ibid., 14.

6. Preston N. Williams, "Afro-American Religious Ethics," in *The Westminster Dictionary of Christian Ethics,* ed. James F. Childress and John Macquarrie (Philadelphia: Westminster Press, 1986), 12.

7. William M. Finnin Jr., "Ethics of Universal Wholeness: An Assessment of the Work of Preston N. Williams," *Iliff Review* 36 (Spring 1979): 28; citing Williams, "Criteria for Decision-Making for Social Ethics in the Black Community," *Journal of the Interdenominational Center* 1 (Fall 1973): 67; emphasis added.

8. Cornel West, *Race Matters* (Boston: Beacon Press, 2001), 111.

9. Ibid., 44. See also Cornel West, "Black Leadership and the Pitfalls of Racial Reasoning," in *Race-ing Justice, En-gendering Power: Essays on Anita Hill, Clarence Thomas, and the Construction of Social Reality,* ed. Toni Morrison (New York: Pantheon Books, 1992), 390–401.

10. West, "Black Leadership and the Pitfalls of Racial Reasoning," 390–401.

11. Robin D. G. Kelley, *Freedom Dreams: The Black Radical Imagination* (Boston: Beacon Press, 2002), 154.

12. Among the many works of womanist ethicists, those that have been particularly insightful for me are Emilie M. Townes, *Womanist Ethics and the Cultural Production of Evil* (New York: Palgrave Macmillan, 2006); Traci C. West, *Disruptive Christian Ethics: When Racism and Women's Lives Matter* (Louisville: Westminster John Knox, 2006); and Stacey M. Floyd-Thomas, *Mining the Motherlode: Methods in Womanist Ethics* (Cleveland: Pilgrim Press, 2006). The writings of my colleagues and friends Jamie Phelps and Shawn Copeland have been very influential, as the notes in this book attest.

13. See also Enoch Oglesby, who examines King's commitment to the "Beloved Community" and concludes that the formation of an inclusive community is the "intentional focus" of the black church's socio-ethical reflection (in his *Ethics and Theology from the Other Side: Sounds of Moral Struggle* [Lanham, Md.: University Press of America, 1979], 146).

14. Paris, *Social Teaching of the Black Churches,* 10, 11.

15. Bishop C. M. Tanner (1900), cited by Paris, *Social Teaching of the Black Churches,* 19–20.

16. Cheryl A. Kirk-Duggan, *Exorcising Evil: A Womanist Perspective on the Spirituals* (Maryknoll, N.Y.: Orbis Books, 1997), 87.

17. Here I am trying to express an insight that I first discovered in the work of my colleague Jamie Phelps, who states that one of the criteria of Black Catholic theology is what she calls, "orthopathy." By this, she means "emotional feeling, and passion that is characteristic of African-American life and is found in the biblical tradition, particularly in the prophetic traditions of Amos and Hosea as well as in the Marcan Gospel. It is this emotional, feeling and passionate aspect of African-American faith that gives rise to the search for authentic doctrine (orthodoxy) and authentic action (orthopraxis)." Phelps acknowledges her indebtedness to Toinette Eugene for her first exposure to this concept. What I am attempting to do in this essay is to show that African American understandings of justice are based in a fundamental passion, what I am calling a "vision." Through this excavation, I hope to uncover the operative "orthopathic" characteristics of justice in the black cultural tradition. See Jamie T. Phelps, "The Sources of Theology: African-American Experience in the United States," in *Black and Catholic: The Challenge and Gift of Black Folk,* ed. Jamie T. Phelps (Milwaukee: Marquette University Press, 1997), 173, at n. 17.

18. Kelley, *Freedom Dreams,* xii. In the same work, he poses this theme again, in the form of a question: "What are today's young activists dreaming about? We know what they are fighting against, but what are they fighting for?" (8). These critical questions highlight the importance of dreams, visions, and transrational imagination in the quest for justice…and its right understanding.

19. There are many versions of this spiritual, with different verses. Such variations are common in the genre of the spirituals, as the enslaved bards both freely borrowed from each other and interchanged the lyrics of one spiritual with another. The version given above is an amalgam from two sources: Kirk-Duggan, *Exorcising Evil,* 64; and a CD recording by Alice Parker, "Listen, Lord" (Gothic Records, 2004).

20. Kirk-Duggan, *Exorcising Evil,* 64 and 81. Kirk-Duggan states that these lyrics were adapted by members of the Student Nonviolent Coordinating Committee (SNCC), a group of younger student radicals in the 1960s civil rights movement.

21. Ibid., 81.

22. Hughes, *Selected Poems,* 275.

23. Kenneth L. Smith and Ira G. Zepp Jr., *Search for the Beloved Community: The Thinking of Martin Luther King Jr.* (Valley Forge, Pa.: Judson Press, 1988), 129.

24. Lewis V. Baldwin, *Toward the Beloved Community: Martin Luther King Jr. and South Africa* (Cleveland: Pilgrim Press, 1995), 175.

25. Citations from King's works, unless otherwise noted, are from James Melvin Washington, ed., *Testament of Hope: The Essential Writings of Martin Luther King Jr.* (New York: Harper and Row, 1986). They will be referenced by the title given in this collection, followed by the page number. Hence, King, "Where Do We Go from Here?" 617.

26. King, "A Testament of Hope," 317.

27. Martin Luther King Jr., *The Autobiography of Martin Luther King Jr.*, ed. Clayborne Carson (New York: Warner Books, 1998), 262.

28. Ibid., 337.

29. "The Beloved Community of Martin Luther King Jr.," available at *www.thekingcenter.org/prog/bc/index.html*. Accessed October 19, 2005. I believe that history will acknowledge the special debt we owe to King's wife, Coretta Scott King. She guarded her husband's legacy against attempts to reduce it to mere comforting rhetoric. But more than this, through the King Center in Atlanta, she extended her husband's vision to incorporate struggles against sexism and homophobia as integral to the realization of the Beloved Community for which she and her husband sacrificed so much. Her inspiring activism in this regard is another demonstration of the inclusive impulse that animates the African American understanding of justice. Her extension of her husband's vision illustrates how a deep appreciation of the essential worth of human personality demands an intentional struggle against all forms of human subordination. Nothing less will bring about the realization of the Beloved Community.

30. On this point, see Robert Michael Franklin, "In Pursuit of Justice: Martin Luther King Jr. and John Rawls," *Journal of Religious Ethics* 18 (Fall 1990): 57–77; and David W. Wills, "Racial Justice and the Limits of American Liberalism," *Journal of Religious Ethics* 6 (Fall 1978): 187–200.

31. Johannes Messner, *Social Ethics: Natural Law in the Western World* (St. Louis: B. Herder Book Co., 1965), 322.

32. Eberhard Welty, *A Handbook of Christian Social Ethics*, vol. 1 (New York: Herder & Herder, 1960), 300.

33. Ibid., 306.

34. Messner, *Social Ethics*, 322; emphasis added.

35. National Conference of Catholic Bishops, *Economic Justice for All*, 70.

36. Welty, *A Handbook of Christian Social Ethics*, 306; and Messner, *Social Ethics*, 322.

37. "Obama Warns of Black 'Quiet Riot,' " *Chicago Tribune* (June 6, 2007), sec. 1, 4.

38. Gustavo Gutiérrez, *On Job: God-Talk and the Suffering of the Innocent* (Maryknoll, N.Y.: Orbis Books, 1987), 24.

39. W. E. B. Du Bois, "Of the Sorrow Songs," in his *The Souls of Black Folk* (New York: Signet Class Penguin Books, 1969), 274.

40. James Cone, *The Spirituals and the Blues: An Interpretation* (Maryknoll, N.Y.: Orbis Books, 1991), 86.

41. Vaclav Havel, *Disturbing the Peace* (New York: Vintage Books, 1991), 181; emphasis added.

42. This distinction, while critically important, merits an important caution: those who strive to defend the status quo will always characterize and dismiss revolutionary hopes as implausible or irresponsible, perhaps "impossible," "naïve," or "nonsensical." Thus one has to be alert to the possibility of ideological uses of the term "irresponsible" as a means of thwarting the potential for profound societal change.

43. This is my reading of the classic understanding of hope as the expectation of the attainment of a "difficult good," in other words, where social progress is neither automatic nor inevitable, but rather painful, slow, difficult, and uncertain, though not thoroughly excluded. To put this another way, hope presupposes that the world, and human beings, are neither utterly evil nor completely good, but a mixture of good and evil. There is no room for hope in an irredeemably evil universe...nor need for it in one completely good.

44. Thus, for example, one cannot "hope" that in leaping off a building one will not fall to the ground, as human activity can in no way change the inevitable outcome; human action in such a situation is pretty well determined.

45. Liberationist theologians and ethicists sometimes articulate this concept by speaking of "subversive memory," that is, the recovery and retelling of certain past insights and historical events — repressed in the interests of the dominant parties of a society — which can show the possibilities inherent in the present situation.

46. Cone, *The Spirituals and the Blues,* 86; emphasis added.

47. "In the blues, stark, full, human passions expressed a fundamental and universal emotion of the human heart, a kind of disillusionment without defeat that might be called existential." See Charles Joyner, "A Single Southern Culture: Cultural Interaction in the Old South," in *Black and White Cultural Interaction in the Antebellum South,* ed. Ted Ownby (Jackson: University Press of Mississippi, 1993), 18.

48. Kalamu ya Salaam, *What Is Life? Reclaiming the Black Blues Self* (Chicago: Third World Press, 1994), 13–14.

49. This discussion is taken from James H. Cone, "The Blues: A Secular Spiritual," *The Spirituals and the Blues,* 104–10.

50. John Rawls, *A Theory of Justice* (Oxford: Oxford University Press, 1971), 11.

5: The Vocation of the Black Catholic Theologian

1. John LaFarge, *The Catholic Viewpoint on Race Relations* (Garden City, N.Y.: Hanover House: 1956). His perspective was summarized and critiqued in the second chapter of this book.

2. Denise M. Ackermann, *After the Locusts: Letters from a Landscape of Faith* (Grand Rapids, Mich.: Wm. B. Eerdmans, 2003), 39.

3. William M. Banks, *Black Intellectuals: Race and Responsibility in American Life* (New York: W. W. Norton, 1996), xvi.

4. Vincent Harding, "The Vocation of the Black Scholar and the Struggles of the Black Community," *Harvard Educational Review* (1974): 2–29, at 5.

5. Ibid., 6.

6. Ibid., 7, and passim. Observe how this echoes the dimension of "struggle" highlighted as a core dimension of the black cultural experience in chapter 1.

7. Mari Evans, *Continuum: New and Selected Poems* (Baltimore: Black Classic Press, 2007), 22–23. Used with permission of the author.

8. Harding, "The Vocation of the Black Scholar and the Struggles of the Black Community," 20. Note that this truth is not an abstract, timeless notion, but one that is discovered and verified in the midst of struggle and action for the sake of justice.

9. Ibid., 13.

10. I argue this point in chapter 1.

11. Black scholars are, in Antonio Gramsci's words, "organic intellectuals." Unlike "traditional intellectuals" who see themselves as functioning somewhat autonomously from society and its influences (the stereotype of the "ivory tower" academic), the Italian social theorist Gramsci describes the "organic intellectual" as one who is intimately involved in a movement for social change and contributes the intellectual justification and analysis necessary for the new ideas upon which a more just society can be founded. He or she also provides the sophisticated critique of the dominant social ideas and values that shore up unjust social situations. In both of these tasks, the organic intellectual contributes to developing the new consciousness essential to a new social order. For a discussion of Gramsci's notion of the "organic intellectual," see Barry Burke (1999, 2005), "Antonio Gramsci, Schooling and Education," *The Encyclopedia of Informal Education,* available at *www.infed.org/thinkers/et-gram.htm.* Accessed July 20, 2009.

12. There are many debates within this tradition both supporting and disputing Harding's thesis that black scholarship must serve an advocacy

role in the quest for black freedom and justice. Banks's work is a masterful recounting of these disputes and debates.

13. Harding, "The Vocation of the Black Scholar and the Struggles of the Black Community," 14 and 16. He lists as examples fear, lack of self-discipline, failure to believe in ourselves, and an excessive desire for public recognition. I would offer Malcolm X as an example of someone who relentlessly criticized the values of white society, yet also offered searing critiques of self-destructive forces within the black community. See, for example, *Malcolm X Speaks*, ed. George Breitman (New York: Grove Weidenfeld, [1965] 1990).

14. James H. Cone, *My Soul Looks Back* (Maryknoll, N.Y.: Orbis Books, 1986), 77–78; emphasis added. Gustavo Gutiérrez, a seminal Latin American liberation theologian, likewise declares: "We make no attempt at an aseptic — and elusive! — 'objectivity.' We shall not be filling the columns of our ledger with cold analysis. What we enter there will be facts, yes, but facts with which we are passionately involved" (*The Power of the Poor in History* [Maryknoll, N.Y.: Orbis Books, 1983], 77).

15. Peter Paris, "The Ethics of African American Religious Scholarship," *Journal of the American Academy of Religion* 64, no. 3 (1996): 483–97, at 489.

16. Audre Lorde, "There Is No Hierarchy of Oppressions," in *Dangerous Liaisons: Blacks, Gays, and the Struggle for Equality*, ed. Eric Brandt (New York: New Press, 1999), 306–7.

17. bell hooks and Cornel West, *Breaking Bread: Insurgent Black Intellectual Life* (Boston: South End Press, 1991), 49.

18. Cornel West, *Race Matters* (Boston: Beacon Press, 1993), 46.

19. Ibid., 43.

20. Paris, "The Ethics of African American Religious Scholarship," 489.

21. One often hears an injunction that the Catholic theologian is to *sentire cum ecclesia*, that is, to "think with the church" and to harmonize one's theological contribution with the normative faith claims taught by official authorities. I believe this is too narrow an understanding. Rather, the Catholic theologian, in order to serve the faith community well, must also *sentire pro ecclesia*, that is, to think *on behalf of and for the sake of the church* in its quest for a less and less imperfect understanding of the infinite love and claim that our God has laid upon it. At times this will entail a stance of critical loving critique of some of the church's concrete practices or current official stances — never out of intellectual arrogance or hubris, but out of deep concern for the adequacy of its internal life and moral witness.

22. Mark D. Jordan, *Telling Truths in Church: Scandal, Flesh, and Christian Speech* (Boston: Beacon Press, 2003), 110, at n. 1.

23. M. Shawn Copeland, "Guest Editorial," *Theological Studies* 61 (December 2001): 607.

24. M. Shawn Copeland, "Theology as Intellectually Vital Inquiry: A Black Theological Interrogation," *CTSA Proceedings* 46 (1991): 51. Copeland elaborates upon the challenges the virulent residue of white racism poses for the entire guild of Catholic theologians regardless of race in her essay, "Racism and the Vocation of the Christian Theologian," *Spiritus* 2 (2002): 15–29.

25. Shawn Copeland describes the commonality and distinctiveness of black Catholic theology with her characteristic lucidity and precision as follows: "Black Catholic Studies involves a three-fold movement: retrieval, critique, and construction.... First, as a division of African American Religious Studies, Black Catholic Studies retrieves, critiques, and evaluates the intellectual, aesthetic, moral, and religious sensibilities and expressions of people of African descent. Second, Black Catholic Studies retrieves, critiques, and evaluates the theological and doctrinal traditions, customs, and expressions of the Catholic Church. Third, Black Catholic Studies synthesizes the decisions and products of the first and second movements: from these materials, Black Catholic scholars construct a distinctive religious, intellectual, and moral horizon or world view." Copeland presented this description in a lecture at the Institute for Black Catholic Studies, Summer 1994.

26. I borrow this term from a personal conversation with my colleague Shawn Copeland.

27. In no particular order: Jamie Phelps (Institute for Black Catholic Studies at Xavier University), M. Shawn Copeland (Boston College), Stephanie Mitchem (University of South Carolina), Diana Hayes (Georgetown University), Philip Linden (Xavier University of New Orleans), Gerald Boodoo (Duquesne University), Jessica Murdoch (Villanova University), Teresia Hinga (Santa Clara), Carmichael Peters (Chapman University), LaReine-Marie Mosely (Loyola University Chicago), Paulinus Odozor (University of Notre Dame), James Okoye (Catholic Theological Union), Cyril Orji (University of Dayton), Edward Braxton (Bishop of Belleville, Ill.), Wilton Gregory (Archbishop of Atlanta), Toinette Eugene (formerly of the Diocese of Oakland, Calif.), Anna Perkins (University of the West Indies), Shawnee Daniels-Sykes (Mount Mary College), Lilan Dube (University of San Francisco), and Bryan Massingale (Marquette University).

28. The historians are Cyprian Davis (St. Meinrad Seminary and School of Theology), Thaddeus Posey (formerly of the University of St. Thomas in St. Paul), Diane Batts Morrow (University of Georgia), Nick Creary

(Ohio University), Katrina Sanders (University of Iowa), Anthea Butler (University of Rochester), and Cecilia Moore (University of Dayton). The canon lawyers are Leonard Scott (Diocese of Camden), Reginald Whitt (Law School of the University of St. Thomas in St. Paul), Arthur Anderson (Chicago), and James Herring (St. Norbert Archabbey). In addition, Joseph Perry (auxiliary bishop of Chicago) has the J.C.L. in Canon Law.

29. For example, Donald Sterling (spirituality), Edward Branch (spiritual development/campus ministry), Clarence Williams (racial and ethnic diversity), Eva Marie Lumas (catechesis), Maurice Nutt (preaching), George Franklin (preaching), Paul Marshall (spirituality), J. Glenn Murray (liturgy), Freddy Washington (pastoral ministry), Joyce Gillie Cruse (spirituality), Kathleen Dorsey Bellow (liturgy), Kimberly Lymore (pastoral ministry), Oralissa Martin (African American youth), and C. Vanessa White (spirituality).

30. The Black Catholic Theological Symposium is a national Roman Catholic interdisciplinary theological society. It is the principal learned society for the study of black Catholicism, especially as it exists in the Western diaspora (specifically in North America). Founded in 1978, the Symposium has been meeting annually since 1991. Further information about the Symposium and its activities can be found at its website *www.bcts.org*.

31. For example, Charles Payne (psychology), Joseph Brown (African American literature), Roy Lee (education), Giles Conwill (anthropology), Addie Lorraine Walker (religious education), Sue Houchins (African American, Women, and Gender Studies), Kevin Johnson (music), Robert Bartlett (leadership studies), Patrick Wells (health sciences), Eva Regina Martin (African American literature), and Kimberly Flint-Hamilton (classics).

32. The Institute for Black Catholic Studies of Xavier University of New Orleans is a summer program that trains ministers and leaders for service to the black Catholic community, primarily though not exclusively in the United States. It is a holistic learning experience, incorporating teaching, research, community service, and communal worship. It is the only institution in the Western hemisphere to offer, among other programs, a master's degree in Black Catholic Studies. More information about the Institute is available at its website *www.xula.edu/ibcs/index*.

33. Joseph Davis, "Black Catholics and the Bicentennial," *Origins 5* (1975): 413. See also *We Walk by Faith and Not by Sight: The Church's Response to Racism in the Years Following* Brothers and Sisters to Us: *A Research Report Commemorating the 25th Anniversary of* Brothers and Sisters to Us (Washington, D.C.: United States Conference of Catholic Bishops, 2004). An executive summary of this report is available at the Conference's Committee on African American Catholics website *www.usccb.org/saac*.

34. For example, the nucleus of chapter 1 on "culture" was formulated in response to an invitation from the National Black Catholic Congress in 1999 to address the questions: What do we mean by "white church culture" and how is it an impediment to African American evangelization? Also, the analysis of the black Catholic experience and the challenges facing this community originated from invitations to address the annual joint convention of black Catholic priests, sisters, deacons, and seminarians in 2008 and a conference of lay pastoral leaders in 2007. Such research and presentations for these particular pastoral concerns are genuine scholarship, though not of the kind prized by the academy — whose elitist tendencies deem such works as "popular" or relegate them to the less valued category of "service."

35. Dwight N. Hopkins, *Introducing Black Theology of Liberation* (Maryknoll, N.Y.: Orbis Books, 1999). One could also point to the edited work of Cornel West and Eddie S. Glaude Jr., *African American Religious Thought: An Anthology* (Louisville: Westminster John Knox Press, 2003). Note that this anthology, despite its omission of black Catholics, has been hailed as "comprehensive" (see back cover). It should be mentioned that James H. Cone is a conspicuous exception; he has been in intentional dialogue with black Catholic theologians and has expressed critical appreciation for our project. See James H. Cone, "Black Liberation Theology and Black Catholics: A Critical Conversation," *Theological Studies* 61 (December 2000): 731–47.

36. Juan Williams, *This Far by Faith: Stories from the African American Religious Experience* (San Francisco: HarperCollins, 2003). The description "seminal" is found on this work's back cover. A welcome exception to this pattern of omission is Anthony B. Pinn's *The African American Religious Experience in America* (Miami: University Press of Florida, 2007).

37. One of the reasons often given for such omission is that there is a lack of resources for such engagement. Given the existence of four anthologies on black Catholic thought edited by black Catholics, this reason is more than a little bewildering (to say the least). Such works include Jamie T. Phelps, ed., *Black and Catholic: The Challenge and Gift of Black Folk* (Milwaukee: Marquette University Press, 1997); Diana L. Hayes and Cyprian Davis, eds., *Taking Down Our Harps: Black Catholics in the United States* (Maryknoll, N.Y.: Orbis Books, 1998); Cyprian Davis and Jamie Phelps, eds., *Stamped with the Image of God: African Americans as God's Image in Black* (Maryknoll, N.Y.: Orbis Books, 2003); and M. Shawn Copeland, ed., *Uncommon Faithfulness: The Black Catholic Experience* (Maryknoll, N.Y.: Orbis Books, 2009). One should also note the anthology edited by William J. Kelly, S.J., *Black Catholic Theology: A Sourcebook* (New York:

McGraw-Hill, 2000). Moreover, since 2007 there is the annual *Journal of the Black Catholic Theological Symposium,* which publishes the significant papers delivered at its annual gatherings. In view of these resources, not to mention the monographs and other publications of black Catholic scholars, the pattern of omission and nonengagement is all the more "curious."

38. Jon Nilson, *Hearing Past the Pain: Why Catholic Theologians Need Black Theology* (Mahwah, N.J.: Paulist Press, 2007); and Laurie M. Cassidy and Alexander Mikulich, eds., *Interrupting White Privilege: Catholic Theologians Break the Silence* (Maryknoll, N.Y.: Orbis Books, 2007).

39. In a future work I hope to examine the "dark night" as this has been understood in the Christian mystical tradition and show its relevance for understanding the religious experience and growth in holiness for African American believers. That work is tentatively titled "The Dark Nights of Malcolm X (and Other Black Spiritual Seekers)."

40. Phrase taken from Copeland, *Uncommon Faithfulness.*

41. West and hooks, *Breaking Bread,* 16–17.

42. As chronicled in Cyprian Davis's seminal work, *The History of Black Catholics in the United States* (New York: Crossroad, 1990).

Epilogue

1. Kenneth L. Smith and Ira G. Zepp Jr., *Search for the Beloved Community: The Thinking of Martin Luther King Jr.* (Valley Forge, Pa.: Judson Press, 1998), 130.

2. Citations from King's works, unless otherwise stated, are from James Melvin Washington, ed., *A Testament of Hope: The Essential Writings of Martin Luther King Jr.* (New York: Harper and Row, 1986). They will be referenced by the title given in this work, followed by page number. Hence, King, "The Ethical Demands for Integration," 118.

3. King offers a serious critique of tokenism as a delay tactic that avoids the demands of integration in "The Case against 'Tokenism,' " 106–11.

4. Smith and Zepp, *Search for the Beloved Community,* 131.

5. King, "A Testament of Hope," 317.

6. Smith and Zepp, *Search for the Beloved Community,* 131.

7. King, "The Ethical Demands for Integration," 118.

8. King, "Nonviolence: The Only Road to Freedom," 61.

Resources for Further Reflection
and Understanding

The literature on racism and white privilege is quite voluminous. I am limiting myself to a list of ten works (listed alphabetically by author) that can be of help particularly for the nonspecialist who wishes to further explore the issues raised in my text, and especially the connections between Catholic faith and racial justice.

Barndt, Joseph R. *Understanding and Dismantling Racism: The Twenty-first Century Challenge to White America.* Minneapolis: Fortress Press, 2007. This is one of the primary texts I use in my college course. Written by a longtime white racial justice activist with a history of faith-based involvement, it is a very complete (and unsparing) overview.

Bonilla-Silva, Eduardo. *Racism without Racists: Color-Blind Racism and the Persistence of Racial Inequality in the United States.* 2nd ed. New York: Rowman and Littlefield, 2006. This is an essential text for understanding how racial inequality can remain such a potent force despite the widespread denials by individual whites of any racist intent. The author provides an illuminating exposé of the various strategies used by many whites to minimize the existence of racial injustice and their participation in it. He concludes by charting a likely path for the evolution of race relations in the United States.

Cassidy, Laurie M., and Alex Mikulich, eds. *Interrupting White Privilege: Catholic Theologians Break the Silence.* Maryknoll,

N.Y.: Orbis Books, 2007. This is a pathbreaking work in Catholic theology, as leading and rising white theologians forthrightly engage a subject that has received scant attention from professional theologians.

Catholic Charities USA. *Poverty and Racism: Overlapping Threats to the Common Good.* Alexandria, Va.: Catholic Charities USA, 2007. (In the interest of full disclosure, I was the principal author of this text). This is a concise overview of the interrelationship between white privilege and economic disadvantage, with a series of concrete actions necessary for achieving the economic justice called for by Catholic social teaching. It is one of the most forthright treatments issued by a national Catholic organization. Catholic Charities is to be commended for its foresight and courage in tackling an issue that other Catholic groups have chosen to avoid or mute.

Copeland, M. Shawn, ed. *Uncommon Faithfulness: The Black Catholic Experience.* Maryknoll, N.Y.: Orbis Books, 2009. This is the latest anthology of black Catholic thought by its most prominent theologians, ethicists, and scholars. The volume surveys the existential concerns of this faith community — from ecclesial exclusion to HIV/AIDS — and demonstrates the range of black Catholic intellectual thought in the first part of the twenty-first century.

Davis, Cyprian. *The History of Black Catholics in the United States.* New York: Crossroad, 1991. Perhaps the most essential text for understanding the situation of black Catholics. Davis masterfully recounts this little-known history and convincingly demonstrates that there has never been an American Catholic Church without persons of African descent who made valuable contributions to a faith community that extended them only a tentative embrace.

Melczek, Bishop Dale J. *Created in God's Image: A Pastoral Letter on the Sin of Racism and a Call to Conversion.* Available online at *www.dcgary.org/bishop-pastoral-letters.htm.* Written by the bishop of Gary, Indiana, in my judgment this is the best pastoral letter written by a U.S. bishop on this topic. Informed by contemporary social science, it lays out the ethical and spiritual challenges of being a follower of Christ in a society of white privilege. What is more remarkable is that this letter was part of a three-year process of intentional engagement by the entire diocese with this pressing social evil. Melczek and the Diocese of Gary have provided the U.S. Catholic Church with what must be ranked as among the "best practices" when it comes to Catholic engagement with racism.

Nothwehr, Dawn M. *That They May Be One: Catholic Social Teaching on Racism, Tribalism, and Xenophobia.* Maryknoll, N.Y.: Orbis Books, 2008. Nothwehr, a Franciscan sister and Catholic ethicist, has edited a collection of official statements by Catholic Church leaders worldwide on issues of racism and racial intolerance. This compendium illustrates how this issue is of increasing importance for the global Catholic social justice agenda.

Williams Jr., Clarence E. *Racial Sobriety: Becoming the Change You Want to See.* Detroit: Institute for the Recovery from Racisms, 2007. Father Williams is one of the foremost educators about racism and cultural diversity in the Catholic Church. This work takes an approach slightly different from mine, but nevertheless complementary, as Williams focuses on the harm experienced by both whites and persons of color who live in a racist society. He then outlines a program for personal recovery from attitudes of racial collusion and complicity. Adopting a very pastoral tone, Williams very competently shows the conversion journey that both whites and people of color — as individuals and groups — must undertake if they are to be in genuine solidarity with one another.

Wise, Tim. *White Like Me: Reflections on Race from a Privileged Son.* 2nd ed. New York: Soft Skull Press, 2007. I admit that this work was not among my initial ten choices, until I thought about the text that has had the most profound impact upon my white college-age students. Hands down, it is this one. After reading this work and/or hearing this author, they "get it." A work of anecdote rather than social analysis, antiracism activist

Wise gives an "insider's account" of what it means to grow up with racial privilege, and the moral imperative of standing against it. Profoundly experiential, it is a very frank account that spares neither himself nor his family in accounting for the impact of race privilege and how it affects the white sense of self. Informed by the perspectives of African American authors such as James Baldwin, this is a candid examination of the issue in a very accessible way. (My students have also found valuable his most recent work, *Between Barack and a Hard Place: Racism and White Denial in an Age of Obama* [San Francisco: City Lights Publishers, 2009], which powerfully challenges the idea that an African American president heralds the arrival of a "post-racial" America).

Though I promised to limit the list to only ten works, the following deserve at least an "honorable mention": Beverly Daniel-Tatum, *"Why Are All the Black Kids Sitting Together in the Cafeteria?": A Psychologist Explains the Development of Racial Identity,* rev. ed. (New York: Basic Books, 2003); and Allan G. Johnson, *Privilege, Power, and Difference,* 2nd ed. (New York: McGraw-Hill, 2006). Both works are valuable resources for exploring racial and cultural diversity. A major plus is that they are written in an accessible style. The Johnson text is a welcome exploration of the various forms of social privilege (such as race, class, gender, sexual orientation, and ability). I have used both as texts in my classes and highly recommend them. A final suggestion is Joe Feagin and Eileen O'Brien, *White Men on Race: Power, Privilege, and the Shaping of the Cultural Consciousness* (Boston: Beacon Press, 2003). This work, based on in-depth interviews with about one hundred upper-class white males, provides revealing and at times disturbing insights into the racial consciousness of those who exercise influence in American society. The authors show how the "white sense of self" concretely expresses itself in daily U.S. life.

Index

CPSIA information can be obtained
at www.ICGtesting.com
Printed in the USA
LVHW031927080720
660120LV00003B/334